Perfect Order

Perfect Order

RECOGNIZING COMPLEXITY IN BALI

J. Stephen Lansing

PRINCETON UNIVERSITY PRESS

PRINCETON AND OXFORD

Copyright © 2006 by Princeton University Press

Published by Princeton University Press, 41 William Street, Princeton, New Jersey 08540

In the United Kingdom: Princeton University Press, 3 Market Place, Woodstock, Oxfordshire OX20 1SY

Library of Congress Cataloging-in-Publication Data

Lansing, John Stephen.
  Perfect order : recognizing complexity in Bali / J. Stephen Lansing.
    p. cm.—(Princeton studies in complexity)
  Includes bibliographical references and index.
  ISBN-13: 978-0-691-02727-2 (hardcover : alk. paper)
  ISBN-10: 0-691-02727-7 (hardcover : alk. paper)
  1. Balinese (Indonesian people)—Rites and ceremonies. 2. Caste—Indonesia—Bali
(Province) 3. Bali (Indonesia : Province)—Civilization. 4. Rice—Irrigation—
Indonesia—Bali (Province) 5. Social systems. I. Title. II. Series.
  GN635.I65L348 2006
  959.8'6—dc22   2005016527

British Library Cataloging-in-Publication Data is available

This book has been composed in Sabon

Printed on acid-free paper. ∞

pup.princeton.edu

Printed in the United States of America

10 9 8 7 6 5 4 3 2 1

For Thérèse de Vet

Contents

Acknowledgments

FOR ANTHROPOLOGISTS WRITING about their fieldwork experiences, the question of how to acknowledge the contributions of those who helped them with their research has become rather troublesome. Are we really authors, or merely ventriloquists? Can we claim any special status for our interpretations? How much credit is due to ourselves, and how much to our "informants"?

The answers to these questions are a little different for this book than for conventional ethnographies, which are traditionally based on the insights of a lone researcher. I stopped thinking of myself as a lone researcher around 1985, when I began to collaborate with a systems ecologist, James N. Kremer, in a series of studies of irrigation systems in Bali. This proved to be so rewarding that I soon began to cultivate collaborative relationships with other researchers, both foreign and Balinese. Not all of these projects were successful, but in time they produced a variety of results, from doctoral dissertations to articles, books, documentary films, seminars, classes, and reports to government agencies. I've listed some of them in an appendix, partly to acknowledge the nature and extent of my debt to my colleagues, but also as a reference for readers.

This book represents my own distillation of some of the results of these team efforts. My role usually involved helping to plan and organize them, and contributing as an anthropologist to the work we did. But one of the themes of this book is the usefulness of the concept of "emergence," the idea that the parts can sometimes be greater than the whole. While many of our research projects had immediate, short-term goals, we also saw them as pieces of a larger puzzle. Somewhere in my mind, I was engaged in a long-running conversation about Bali with social scientists whose work I admire: Clifford Geertz, Jürgen Habermas, Roy Rappaport, V. E. Korn, Jean-François Guermonprez, the late Gusti Ngurah Bagus, Valerio Valeri, Lyndal Roper, James J. Fox, Ann Stoler, Robert Hefner, Louis Dumont, Janet Hoskins, Michael Dove, Robert Axelrod, even Karl Marx. At the same time, I was engaged in another sort of mental (and sometimes real) dialogue with ecologists James Kremer, Lisa Curran, Vanda Gerhart, and Simon Levin. Another conversation began in the 1990s with complexity theorists: John Holland, Christopher Langton, Stuart Kauffman, John Miller, Walter Fontana, Erica Jen, and most recently David Krakauer.

But the main point I wish to make is with regard to my conversations with Balinese colleagues. Of course much of what we talked about had to do with the practical task of carrying out research on specific topics: what questions should be asked, by whom, and so forth. Very often our projects had overlapping purposes. For example, Dean Nyoman Sutawan of the Faculty of Agronomy of Udayana University, and faculty members Wayan Windhia and Ni Luh Kartini, shared my interest in the ecological basis of Balinese rice agriculture, both in terms of short-term practical implications for agricultural policy and as an intellectual puzzle. Gusti Ngurah Aryawan, Wayan Sumarma, and Nyoman Widiarta of the Laboratory for Food Crop Protection worked with me, Kremer, and Lisa Curran's graduate student Daniel Latham in a series of studies of the population dynamics of insect pests in the rice paddies. Guru Nyoman Sukadia, an Elder of the supreme water temple Pura Ulun Danu Batur, became so interested in the questions that I and several Balinese scholars (Putu Budiastra of the Bali Museum, Ngurah Oka Supartha) were asking about the history of the temple that he began to collect and publish materials himself. Yves Bellekens, a Belgian irrigation specialist at the Asian Development Bank, began his work in Bali as the head of ADB project evaluation teams. Later on, he and his former professor Lucas Horst of Wageningen University began to take a more academic interest in the history of irrigation engineering in Bali, which brought them into touch with us.

When I say "us," I refer in particular to Wayan Alit Arthawiguna ("Alit") and later on Sang Putu Kaler Surata ("Kaler"). Alit is a senior researcher at the Ministry of Agriculture research center in Bali, and Kaler is a conservation biologist and lecturer at Mahasaraswati College in Tabanan. The three of us formed a sort of core team, involved in every aspect of the research that went into this book. Alit and Kaler spent some time with me at the Universities of Michigan and Arizona, and Alit wrote his doctoral dissertation on subak ecology. His studies of the runoff of nitrogen fertilizer from the paddies to the coastal zone led us to wonder about the effects on coral reefs, a question that brought Guy Marion (then a Stanford undergraduate) and Richard Murphy (Cousteau Society) to Bali to work with us. Guy took coral samples from Balinese reefs with Kremer's help and analyzed them at Stanford with assistance from Robert Dunbar. The results of these and other studies persuaded us of the need to try to undo some of the problems caused by ill-informed development schemes. Besides publishing our results, we also began to carry out training programs in data collection and analysis for agricultural extension agents and students in Bali.

David Suzuki filmed this part of the story for a television series, *The Sacred Balance*, and so did volcanologist Jacques Durieux for European television, for a series produced by André Singer. Alit also arranged for occasional televison coverage of our ecological work on Bali TV and in the newspapers.

We also worked closely with several archaeologists. John Schoenfelder first joined us as a graduate student, and subsequently wrote his dissertation at UCLA on the role of irrigation in Balinese state formation. Vernon Scarborough brought me to his field site in Belize to explore parallels between Balinese and Mayan systems of water control. Subsequently he and Schoenfelder carried out fieldwork in Bali, with continuing assistance from Balinese archaeologist Wayan Ardika. We also benefited greatly from a continuing correspondence with Jan Wisseman Christie.

Several other Balinese collaborators played a vital role in our studies of ritual and politics, not only by suggesting new lines of research but by joining in our discussions about the results: Pedanda Gde Sidemen of the Griya Taman Sari, Sanur; Gusti Ngurah Penatih of Kedisan; Wayan Pageh Sugriwa of Sebatu; Guru Badung and Guru Nengah Teka of Batur.

I am also very grateful to those who have offered critical comments on this manuscript: William Durham, Thérèse de Vet, Carol Lansing, John Lansing, Vernon Scarborough, Robert Hefner, and Ann Kinzig. Finally, I wish to express my thanks to several institutions for their support, beginning with the National Science Foundation, which was our major source of funding, and the James S. McDonnell Foundation. Additional support was provided by the United Nations Food and Agriculture Organization, with special thanks due to Ronny Adhikarya, and to the World Wildlife Fund office in Bali, in particular Ketut Sarjana Putra and Timothy Jessup. The Center for Advanced Study in the Behavioral Sciences provided a sort of scholar's paradise in which to write this book in 2000–2001; special thanks are due to Lynn Gale for helping me to rethink some of the mathematical issues. My indebtedness to my colleagues at the Santa Fe Institute will be clear to readers of this book; here I wish to express further thanks to Ellen Goldberg, George Gumerman, Bae Smith, Marcus Daniels, Shannon Larsen, and Ginger Richardson. Finally, I wish to express my gratititude to my colleagues at the University of Arizona, especially Thomas Park, James Greenberg, Tatiana Karafet, Joseph Watkins, Steve Kuhn, Mary Stiner, John Olsen, Michael Hammer, Mark Nichter, and Alan Redd; to my graduate research assistants John Murphy, Katherine Holmsen, and Kay McElveen; and to Norma Maynard, Cathy Snider, Ellen Stamp, Mary Stephenson, Barbara Fregoso, Caroline Garcia, and Dirk Harris for their efforts in support of "antichaos."

The University of Arizona provided a stimulating intellectual environment and gave me the freedom to carry out extended fieldwork in Bali. I am most grateful to my colleagues for taking up the slack when I was away. Research in Indonesia was sponsored by the Ministry of Agriculture and the Indonesian Institute of Science, with the helpful support of the Consulate General of the Republic of Indonesia in Los Angeles. Credit for the research results reported in this book is thus widely shared, but responsibility for any errors that may have crept in is mine alone.

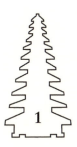

Introduction

> The transition from *myth* to *reason* remains a problem even for
> those who recognize that myth too contains reason.
> —Marcel Detienne, *The Masters of Truth in Archaic Greece*

WHEN ANTHROPOLOGISTS TRY to evoke an exotic non-Western society
like that of Bali, the result may look like a dance of marionettes. Customarily we begin by highlighting the unusual, the strange symbols and
beliefs that are most unlike our own. Through the alchemy of our own
words we imprint these symbols on our subjects' minds, and then they
are made to dance. This approach can sometimes be fruitful: the celebrated French theater director Antonin Artaud wrote that he drew much
of his inspiration from Balinese performances that he witnessed at the
Paris World's Fair in 1937, and saw no need to complicate his first impressions by further study. But if we are interested in a less superficial encounter there is an alternative. Suppose, in a playful spirit, we turn the
question around and ask what Western social science might look like
from a "magical" Balinese perspective?

Picture a scene in a *griya*, the residence of a Balinese high priest. Inside
a walled stone courtyard, he sits engrossed in transcribing a fourteenth-
century manuscript borrowed from a colleague, surrounded by the para-
phernalia of his daily rituals: silver bowls and bells, jars filled with holy
water, and woven baskets filled with flower petals used to make offerings.
To become a high priest, he has undergone years of apprenticeship to a
senior Brahmin priest, reading and discussing the ancient literature of
Hindu and Buddhist philosophy. When the mentor believes that the student is ready, a funeral ceremony is performed in which the student symbolically undergoes his own death, cutting his ties to ordinary human life
so that he can concentrate on the cultivation of his mind. But not all of
his studies are directed toward personal enlightenment; the apprentice

also learns how to perform rituals for the benefit of the community. I have had many conversations over the years with these "twiceborn" priests, hoping to gain insights into Balinese ideas about the sorts of questions that interest social scientists. Not infrequently they ask me to reciprocate. Like them, I have had to undergo a long apprenticeship in an intellectual tradition, Western social theory, that explores many of the same topics they have studied. In the past these conversations sometimes became uncomfortable for me: should I admit that I regard much of their belief system as mere magic, with no foundation in reality? But as my knowledge of Balinese philosophical literature grew, I realized that my first impressions were superficial, and I began to see ways to keep the conversation alive.

The concept of magic is important for Western science, which often sees itself as engaged in a centuries-old battle against superstition. From this perspective, magic is the antithesis of rational thought. This opposition is particularly important for the social sciences. In a recent book (*Sources of the Self: The Making of the Modern Identity*), philosopher Charles Taylor argues that in the Western world, the loss of a magical worldview was the essential precondition for the appearance of the modern sense of the self: "The decline of the world-view underlying magic was the obverse of the rise of the new sense of freedom and self-possession. From the viewpoint of this new sense of self, the world of magic seems to entail a thralldom, an imprisoning of the self in uncanny external forces, even a ravishing or loss of self."[1] According to Taylor, the need for a specifically *social* science comes from our recognition that the human mind is not fully rational, because it is constrained by being embodied and by living in the world. The task of social science is to make us cognizant of such constraints and, by so doing, help us to gain mastery over them.

Yet most of this would seem very familiar to a Balinese schooled in the disciplines of *Saivasiddhanta* and Buddhist philosophy. Both of these philosophical traditions have flourished for more than a millennium in Bali. They emphasize the liberation of the mind through awareness of the constraints imposed on it by the fact of being embodied in the material world. The real differences between the perspectives of Western social

---

[1] Charles Taylor, *Sources of The Self: The Making of the Modern Identity*, Cambridge, Mass.: Harvard University Press, 1989: 192. Similar arguments are developed by Keith Thomas in *Religion and the Decline of Magic*. Other historians have underscored the ways in which magic and alchemy were intertwined with science in early modern Europe, for example in Isaac Newton's keen interest in the mathematical basis of astrology. But this approach only serves to heighten the significance of the decline of magic as a prerequisite for the rise of science and modernity, except for those historians who challenge the distinction between early modern science and magic.

scientists and Balinese priests are not a simple matter of superstition versus science. Instead they reflect profoundly different ideas about the nature of society. Social science is comparative; it assumes that the world is a human creation and that social institutions are malleable. Comparisons, either between different societies or the same society in different historical periods, show how different social outcomes are produced. This idea was first articulated in Europe in the eighteenth century. "Civilization," for example, is derived from a French word that was first used in the plural form for the comparison of different societies in 1819.[2] But for a Balinese priest, the idea of a comparative social theory begins with a false premise. Balinese Brahmanical ideas of society are founded on the concept of caste. In a caste system, every person inherits his or her caste status at birth, and differences between castes are taken to be facts about the world, not about history. So for a Brahmin scholar, the basic framework of the social world is a given, and the idea of a comparative sociology seems merely odd.

But the conversation need not end there. After all, the social scientist's preferred method of comparison is at best indirect. Balinese literature is full of stories about different societies, which are studied for their insights into the workings of the social world. Why do some kingdoms—or some individuals—prosper while others do not? Why do conflicts arise, what makes them intensify, and how are they successfully resolved? The answers must lie in the actions of the people, and according to Balinese ideas, ultimately those actions are driven by people's sense of themselves. A great deal of Balinese philosophical literature, and much serious art including drama, painting, and poetry, explores the relationship between levels of mental development and behavior in the world. Thus the shape of an eye in a traditional Balinese drawing or painting expresses the level of emotional self-mastery of its owner. From the priest's perspective, a comparison between societies is like the beginning of a historical chronicle, a mere setting of the stage. The place to focus one's analytical powers—the heart of the matter—is in the ways the main characters display their shifting levels of consciousness and engagement with the world.

The Western social theory I studied is preoccupied with a different story: the emergence of modern society, the coming into being of a new kind of person. That is the story Taylor tells, but it is as old as social science itself, and has roots in a Christian worldview. The modern West is unique, according to this view, because only in the modern world is the

---

[2] Formerly "civilization" was a technical legal term, referrring to the conversion of a criminal prosecution into a civil matter. See Philippe Beneton, *Histoire des mots: Culture et Civilization*, Paris: Presses de la Fondation Nationale des Sciences Politiques, 1975.

self free to discover its own nature. Premodern societies see society as part of the natural order of the cosmos. The achievement of Western science has been to strip away superstition, to reveal that society is our own creation, not that of the gods. What Taylor calls "inwardness," the modern sense of the self as an autonomous agent and a historical being, is bound up in this recognition. Social science is thus a form of self-knowledge, as historical events are mined to discover the stages of the emergence of modern selfhood. In the European tradition of Hegel, Marx, and Weber, these stages are correlated with the development of democratic social institutions. Hegel's argument, which laid the foundation for nineteenth-century European social theory, is that social institutions reflect a society's level of maturity and self-awareness. It follows that genuine self-knowledge is available only to members of modern societies. Indeed, this tradition makes modern Western social scientists into uniquely privileged observers.

But a Balinese Brahmin priest also regards himself as a uniquely privileged observer, and for quite similar reasons. Like the social scientist, he lays claim to theoretical knowledge about human nature that is abstracted from observations of the world. Still, from the perspective of the social scientist, the priest's views and his own are not on an equal footing, because the Brahmin's views are contained within the horizons of his "premodern" worldview. This idea was perhaps most fully articulated by the French anthropologist Louis Dumont, author of a celebrated book on the caste system in South Asia (*Homo Hierarchicus*) and another on the modern West (*Homo Aequalis*). Dumont does not question the advanced historical vantage point of the West, or the "premodern" limitations of the Brahmanical worldview. But he argues that it is worth paying close attention to the East, because the caste system offers a chance to glimpse a universal aspect of human society, the principle of hierarchy, in a pure form unalloyed by modern ideas about equality. *Homo hierarchicus* still exists in the modern West, according to Dumont, but we have trouble recognizing him precisely because our ideology celebrates his downfall. Yet "caste has something to teach us about ourselves: . . . the castes teach us a fundamental social principle, hierarchy. We, in our modern society, have adopted the principle contrary to it, but it is not without value for understanding the nature, limits and conditions of realization of the moral and political egalitarianism to which we are attached."[3]

So for Dumont hierarchy is to the East what equality is to the West, the fundamental principle on which society is organized. The proposition could hardly be clearer. But is it true? A concern with hierarchy is certainly part of the outlook on life of a "twice-born" Balinese Brahmin

---

[3] Louis Dumont, *Homo Hierarchicus* (2nd ed.), Paris: Gallimard, 1979: 2.

priest. The farmers who visit him to ask for his assistance must speak to him in a language register called "High Balinese," filled with honorific terms, and he is supposed to respond to them in the unflattering vocabulary of Low Balinese. In this way, hierarchy is built into the fabric of daily life and the Balinese language. But if asked whether the concept of *Homo aequalis* is strange and unfamiliar to him, a priest might point out that the same farmers are obligated, as members of their village communities, to attend monthly assemblies where the community's affairs are decided by means of extended discussion followed by democratic vote. In those assemblies, every speaker must use the self-deprecating high register of the Balinese language, thus affirming both the personal dignity and the jural equality of his fellow villagers. Failure to use this register is understood to signify disrespect for the community, and is subject to formal sanctions. Farmers also belong to organizations devoted to the management of rice terraces for which we must use the Balinese word *subak*, because no equivalent term exists in English. Subaks are egalitarian organizations that are empowered to manage the rice terraces and irrigation systems on which the prosperity of the village depends, and they too have frequent meetings that are governed by the same strict democratic etiquette. Between them, the village and subak assemblies govern most aspects of a farmer's social, economic, and spiritual life. Thus the average Balinese farmer undoubtedly has more experience of direct democratic assemblies than the average Frenchman. These Balinese democratic institutions are not recent innovations; there are references to subaks and to village assemblies in thousand-year-old inscriptions.

Anomalous cases can be useful. Social science has long been fascinated by the Balinese, who have supplied some of the most colorful footnotes for our textbooks. But for the reasons we have just considered, it has proven difficult to get them safely tucked into their proper position in the "premodern" rear guard. The more we understand about Balinese society, the more the Balinese people seem to be marching off in both directions at once, adding new embellishments to their ancient rituals of status while also devoting themselves to the perfection of formal systems of self-governance. I am not the first anthropologist to take note of this paradox: Hildred and Clifford Geertz famously observed that "in Bali, *homo aequalis* and *homo hierarchicus* are engaged in war without end." Clifford Geertz also shares my skepticism about the application of standard social science models to Balinese society. "It is fatally easy," he writes, "to fit the Balinese state to one or another of these familiar models, or to all of them at once. . . . Yet to reduce [it] to such tired commonplaces, the worn coin of European ideological debate, is to allow most of what is most interesting about it to escape from view. Whatever intelligence it may have to offer us about the nature of politics, it can hardly be that big fish eat little fish, or that the rags of virtue mask the engines of privilege."[4]

•   •   •

I would probably have lacked the courage to begin with this rather extravagant introduction had I not witnessed a series of social and environmental crises on Bali whose origins lie in precisely this problem, the failure of a Western social science preoccupied with modernity to adequately encompass the Balinese world. It is worth remembering that topics such as modernity, which appear as theoretical issues in academic classrooms, take on enormous practical significance in those parts of the world, such as Bali, where social scientists have given themselves the mission of promoting "modernization." As John Maynard Keynes wrote in the conclusion to his *General Theory* (1935), when madmen in authority hear voices in the air, they are likely to be listening to some academic scribbler of a few years back. Today, the path from academic scribbles to large-scale social engineering projects is nowhere shorter than in what is called the "developing world," where each new Five Year Plan must reflect the latest ideas about how to accelerate modernization.

Over the past forty years the Balinese have had much to do with Five Year Plans. The experience seems to have bred a profound ambivalence, particularly among the civil servants who are responsible for their actual implementation. On the one hand, Five Year Plans are seen as a good thing; they signify that the governance of the nation has passed from the hands of Western imperialists back to the Indonesians themselves. But in a paradoxical way, the Five Year Plans have actually intensified the involvement of Western advisers in policies related to rural development, compared with the role of the colonial civil services in the past. The explanation for this paradox is that colonial officials had limited practical goals, such as increasing agricultural production, and soon convinced themselves that the management of the rice paddies could be safely left in the competent hands of Balinese farmers. In contrast, the goals of the postcolonial Five Year Plans involved nothing less than wholesale social transformation, the comprehensive modernization of the countryside.

With the advent of the Five Year Plans, in the late 1960s a network of new institutions designed to achieve fundamental changes in the management of agriculture began to appear in Balinese villages. Farmers were urged to follow the advice of the agricultural extension service as a matter of patriotism, as their contribution to national development. It was

---

[4] Clifford Geertz, *Negara: The Theatre State in Nineteenth-Century Bali*, Princeton, N.J.: Princeton University Press, 1980: 123.

foreseen by the architects of the modernization plans that the new methods would come into conflict with preexisting local ideas; indeed they were intended to do so. The planners and consultants were prepared to believe that the farmers of Bali were already practicing effective techniques for managing irrigation and growing rice. But however successful such systems might be from a practical perspective, they were not designed to accomplish the broader goals of modernization. Five Year Plans were seen as an extension of the nationalist agenda: why should social and economic change be haphazard, when it could be intelligently guided?

With a long history of rice cultivation and a functioning infrastructure of roads, schools, and government offices, Bali was an obvious choice for field-testing and implementation of the modernization drive in Indonesia. Existing programs to boost rice production were augmented, and were embedded within a larger framework designed to accelerate the spread of capitalism and the adoption of new technology. I began to observe the results of these policies in 1971, when as an undergraduate I spent five months living in a Balinese village. Some farmers were already having second thoughts about the modernization drive, although they told me that they had initially been willing participants. When I returned a few years later, the resistance of the farmers was increasing, but so was the scale of the modernization program. While the new technologies were often ill suited to Balinese conditions, any reluctance to adopt them was taken as a sign of backwardness or even a lack of patriotism. It did not help that the "traditional" Balinese systems of agricultural management were inextricably linked to the Balinese religion. To plant native Balinese rice instead of the hybrid "Green Revolution" varieties endorsed by the extension service was to place oneself in opposition to the whole agenda of forward-looking nationalism and modernization.

The strength of sentiments on both sides of this issue was brought home to me when I attempted to alert foreign consultants in charge of the modernization programs to practical problems that the farmers were encountering as these plans were implemented. By the mid-1970s, harvests were failing in some regions as a consequence of explosions in the populations of rice pests and chaos in irrigation scheduling. Expensive new irrigation machinery installed in the weirs and canals at the behest of the consultants was being torn out by the farmers as soon as they felt that it was safe to do so. The explanation for these problems, I suggested, was that the traditional Balinese system of water management had simply gone unnoticed by the consultants. This system had been extensively studied by scholars during the colonial era, but their descriptions were mostly published in obscure Dutch academic journals, and so were easily overlooked. Moreover, traditional Balinese techniques for water control and terrace management are based on principles nearly opposite to those of the top-down control structures favored by the planners. The Balinese manage things from the bottom up, by means of nested hierarchies of water temples that cooperate in setting irrigation schedules. To a planner trained in the social sciences, management by water temples looks like an arcane relic from the premodern era. But to an ecologist, the bottom-up system of control has some obvious advantages. Rice paddies are artificial aquatic ecosystems, and by adjusting the flow of water farmers can exert control over many ecological processes in their fields. For example, it is possible to reduce rice pests (rodents, insects, and diseases) by synchronizing fallow periods in large contiguous blocks of rice terraces. After harvest, the fields are flooded, depriving pests of their habitat and thus causing their numbers to dwindle. This method depends on a smoothly functioning, cooperative system of water management, physically embodied in proportional irrigation dividers, which make it possible to tell at a glance how much water is flowing into each canal and so verify that the division is in accordance with the agreed-on schedule.

Modernization plans called for the replacement of these proportional dividers with devices called "Romijn gates," which use gears and screws to adjust the height of sliding metal gates inserted across the entrances to canals. The use of such devices makes it impossible to determine how much water is being diverted: a gate that is submerged to half the depth of a canal does not divert half the flow, because the velocity of the water is affected by the obstruction caused by the gate itself. The only way to accurately estimate the proportion of the flow diverted by a Romijn gate is with a calibrated gauge and a table. These were not supplied to the farmers, although $55 million was spent to install Romijn gates in Balinese irrigation canals, and to rebuild some weirs and primary canals.

The farmers coped with the Romijn gates by simply removing them or raising them out of the water and leaving them to rust. This naturally upset the consultants when they eventually became aware of it. "Everybody can criticize and damage a project," a senior official complained, "but only few people can overcome those difficult problems and make the project viable."[5] Still, problems like this were not unexpected, and were viewed as merely practical difficulties in the transition to modern agricultural practices. Meanwhile, the modernization drive continued. In

[5] Letter to the Vice President (Projects) from Director, IRDD, 2 October 1984, Asian Development Bank. Professor Lucas Horst comments on the consequences of this error by the irrigation engineers in *The Dilemma of Water Division: Considerations and Criteria for Irrigation System Design*, Colombo: International Irrigation Management Institute, 1998.

a program called "Massive Guidance," an agricultural credit system was developed to promote the use of chemical pesticides and fertilizers. Dozens of warehouse complexes were built in rural Bali in order to make seeds and agrochemicals (bundled into "technology packets") available to the farmers on credit. The cost of the technology packets was recouped by deducting it from the farmers' profits when they returned to the warehouses to sell their harvests.

At first, "Massive Guidance" appeared to be a success. Farmers easily fell into a routine of purchasing "technology packets" and selling their crops for cash, which could be used to purchase consumer goods such as motorcyles. But it turned out that there were hidden environmental costs. Rice pests soon acquired resistance to pesticides. The agricultural service responded by prescribing more pesticides. Within a few years resistant pests such as the brown leafhopper were devastating rice crops, in some areas consuming the entire harvest. While the extension service turned to aerial pesticide-spraying campaigns, the farmers found a more effective solution by returning to the old system of coordinated region-wide fallow periods, organized by water temples. Pesticide usage declined, but meanwhile it was becoming apparent that the technology packets were triggering another major environmental crisis. The fertilizer contained in these packets included phosphate and potassium, minerals that are naturally abundant in the volcanic soil of Bali. Monsoon rains falling on the island leach these nutrients from the soil, and irrigation canals continuously transport them to the rice paddies. The result is a very efficient hydroponic system of fertilization, which in the past enabled the farmers to grow crops in the same fields for centuries without harming the land. But this natural system of fertilization was ignored by the designers of the "technology packets." A few years ago my colleagues and I began to measure nutrient concentrations in the paddies and irrigation canals, before and after fertilization. We found that most of the superfluous fertilizer flows out of the paddies and back into the rivers. By the time the rivers reach the sea, they contain very high levels of nitrogen and phosphate, which pollute the coastal zone. Many coral reefs located near the mouths of these rivers are dead or dying, blanketed with algal growths triggered by the excess nitrogen.

Altogether, the cumulative impact of modernization schemes such as Romijn gates and technology packets has been devastating to the ecology of the rice terraces, and to the social institutions that the Balinese have traditionally used to manage them. Yet these "environmental" and social problems are still not perceived by planners as serious issues. "Massive Guidance" is only incidentally about farming; its purpose is to promote the modernization of the countryside, and so questions like the effects of agrochemicals on the environment are seen as peripheral, while the breakdown of traditional systems of management may actually be viewed as a good thing. The task that the planners have set themselves is to graft modernization programs onto whatever happens to be growing in the hinterlands. Oil palm plantations or copper mines could accomplish the same ends, if the island were endowed with different resources. Simply put, if "technology packets" lead to blighted reefs, it is the price of progress. It seems that the economist Keynes was right: "the ideas of economists and political philosophers, both when they are right and when they are wrong, are more powerful than is commonly understood. Indeed the world is ruled by little else."

Over the past few decades I have had many conversations with planners and consultants about their projects in Bali. Whenever possible I have seized the opportunity to invite them to visit a water temple and talk with the farmers directly. This never worked out quite as I had hoped: the consultants were usually delighted to make these trips, but they had to be scheduled so as not to conflict with the planner's real work, which always took place in hotels and government offices. Gradually I came to understand that the consultants saw their job as energizing the civil service. The views of the farmers, and indeed all the particularities of the Balinese case, are largely irrelevant to this task. When I returned the consultants to their hotels, the image that often came to mind was that of a team of specialists vigorously treating a patient for what might prove to be the wrong disease. Why, I wondered, do the consultants believe that the details don't matter?

In retrospect the answer seems embarrassingly obvious. From the perspective of conventional Western social science, the details of how "traditional" societies like Bali are organized really don't matter. The great social theorists from Marx to Durkheim, Weber, and Parsons were unanimous in their view of "traditional society" as an uncomplicated world held together by the bonds of kinship. One finds this view articulated today by the leading contemporary European social theorist, Jürgen Habermas. In his major work, *The Theory of Communicative Action*, Habermas explains that in traditional societies "the system of kinship relations forms something like a total institution."[6] According to Habermas, the central problem for the social theorist is to comprehend the patterns of change by which this simple world has been transformed. "Traditional" societies are merely the baseline from which modernity began to emerge, while fully modern societies are theaters of continual change. Consequently, the task for practicing social scientists in a place

---

[6] Jürgen Habermas, *The Theory of Communicative Action*, vol. 2, translated by Thomas McCarthy, Boston: Beacon Press, 1981: 157.

like Bali is to work with the agents of change, the modernizing civil service.

This perspective also creates a division of academic labor in the social sciences, reserving the study of "traditional" societies for anthropologists. It is in keeping with this division of labor that we anthropologists should spend our time tranquilly in the villages talking to farmers about topics like magic and kinship while other social scientists are busy helping the civil service invent the future. Still, as the anthropologist Marshall Sahlins observed a few years ago, it would be rather pathetic if anthropology never discovered anything that might complicate this view: "a hundred years of thought and fieldwork, all that mental and physical discomfort, would have been largely for nothing—an immense detour into the uncharted hinterlands of mankind that merely brought us back to the starting point."[7] My intention here, as the reader will have gathered, is to complicate this picture. I ask the reader's indulgence for beginning this book with so much indecorous hand-waving to signal its broader messages. My excuse is that otherwise it is likely to become the written equivalent of those field trips for the consultants, just another anthropological entertainment.

• • •

This book began with a question posed by a colleague. In 1992 I gave a lecture at the Santa Fe Institute, a recently created research center devoted to the study of "complex systems." My talk focused on a simulation model that my colleague James Kremer and I had created to investigate the ecological role of water temples. I need to explain a little about how this model came to be built; if the reader will bear with me, the relevance will soon become clear.

Kremer is a marine scientist, a systems ecologist, and a fellow surfer. One day on a California beach I told him the story of the water temples, and of my struggles to convince the consultants that the temples played a vital role in the ecology of the rice terraces. I asked Jim if a simulation model, like the ones he uses to study coastal ecology, might help to clarify the issue. It was not hard to persuade him to come to Bali to take a look. Jim quickly saw that a model of a single water temple would not be very useful. The whole point about water temples is that they interact. Bali is a steep volcanic island, and the rivers and streams are short and fast. Irrigation systems begin high up on the volcanoes, and follow one after another at short intervals all the way to the seacoast. The amount

---

[7] Marshall Sahlins, *Culture and Practical Reason*, Chicago: University of Chicago Press, 1976: 2.

of water each subak gets depends less on rainfall than on how much water is used by its upstream neighbors. Water temples provide a venue for the farmers to plan their irrigation schedules so as to avoid shortages when the paddies need to be flooded. If pests are a problem, they can synchronize harvests and flood a block of terraces so that there is nothing for the pests to eat. Decisions about water taken by each subak thus inevitably affect its neighbors, altering both the availability of water and potential levels of pest infestations.

Jim proposed that we build a simulation model to capture all of these processes for an entire watershed. Having recently spent the best part of a year studying just one subak, the idea of trying to model nearly two hundred of them at once struck me as rather ambitious. But as Jim pointed out, the question is not whether flooding can control pests, but rather whether the entire collection of temples in a watershed can strike an optimal balance between water sharing and pest control.

We set to work plotting the location of all 172 subaks lying between the Oos and Petanu rivers in central Bali. We mapped the rivers and irrigation systems, and gathered data on rainfall, river flows, irrigation schedules, water uptake by crops such as rice and vegetables, and the population dynamics of the major rice pests. With these data Jim constructed a simulation model (Figure 1). At the beginning of each year the artificial subaks in the model are given a schedule of crops to plant for the next twelve months, which defines their irrigation needs. Then, based on historic rainfall data, we simulate rainfall, river flow, crop growth, and pest damage. The model keeps track of harvest data and also shows where water shortages or pest damage occur. It is possible to simulate differences in rainfall patterns or the growth of different kinds of crops, including both native Balinese rice and the new rice promoted by the Green Revolution planners. We tested the model by simulating conditions for two cropping seasons, and compared its predictions with real data on harvest yields for about half the subaks. The model did surprisingly well, accurately predicting most of the variation in yields between subaks. Once we knew that the model's predictions were meaningful, we used it to compare different scenarios of water management. In the Green Revolution scenario, every subak tries to plant rice as often as possible and ignores the water temples. This produces large crop losses from pest outbreaks and water shortages, much like those that were happening in the real world. In contrast, the "water temple" scenario generates the best harvests by minimizing pests and water shortages.

Back at the Santa Fe Institute, I concluded this story on a triumphant note: consultants to the Asian Development Bank charged with evaluating their irrigation development project in Bali had written a new report

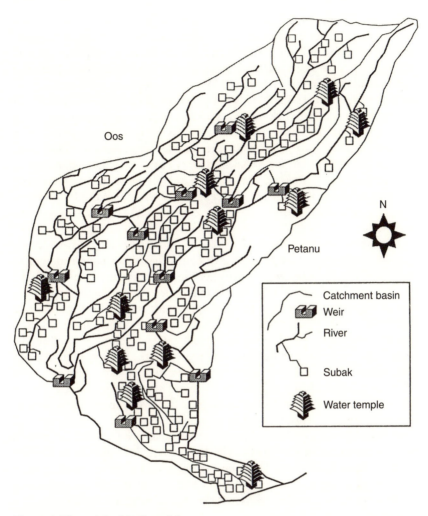

Figure 1. The original Bali model.
This map shows the approximate locations of catchment basins, irrigation systems, and 172 subaks located in the watersheds of the Oos and Petanu rivers in central Bali. Map is not to scale.

acknowledging our conclusions. There would be no further opposition to management by water temples. When I finished my lecture, a researcher named Walter Fontana asked a question, the one that prompted this book: could the water temple networks self-organize? At first I did not understand what he meant by this. Walter explained that if he understood me correctly, Kremer and I had programmed the water temple system into our model, and shown that it had a functional role. This was not terribly surprising. After all, the farmers had had centuries to experiment with their irrigation systems and find the right scale of coordination. But what kind of solution had they found? Was there a need for a Great Designer or an Occasional Tinkerer to get the whole watershed organized? Or could the temple network emerge spontaneously, as one subak after another came into existence and plugged in to the irrigation systems? As a problem solver, how well could the temple networks do? Should we expect 10 percent of the subaks to be victims of water shortages at any given time because of the way the temple network interacts with the physical hydrology? Thirty percent? Two percent? Would it matter if the physical layout of the rivers were different? Or the locations of the temples?

Answers to most of these questions could only be sought if we could answer Walter's first large question: could the water temple networks self-organize? In other words, if we let the artificial subaks in our model learn a little about their worlds and make their own decisions about cooperation, would something resembling a water temple network emerge? It turned out that this idea was relatively easy to implement in our computer model. We created the simplest rule we could think of to allow the subaks to learn from experience. At the end of a year of planting and harvesting, each artificial subak compares its aggregate harvests with those of its four closest neighbors. If any of them did better, copy their behavior. Otherwise, make no changes. After every subak has made its decision, simulate another year and compare the next round of harvests. The first time we ran the program with this simple learning algorithm, we expected chaos. It seemed likely that the subaks would keep flipping back and forth, copying first one neighbor and then another as local conditions changed. But instead, within a decade the subaks organized themselves into cooperative networks that closely resembled the real ones.[8]

This discovery prompted a new question. Were the temple networks a solution, or a device for finding solutions? In other words, had the subaks solved a problem, or built themselves a problem solver? In some ways, the networks looked like a problem solver. For example, if we fiddled with the environmental conditions in the simulation—for example,

---

[8] In subsequent experiments we found that varying the environmental conditions—for example, by changing the rainfall patterns—led to slightly different network configurations. But as long as rice could grow in our artificial fields, adaptive networks always emerged.

by reducing rainfall—the networks would adapt by adjusting the patterns of synchronized cropping among the subaks. For this system to work in the real world, the subaks would need to be able to rapidly alter the scale at which they cooperated with their neighbors. While we were thinking about this question and experimenting with the model, Fontana and other researchers at the Santa Fe Institute were asking more basic questions about the nature of networks, which turned out to be relevant. There is an interesting distinction between networks created by engineers, such as the wiring system of a car or an airplane, and those that evolve, such as immune systems. An airplane's control system is designed to keep the plane flying by solving many specific problems. Each type of plane has its own wiring system; the network that controls a Boeing 727 would not work on an Airbus, and making changes in midair would not be a good idea. Immune systems are different, not only because they are produced by natural selection, but also because they must be able to cope with a much larger range of problems. They cannot specialize in defeating a single type of virus; instead they must have the ability to adapt to whole classes of possible invaders. Consequently, natural selection does not focus on optimizing one solution, but rather on improving the features of the system that enable it to learn and adapt. If real water temple networks were not created by a Great Designer, but rather came into existence by a process of trial and error like those modeled in our computer simulations, then they might be more like immune systems than the wiring of an aircraft. A self-organizing water temple network would need to be able to cope with many fluctuating environmental variables. Hence there would be rewards for temples that could function as efficient nodes or components in networks.

The analogy with self-organizing networks like immune systems had a further implication. Water temples are physically located at or near the main components of the irrigation systems. Most of the time they stand empty. Thus one can think of them as a sort of map of the hydrology of the watershed: the lakes, rivers, dams, canals, and blocks of terraces. This map acquires functionality when groups of farmers decide where to position themselves on it and exert control. The ability to shift the scale at which synchronized irrigation occurs is what gives temple networks their ability to manage the ecology. With that ability, the temple networks become flexible problem solvers.

Whether or not this was how things actually worked in the real world, it was an interesting idea. In the model world, or as they say in Santa Fe, *in silico*, the functionality of the temple networks is based on their capacity for dynamic behavior. The faster they can react by reconfiguring themselves into different patterns, the better they do at managing the ecology.[9] This was a model for an intrinsically dynamic social institution. The capacity of water temple networks to solve problems at the global (watershed) scale could emerge from decisions taken at local scales. The success of the temple networks would depend on their ability to gather and respond to information from local environments. But most critically it would depend on cooperation. Farmers would have to be willing to cooperate with different-size groups in sharing their most precious resource, water. But if they could manage to sustain such cooperation, the simulations showed that something rather magical could occur. If each local group of farmers acts in its own interests and responds to purely local conditions, all the groups benefit as a solution for the entire watershed emerges. In the simulations, subaks begin by experimentally cooperating with their closest neighbors. Patches of cooperation appear and grow, adjusting their borders and irrigation schedules until the entire watershed is connected. The system grows from the bottom up, and rapidly adapts until globally optimal patterns of behavior emerge. Once the networks are in place, from year to year they can cope with changes in local environmental conditions.

The sheer inevitability of the appearance of networks in the model world naturally led us to wonder about the real world. We imagined a historical scenario for Bali that might have begun with the appearance of a few small irrigation systems. As irrigation expanded, these systems would have come into contact with their neighbors and begun to interact. The ability to vary the scale of water control in response to changing conditions would have been the key to success. If water temples began to function like nodes in a network, then an efficient and adaptable system of control could have emerged with no need for centralized planning. The real world was bound to be a lot messier than our computer simulations, but this scenario gave us a place to begin.

So about a year after the lecture at the Santa Fe Institute, with support from the National Science Foundation Kremer and I were able to return to Bali to take a fresh look at water temples. By then the question of the

---

[9] An illustration may help to clarify this point. Imagine a jigsaw puzzle of a watershed with perhaps hundred subaks, where each color signifies a cropping plan for the year: yellow might mean "plant a particular rice variety the week of February 15, and a different rice variety the week of July 20." Groups of subaks up and down the river choose this plan, while others adopt different plans, symbolized by different colors. The result, for the whole watershed, is a patchwork of colors. An enormous variety of different-size and different-color patches is possible, but nearly all of them would lead to widespread water shortages and pest outbreaks. Very few patterns will produce the abundant harvests for whole watersheds that the farmers actually enjoy. And the scale and color of the patches for optimal solutions will vary from year to year as environmental conditions change, or new irrigation systems come into existence.

functional role of water temples had become rather urgent at the Ministry of Agriculture research centers in Bali. We began to collaborate with members of their research staff. One question soon led to another, and before long we were joined by colleagues from other disciplines, from archaeology to computer science. This book describes the questions that we asked and the answers that we found.

• • •

Our first question was whether the conceptual model of self-organizing temple networks bore any resemblance to the actual history of irrigation development in Bali. There is a decades-old controversy among historians and anthropologists about the management of Balinese irrigation systems in the past. Were they entirely controlled by the subaks, and therefore decentralized? Or did the rajahs exert some form of centralized control? The fact that such a straightforward question could be debated for so long suggests that neither of these alternatives is entirely correct, and our model suggested a third alternative. But the model was based on contemporary data; whether it might illuminate the past would depend on the answers to several historical questions. For example, when did irrigation begin in Bali? How was it organized in the ancient kingdoms? When did subaks and water temples appear, and what was the scope of their authority?

We approached these questions from two directions. First, we reevaluated what is already known about the archaeology of water control, not only in Bali but also in neighboring agrarian kingdoms. Second, we undertook our own archaeological studies at the site of an ancient water temple and irrigation system. Chapter 2 describes our results, and suggests a historical explanation for the origins of the subaks and water temples. The argument turns on a point-by-point comparison of the history of water control in Bali with parallel developments on the neighboring island of Java. I have tried to make this comparison interesting for readers who are not archaeologists, but despite my best efforts it is not hard to get lost in the details. Readers who are not particularly interested in the historical origins of the subaks and water temples may prefer to read the summary at the end of the chapter and continue on to chapter 3.

In chapter 3, we return to the question of the ecological effects of water temple networks, and the basis for cooperation among the farmers. Kremer's model of 172 subaks in the Oos and Petanu watersheds was designed to capture the effects of temple networks at a gross scale. Clearly, the next step was to see whether its predictions were borne out in the actual management of the rice terraces. We decided to study fourteen subaks that form the congregation of one large water temple, the

Masceti Pamos Apuh, which is located in the same region as our archaeological excavations. By putting one small network of subaks and water temples under the microscope, we hoped to discover whether these networks really function as problem solvers. This chapter draws on some ideas from systems ecology and game theory, but they are discussed at a level that assumes no prior knowledge of these fields.

Chapter 4 continues the analysis of the fourteen subaks of Masceti Pamos Apuh. The emphasis shifts from ecology to the governance of the subaks. We pursue Karl Marx's fundamental question: who benefits? Does *Homo hierarchicus* really disappear in subak meetings, or does he merely put on some form of disguise? How do these self-governing bodies cope with conflicts and failures?

Chapter 5 continues the analysis of *Homo aequalis* in the subaks, but looks at the question from a Balinese perspective. Subaks devote a great deal of their time and resources to religious activities in the water temples. How are we to understand the relationship between these religious activities—the cult of water temples—and the functional role of the subaks and temple networks? This chapter follows our attempts to comprehend the deeper meaning of these rituals and beliefs, especially those that relate to the democracy of the subaks.

Chapter 6 focuses on Bali's supreme water temple, located on the rim of the central volcano overlooking a crater lake. This temple has the power to alter the decisions of the subaks, and it is governed by priests who are endowed with much greater spiritual authority than ordinary water temple priests. The very existence of such a temple appears to contradict the idea of water temple networks as decentralized, self-governing institutions. Fieldwork was aimed at resolving this puzzle. The results helped clarify not only the role of this temple but the deeper meaning of the water temple cult.

Chapter 7 concludes with a summary of what we learned from this series of investigations, and some reflections on the implications. To help orient the reader, I will foreshadow some of these conclusions here. The water temples of Bali went mostly unnoticed until the Green Revolution in agricultural interfered with their role in the management of rice terrace ecology. But even after their functional role became apparent, they proved to be difficult to comprehend from within the horizons of Western social science. Water temple networks depend on unprecedented levels of cooperation among farmers; they actively manage the ecology of the rice terraces at the scale of whole watersheds, and they appear to be organized as dynamical networks. Moreover, a great deal of what goes on in them falls into the Western category of "religion" or even "magic." But from the perspective of Balinese farmers, these "magical" ideas and practices provide indispensible tools for governing the subaks, the rice paddies, and their own inner worlds. Water temple rituals draw on Hindu and Buddhist traditions of thought to create the preconditions for a robust system of self-governance. The wedding of these ideas with the managerial capacity of temple networks provides powerful tools for communities to impose an imagined order on the world. However, the farmers' recognition that such tools exist is coupled with an awareness of the ease with which they can fail. A certain kind of self-mastery, and awareness of interdependencies, is understood to be a prerequisite for governing both the social and natural worlds. These Balinese ideas about selfhood contrast with the celebration of the emergence of the autonomous subject in Western social thought. (A darker vision, perhaps most cogently expressed by the scholars of the Frankfurt School, associates the triumph of the unitary subject with rise of totalitarian rationality. But these two versions of the story of the emergence of the subject, which seem to us so far apart, draw similar connections between objective economic conditions and the subjective awareness of individuals.) The world of the water temples, I suggest, has different lessons to impart.

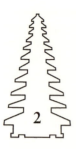

2

Origins of Subaks and Water Temples

IN AN AFTERWORD he wrote to an earlier book of mine about Balinese water temples, Valerio Valeri commented on the apparent detachment of the princes of Bali from the productive system of irrigated rice terraces. Why didn't the kings claim these important resources for themselves? Valeri observed that "the puzzle exists because we do not understand a political ideology that discourages the indefinite expansion of kingly power, especially in the direction of the basic grounds of its existence."

This question recurs in the literature on Balinese kingship and society. In 1932 the great Dutch ethnographer V. E. Korn described "the lack of a powerful government over the whole realm" as the "great failing" of Balinese kingdoms. More recently, Clifford Geertz offered a solution in *Negara: The Balinese Theatre State in the Nineteenth Century*. In broad terms, Geertz's answer was that Balinese kings were the prisoners of an ancient cult of divine kingship, according to which the ruler derived his authority from his identification with a god. This cult required the monarch to make a convincing display of his supernatural powers; as Geertz puts it, "if a state was constructed by constructing a king, a king was constructed by constructing a god."[1] Thus the performance of extravagant rituals became "the measure of the king's divinity [and] the realm's well-being." According to Geertz, Balinese kings nominally owned everything in their kingdoms, but as a practical matter, their interest in the agrarian economy was largely confined to the amount of wealth and manpower that could be extracted from it to fuel the rituals of the "theater state." Since by the nineteenth century the island was home to half a dozen would-be Universal Monarchs, there was inevitably a competition among them

[1] Clifford Geertz, *Negara: The Theatre State in Nineteenth-Century Bali*, Princeton, N.J.: Princeton University Press, 1980: 124.

to put on the most convincing displays: "kings were all Incomparable, but some were more Incomparable than others, and it was the dimensions of their cult that made the difference." This fragmentation of kingship further weakened the state's grasp on the countryside, especially because each little kingdom was itself divided into smaller domains controlled by local gentry. Geertz's thesis that the "theater state" was largely detached from its material base has been much criticized (S. J. Tambiah calls it a "peculiarly disconnected" situation), but no convincing alternative explanation has yet been proposed.[2] "The 'power' that upheld the theater state remains an enigma," observed the Dutch historian Schulte Nordholt; "from where does it emanate, how is it organized, who controls it?"[3]

It was not my intention to address this question when I set out to study patterns of conflict and cooperation among Balinese farmers in 1995. My interest was not in an exotic royal cult but in cooperation among farming villages, and the problems of the precolonial "theater states" seemed a long way from the rice terraces. Surprisingly, however, the problem of kingship failed to go away. Instead, it reappeared with only the thinnest of disguises in the midst of the water temples and rice-growing villages. It turned out that the cult of kingship was vital precisely because it had failed to be all-encompassing; instead quite a lot of it had been dismantled, carried off, and appropriated by the villagers. For example, Balinese kings are consecrated by a ritual called *abiseka ratu*, which is based on ancient Sanskrit texts.[4] But two high priests of Bali's most important water temple, who are born commoners, are also expected to undergo this supreme rite. The details of both rituals—the consecration of Balinese monarchs, and of water temple priests—are at variance with the Sanskritic originals, but the aim in both cases is indeed to "construct a king." And this is but a single example. The rituals performed in village temples, even the architecture of villages and farmers' houses, all contain significant borrowings from the cult of kingship.

---

[2] As Tambiah observes, "The Geertzian exegesis poses an awesome challenge to conventional Marxist and neo-Marxist paradigms. Geertz is proposing that in Bali (and elsewhere in Southeast Asia, at least) one cannot generate or derive from the local peasant agricultural sector of the society the mode of domination, the semiotics of the ritual action of the rulers, or their passion for status and display." Stanley J. Tambiah, "A Reformulation of Geertz's Conception of the Theatre State," in Stanley J. Tambiah, *Culture and Social Action: An Anthropological Perspective*, Cambridge, Mass.: Harvard University Press, 1985: 252–86.

[3] Henk Schulte Nordholt, *The Spell of Power: A History of Balinese Politics, 1650–1940*, Leiden: KITLV Press, 1996: 7.

[4] For a description of the *abiseka ratu* rite in a twentieth-century Balinese court, see J. L. Swellengrebel, *Een Vorstenwijding op Bali*, Leiden: Mededeelingen van het Rijksmuseum voor Taal-, Land- en Volkenkunde, 1947.

Thus it appeared that the realities of Balinese kingship were not in perfect conformity with the Sanskritic ideal, or even Geertz's model of the "theater state." In 1989 a French anthropologist, Jean-François Guermonprez, showed that the very cult of "divine kingship," centerpiece of the "theater state" model, probably never existed in Bali.[5] In an effort to clarify the relationship of Balinese farmers to their kings, in the 1990s I began to work with several archaeologists: John Schoenfelder, a doctoral candidate from UCLA who had previously studied prehistoric Hawaiian temples; Vernon Scarborough, an expert on water control by the ancient Maya, and Wayan Ardika, a Balinese archaeologist interested in the early kingdoms. Our plan was to carry out what is known as "ethno-archaeological" research, in which anthropological studies of existing social institutions, such as temples and villages, are done in tandem with archaeological investigations of the same topics. The site we chose was Sebatu, a village that is located in the region where the first Balinese kingdoms are thought to have appeared, around the end of the first millennium A.D. From an archaeological perspective Sebatu looked promising: Ardika had recently retranslated a number of royal inscriptions addressed by kings to villages in this area, and the inscriptions provided detailed information on many institutions and practices that continue to exist, such as irrigation systems, land tenure, and temples. By reexamining this evidence from a comparative perspective, and perhaps carrying out some surveys and excavations, we hoped to find a way to anchor the "theater state" more solidly to the material world.

We began by reexamining the comparative evidence on the formation of agrarian kingdoms in the region. Between the fifth and tenth centuries A.D., dozens of little kingdoms came into existence in the islands of Indonesia and the Southeast Asian mainland. Some were focused on trade, like modern Singapore, while others grew up around inland rivers that could be used to grow paddy rice. Most of them survived only for a short time and left few traces, often no more than a few fragmentary inscriptions. The handful of agrarian kingdoms that prospered were situated in the regions that were best suited to rice agriculture. Paddy rice needs an abundant supply of water for flooding the terraces at the beginning of its planting cycle. This requirement was easily met in most of the region. But rice also prefers a dry spell for ripening at the end of the growing cycle, and volcanic soil rich in mineral nutrients. Among the large islands of Indonesia, the best conditions for growing paddy rice were found in Java and Bali.

Summarizing the historical evidence, Hermann Kulke suggests that the successful agrarian kingdoms passed through three successive phases

---

[5] J.-F. Guermonprez, "Dual Sovereignty in Nineteenth-Century Bali," *History and Anthropology* 4 (1989): 189–207.

associated with changes in the control of irrigation.[6] According to Kulke, the first phase began with the creation of small-scale irrigation systems by villagers for their own use. These systems were subject to taxation or other forms of control by local territorial chiefs. Regional kingdoms emerged from competition among the chiefs, with the losers reinstalled as tributary chiefs. Kulke supports Oliver Wolters's view that Hindu and Buddhist royal cults played a vital role by conferring unique status on the king, who would otherwise have been indistinguishable from the other territorial chiefs. By virtue of their ritual sovereignty, kings could convert "a congeries of local political systems into a segmentary state." The appearance of kingship marked the beginning of a second phase, when a new class of religious functionaries appeared, and temples and religious foundations proliferated in the countryside.

Toward the end of the millennium, a third phase of imperial expansion began in the regions that could support the largest rural populations. The imperial phase was marked by the increasing importance of slave labor. Slaves enabled wealthy rulers to construct grand royal capitals. Influenced by the Indian cults of sacred kingship, these sites invariably included royal temples representing a cosmic mountain. In an early study of kingship in Southeast Asia, archaeologist Robert Heine-Geldern offered an explanation for this symbolism: "As the universe, according to Brahman and Buddhist ideas, centers around Mount Meru, so that smaller universe, the empire, was bound to have a Mount Meru in the center of its capital which would be if not the country's geographical, at least its magical center."[7] For example, an edict from the reign of the eleventh-century Khmer king Udayadityavarman II explains that "because the king was aware that the center of the universe was distinguished by [Mount] Meru, he considered it appropriate that there should be a Meru in the center of his own capital."[8]

Thus according to Kulke, the agrarian kingdoms of Southeast Asia were shaped by two major forces: the expansion of a mode of production based on irrigated rice cultivation, and the rulers' need to legitimize

[6] Hermann Kulke, "The Early and the Imperial Kingdom in Southeast Asian History," in David G. Marr and A. C. Milner, eds., *Southeast Asia in the 9th to 14th Centuries*, Canberra: Research School of Pacific Studies, Australian National University, 1986. See also in the same volume Michael Vickery, "Early State Formation in Cambodia."

[7] Robert Heine-Geldern, "Conceptions of State and Kingship in Southeast Asia," *Far Eastern Quarterly* 2 (1942): 17–18.

[8] Quoted from Paul Mus's translation in Paul Wheatley, *The Pivot of the Four Quarters*, Edinburgh: Edinburgh University Press, 1971: 465 (n. 81). Michael Vickery similarly observes that "on top of the temple pyramids of Angkor the divine Devaraja and the 'subtle innerself' (*suksmantaratman*) of his earthly representative met and merged in the divine lingam which bore a name combining god and king."

their authority according to the precepts of the royal cults. An imaginary aerial tour of these kingdoms would reveal broad green plains dotted with innumerable small villages, clustered around the rivers, ponds, and irrigation canals. Temples and elite residences are located near important water resources. Royal capitals such as Angkor resemble "magical diagrams traced in the parchment of the plain," with great temple-mountains at their center.[9]

But if we divert our aerial tour to Bali, a very different picture appears, one that lacks most of the features noted above. The island has an ideal climate for paddy rice, and the volcanic soil is rich in mineral nutrients. But the landscape lacks broad plains and large rivers, and there are no grand capitals with monuments representing the cosmic mountain. Instead the island is dominated by several large active volcanoes, with steep slopes reaching almost to the sea. According to Balinese legend, these symmetrical peaks are fragments of the cosmic mountain that were brought to the island by the Hindu gods. Villages and the comparatively modest palaces of the kings and gentry are located on their slopes. There are no irrigation tanks, but crater lakes at the summits of the volcanoes form natural reservoirs. The flanks of the volcanoes are deeply incised by ravines containing small rivers and streams. Looking more closely into these ravines, one can see small diversionary dams or weirs. The dams begin near the maximum elevation where rice will grow, and are spaced a few kilometers apart along each river until they reach the coast. Each dam diverts the flow from a short stretch of river into a small irrigation tunnel, no taller than a man and about a meter in width. The tunnels angle sidewise and emerge a kilometer or more downslope to flood one or more patches of rice terraces that have been carved into the flanks of the volcanoes. One of these little irrigation systems emerges from a spring enclosed by a water temple in the village of Sebatu, high on the slopes of the central volcano.

• • •

We chose the Sebatu site to follow up on an idea suggested by Ardika, who had already begun to investigate the origins of agriculture in Bali. Farming began in Bali with the arrival of the Austronesians, who colonized the Indonesian archipelago between 4,500 and 3,000 years ago. The Austronesians were farmers and fishermen whose agricultural assemblage included pigs, dogs, and chickens; root and tree crops such as

---

[9] Bernard-Philippe Groslier, *Angkor, Hommes et Pierres*, Paris: Arthand, 1956: 11.

coconuts, bananas, taro, and bamboo; and a tool technology that included stone adzes. Ardika and another archaeologist, Peter Bellwood, estimate that Austronesian farming communities existed in Bali by 2,600±100 years ago. They suggest that the most desirable sites for early Austronesian colonists on Bali would have been coastal swamps, where crops such as taro, bananas, and perhaps swamp rice could have been grown to supplement food obtained from the sea. A little later, pioneering colonists who ventured into the interior could have grown the same crops in places where natural springs had created swamps.

The Sebatu water temple is located in a deep natural depression high on the central volcano, Mount Batur. It contains two natural springs, which today are enclosed by a water temple. If Ardika was right, this little valley would have been an ideal place to grow the suite of crops favored by the Austronesians, and should have been one of the first inland sites to be occupied. Later, with the appearance of paddy rice, it would have been one of the most desirable small sites on the island. An abundant source of springwater could easily have been channeled by a surface canal into another small depression just below the first valley. Building such a canal would have been immeasurably easier than carving irrigation tunnels into the volcanic rock, so this site would likely have been one of the first to be exploited when the farmers began to experiment with irrigation. But the two springs produce considerably more water than is needed to irrigate the two little valleys. The excess flow is now carried by a fragile system of tunnels, canals, and aqueducts that continue for a distance of four kilometers downslope. These presumably represent a later and more technologically sophisticated phase of engineering. There was thus a possibility that this single site would enable us to retrace the entire history of farming, from the time of the first colonists through the development of kilometer-long irrigation tunnels.

We also had another reason for choosing the Sebatu site. Ardika had recently mapped the geographic location of several hundred "Polynesian-style" stone sarcophagi, which were used as burial chambers for chiefs in the period immediately preceding the formation of the first Balinese kingdoms, in the early first millennium A.D. Several contain infant burials, as well as various types of bronze jewelry.[10] Although sarcophagi have been found in many sites around the island, a large concentration

---

[10] The burial of infants in sarcophagi found at Celuk, Busungbiu, and Ambiarsari suggests that status was inherited at birth. A different system of earthenware jar burials and burials without coffins has also been discovered, and provides additional support for the existence of social stratification. See R. P. Soejono, "The Significance of the Excavations at Gilimanuk (Bali)," in R. B. Smith and W. Watson, eds., *Early Southest Asia: Essays in Archaeology, History and Historical Geography*, New York: Oxford University Press, 1979: 185–98.

of them were discovered in the general vicinity of Sebatu. The same is true for the distribution of other artifacts associated with the early kingdoms, such as copper-plate inscriptions, religious sculpture, and architecture. Thus it seemed quite possible that our little valley was located in the region where one of the first Balinese kingdoms emerged, sometime in the first millennium A.D.

The most impressive physical artifacts dating from the age of chiefdoms are stepped stone temples. These structures bear a strong resemble to the temples constructed by Austronesian voyagers in the Pacific, which are commonly known by the Tahitian and Hawaiian term *marae*. Marae are raised rectangular walled courtyards, with a row of upright stones and altars in the innermost courtyard that serve as temporary seats for visiting gods. The marae-like temples of Bali and Java have not been dated by archaeologists, but their physical similarity to Polynesian marae suggests a common origin, and this inference is supported by historical linguistic analysis.[11] The extent of the parallel between Balinese chiefdoms and those that developed in Polynesia is significant, because in Polynesian chiefdoms the power of chiefs was linked to their role in the annual cycles of rituals performed at the marae, in a way that resembles the ritual role of Balinese kings. The religions of Polynesian chiefdoms focused on rituals in which first fruits from both agriculture and fishing were dedicated by chiefs to the gods and ancestors.[12] In Hawaii, the most thoroughly studied Polynesian society, the hierarchy of temples (from small local shrines to the largest marae) defined the hierarchy of chiefs, with the highest-ranking chiefs performing the functions of sacrifier of offerings at the grandest and most imposing marae.

However, the emergence of complex chiefdoms in Hawaii was a purely endogenous process that took place in the absence of contact with other societies. In contrast, early Balinese kingdoms were profoundly influenced by ideas about governance derived from India. Stylistically, there

---

[11] See John Miksic, "Terraced Temple Sites," in Gunawan Tjahjono, ed., *Architecture*, Singapore: Indonesian Heritage Series, Editions Didier-Millet and Archipelago Press, 1998: 74–76.

[12] Nicholas Thomas summarizes the relationship between chiefs and temples in Polynesian societies: "Dependence arises because the hierarchy is linked to an iconography of food production (agriculture and fishing) whereby such activities do not simply happen but are conditional upon certain types of ritual work associated with specific ancestor-gods. The ancestor-gods are thus causes of the life of plants and other elements in the natural world and also of course of the humans who depend on those plants, fish and so on. . . . With respect to any particular object, such as a tract of land, there was a combination of two sets of rights: an abstract or titular ownership on the part of the chief, and contingent but immediate tenure on the part of the users." Nicholas Thomas, *Marquesan Societies Inequality and Political Transformation in Eastern Polynesia*, Oxford: Clarendon, 1990: 28–33.

is an abrupt discontinuity between the Austronesian or "Polynesian-style" artifacts dating from the time of the later chiefdoms and the Indian artifacts that are associated with the early Balinese kingdoms. The latter include stone sculptures of Hindu and Buddhist deities as well as inscriptions written in Indian script, either fully or partly composed in Sanskrit. But the apparent abruptness of this change may be misleading. Although the earliest known Balinese kingdoms date from the ninth century A.D., we found abundant physical evidence for direct contact between Bali and India beginning at least a thousand years earlier.[13] Bronze artifacts dating from the age of chiefdoms, including the largest bronze kettledrum ever found in Southeast Asia, provide indirect evidence for long-distance trade because neither tin nor copper (the raw materials for making bronze) are found in Bali, though they exist elsewhere in the archipelago. Fragments of stone molds used for casting bronze have also been found in close proximity to prehistoric sites in Bali. Altogether, it is clear that long before the first kingdoms appeared, the Balinese were in contact with Indian kingdoms, and that they lived in a stratified agricultural society with temples, metal technology, and long-distance trade. But when did they begin to experiment with water control and paddy rice? Was the development of irrigation the catalyst for the transition to kingship? At what point did the developmental trajectory of Balinese kingdoms begin to veer away from that of other Southeast Asian kingdoms?

These questions prompted our interest in the Sebatu site. But before turning to the story of our excavations, it is necessary to set the stage by summarizing what is known about the transitional era and the first Balinese kingdoms. According to Kulke, the key questions concern the relationship of kings to irrigation development and their support of Hindu and Buddhist cults. Fortunately, because of the unusual system of taxation employed by the early Balinese kings, quite a lot of evidence is available on precisely these topics. Rather surprisingly, the ancient kingdoms did not possess a royal treasury or a centralized system for collecting taxes. Instead, as archaeologist Jan Wisseman Christie explains, "the kings reimbursed everyone from the highest ministers to their barbers and stablehands by giving them the right to collect their own income directly from the villages." This system of "tax farming" led to a proliferation of specific taxes, which might vary from one region or even one village to the next. For example, performing artists were authorized to collect specified fees from villages whenever they performed, the amount varying

[13] J. S. Lansing, T. M. Karafet, M. H. Hammer, A. J. Redd, I. W. Ardika, S.P.K. Surata, J. S. Schoenfelder, and A. M. Merriwether, "An Foreign Trader in Ancient Bali?" *Antiquity* 78, no. 300 (June 2004): 287–93.

depending on the legal status of the performers' troupe. For this system to function, villagers needed to understand their obligations. To that end, the kings issued detailed written charters to the villages in their domains. The oldest was written in A.D. 882, by one of the first Balinese kings. They were composed in several languages (Sanskrit, Old Balinese, and Old Javanese) using an Indian script.[14] There are often periods of overlapping inscriptions issued by different kings, indicating that from time to time several small kingdoms coexisted.

The inscriptions were addressed to specific persons and groups in the villages, and so it is possible to reconstruct the broad outlines of village social organization at the time when the first kingdoms arose. Early Balinese kings treated villages in their realms as quasi-autonomous republics. Villages were identified by the common Austronesian term for village (*wanua*); villagers are called "persons of the wanua" (*anak wanua*). The councils that governed these communities consisted of male elders referred to as *rama*.[15] Village leaders were addressed by titles and

---

[14] Seven inscriptions (*prasasti*) have been discovered dated between A.D. 882 and A.D. 914 and written in the Old Balinese language, with much Sanskrit vocabulary. One inscription, the Blanjong pillar (A.D. 914), is bilingual, with one inscription written in Old Balinese using the Kawi script, whose contents are duplicated in Sanskrit written in Nagari script. Casparis argues that the Nagari script used on this inscription is nearly identical to the "kutila" type of contemporary Indian inscriptions, such as the Bagumra plates of the Rasrakuta king Indrajaya III, dated A.D. 950, and suggests direct influence from India to Bali. J. G. de Casparis, *Indonesian Paleography*, Leiden: Brill, 1975: 37. In general, most Balinese prasasti (except those most recently published) may be found in Casparis or in one of the following sources:

Roelof Goris, *Inscripties voor Anak Wungçu, Prasasti Bali I–II*, Bandung: C. V. Masa Baru, 1954.

P. V. van Stein Callenfels, *Epigrafica Balica*, The Hague: Verhandelingen van het Bataviaansch Genootschap no. 56, 1926: iii–70.

J.L.A. Brandes, "De Koper Platen van Sembiran (Boeleleng, Bali), Oorkonden in het Oud-Javaansch en het Oud-Balische." Bandung: *Tijdschrift voor Indische Taal-, Land- en Volkenkunde* 33 (1889): 16–56.

Less accessible but indispensible for research on ancient farming systems in Bali are Wayan Ardika's translations into Indonesian, which include some more recent inscriptions unknown to the colonial epigraphists:

I Wayan Ardika, *Pertanian pada masa Bali Kuno: Suata Kajian Epigrafi. Laporan Penelitian*, Denpasar: Universitas Udayana, 1994.

I Wayan Ardika and Ni Luh Sutjiati Beratha, *Perajin pada masa Bali Kuno Abad IX–XI*, Denpasar: Fakultas Sastra, Universitas Udayana, 1998.

[15] *Rama* appears to derive from the Proto-Austronesian *ama*, "fathers." Peter Bellwood, James J. Fox, and Darrell Tryon, eds., *The Austronesians: Historical and Comparative Perspectives*, Canberra: Research School of Pacific and Asian Studies, Australian National University, 1995: 11. Wisseman Christie also notes that "in Balinese texts the rggep or married residents were the village decision makers. This distinction is still made in Bali

teknonyms that are still in existence today in many mountain villages. Taxes were calculated in monetary units (gold and silver coins of standardized value), as well as labor and provisions such as foodstuffs. It is apparent from the inscriptions that ancient Balinese kings did not claim ownership of all agricultural land in their kingdoms. Such land could also be owned by individual farmers as well as by villages and religious groups. For example the Bwahan B inscription (A.D. 1025) states that the village of Buwahan is permitted to purchase hunting lands belonging to a king, by the shore of the crater lake on Mount Batur, because the village does not have enough land to pasture cows and collect firewood. The king sold them the land they wanted.[16] The existence of irrigated rice technology and small-scale, village-size irrigation systems is implied in many of the earliest inscriptions. For example, words for farming activities such as plowing and transplanting, identical to the modern vocabulary, are found in one of the oldest inscriptions (A.D. 968).[17] It is also apparent that early kings encouraged the construction of temples and irrigation systems. These two projects were often linked: for example in the Tengkulak A inscription (A.D. 1023), villages that have the duty to support royal temples are permitted to take water from other villages to water their own rice terraces.[18]

Interestingly, early Balinese kings apparently felt no need to choose between the various Hindu and Buddhist sects that existed in their realms; instead they supported all of them. The kings also carried on an ancient Austronesian religious tradition, performing an annual cycle of rites in their temples that were intended to promote the well-being and fertility of

---

Aga villages." Jan Wisseman Christie, "Raja and Rama: The Classical State in Early Java," in Loraine Gesick, ed., *Centers, Symbols and Hierarchies: Essays on the Classical States of Southeast Asia*, New Haven, Conn.: Yale University Monograph Series no. 26, 1983: 37.

[16] Wayan Ardika observes that "the existence of the village as a self-contained entity during the Early State period in Bali is indicated in the inscription of Bwahan B, dated A.D. 1025. This inscription mentions that the village heads of Bwahan met the ruler Cri Dharmawangsa Wardhana Marakata Pangkajasthanottunggadewa. They wanted to buy a piece of the royal hunting ground which lay adjacent to their village. The village lacked sufficient land for herding and collecting firewood, and eventually the king sold them the land which they wanted." I Wayan Ardika, "Bronze Artifacts and the Rise of Complex Society in Bali," master's thesis, Dept. of Anthropology, Australian National University, Canberra ACT, March 1987: 66.

[17] Prasasti Bedulu, A.D. 968 written in Old Balinese. See I Wayan Ardika, *Hak Raja atas Tanah pada masa Bali Kuno*, Denpasar: Fakultas Sastra, Universitas Udayana, 1986: 20–21.

[18] This becomes more frequently mentioned later in the time of Anak Wungcu, in many inscriptions including Dawan, Pandak Bandung, Klungkung A, and Jalan Tengah (Goris 1954).

the realm.[19] The most important instrument available to a king for supporting the temples, monastaries, and priests was a legal device called a
sima grant. This grant lifted other tax burdens from a village in return for
support for a royal temple or other religious establishment, such as a
refuge for traveling monks. As Wisseman Christie notes, an engraved copper inscription proving the existence of a sima grant conferred exemption
from the hordes of minor royal servants seeking to collect their income
from the peasants. The *sima* grants enabled the kings to build and sustain
temples and monasteries linked to the royal cult, by placing responsibility
for supporting these institutions in the hands of councils of village elders.[20]

With regard to royal involvement in irrigation, many inscriptions refer
to a small annual tax for the use of irrigation water, to be paid to specified officials. The standard tax was one *ma*, a 2.4-gram gold coin worth
about one-fifteenth the value of a water buffalo.[21] By the eleventh-century
farmers who wished to construct irrigation canals required royal permis-
son. Later inscriptions illustrate a rather surprising interest by the royal
courts in the smallest details pertaining to irrigation. A few examples
give the flavor: in an inscription dated A.D.1027, it is stated that three
named individuals converted a tract of forest owned by a court official
into rice terraces, and that a different forest was made into terraces by
three other villagers. The inscription also mentions the construction of a
dam by the villagers.[22] Forty-three years later, another inscription instructs the farmers to plant trees around their dam: "So that the dam
will be well cared for, it is permitted to plant there coconut trees, areca
nuts, lontar palm trees, bamboo and all types of long-lived trees including types that have no use." And for three years, the taxes of the farmers
who clear the land for rice are reduced by two-thirds.[23] An inscription

---

[19] For a detailed analysis of the relationship between the religious and secular roles of
Polynesian chiefs, see H.J.M. Claessen, "Ideology, Leadership and Fertility: Evaluating a
Model of Polynesian Chiefship," *Bijdragen tot de Taal-, Land- en Volkenkunde* 156, no. 4
(2000): 707–35.

[20] For example, an inscription dated A.D. 911 instructs the people of the village of Trun-
yan, on the edge of Lake Batur, to carry out annual rituals for the god Bhatara Da Tonta
every August. Trunjan B I, no. 004 in Goris 1954: 125–26. Today, these rituals are still performed on schedule.

[21.] *Ma* literally means bean; J. G. de Casparis suggests that a gold *masa* coin may have
weighed as much as a bean.

[22] Prasasti Batuan, A.D. 1027, "(the) forest possessed by the lord Senapati Kuturan (who
is called) Putuputu, consisting of forest of the size of a sukat, (located) in the ser-territory
(?) of Gurang Pangsug in Baturan [a village now called Batuan], was made into rice terraces by (three named individuals). At Tepasan (forest was turned into rice terraces by) 3
more individuals." My translation into English of an Indonesian translation of the original
Old Javanese text, in Ardika and Beratha 1998: 73–74.

[23] Prasasti Klungkung A (A.D. 1072), no. 439 in Goris 1954.

from A.D. 1181 states that the villagers "are permitted to build more irrigation canals, clear more land and make small canals to create sawah [rice paddies]."[24] Another inscription levies fines on villagers who are expected to work on rice terraces dedicated to the support of a royal temple: "if the [irrigation water for] these rice terraces is stopped for one night there is no fine, but if the terraces are dried for two nights or the dam is damaged the people must report to [the priests] Mpu Sthapaka or Caksu. If such events are not reported the villagers of Lutungan are fined 3 saga."[25] In other inscriptions, the village council is directed to reassign lands belonging to childless couples to the support of such temples after the couples' death.

Altogether, the royal inscriptions provide a richly detailed source of primary information about ancient Balinese kingdoms. Unlike the kings of the largest Southeast Asian kingdoms, the ones Kulke terms "imperial," Balinese kings did not claim to be gods. They also did not build urban centers or large palaces in the shape of "temple mountains." Villages were treated as semiautonomous republics governed by a council of married men, and the expansion of irrigation systems was left in their hands. Kings claimed ownership of forest lands, which could be purchased by villagers, and kings encouraged the conversion of forests into rice paddies. Agricultural land could be owned by villages as communal property, by individual peasants, by temples, court officials, or by the king.[26] Slavery existed but was not the main source of agricultural labor. While the kings encouraged the construction of royal temples and monastic retreats, these projects were actually carried out by village communities as a form of taxation under the system of sima grants. In neighboring Java, as we will see, an administrative level developed between villagers and the royal courts, but this did not occur in Bali. Instead, the courts interacted directly with specific villages, and took an interest in the most minute details of the farmers' activities having to do with the provisioning of royal temples and the payment of agricultural taxes.

[24] Bwahan D (A.D. 1181), no. 623 in Goris 1954.

[25] Ardika 1994: 12.

[26] Antoinette M. Barrett Jones describes similar conditions in tenth-century Javanese kingdoms: "we can draw some general conclusions from the data contained in the inscriptions dealing with the sale of land. Firstly, we notice that in several cases where the sellers of the land are mentioned they are the rama of a village, and on a couple of other occasions they are villagers (anak wanua). The buyers of the land, on the other hand, seem always to be high officials. . . . In the Lintakan inscription the buyer of the land from the village rama is the king himself." Early Tenth-Century Java from the Inscriptions, Dordrecht-Holland: Verhandelingen van het Koninklijk Instituut voor Taal-, Land- en Volkenkunde no. 107, 1984: 146–47.

TERRACING A VOLCANO

Elsewhere in Southeast Asia, as we have seen, the growth of kingship was associated with an increasing royal role in the development of irrigation systems. But the steep, dissected landscape of Bali offered no possibility for the construction of storage tanks or navigable canals, and the technology did not exist to build storage dams. Thus in Bali, the expansion of both irrigation and royal temples remained in the hands of the villagers, with the kings simply offering encouragment to local initiatives. The forces that led to the centralization of power in neighboring kingdoms did not develop in Bali, yet kingship persisted, irrigation expanded, and temples proliferated. The desire to make sense of this apparent paradox led to my collaboration with Vernon Scarborough, an archaeologist well known for his studies of water control in the ancient Mayan kingdoms of central America. Our collaboration got off to a slow start, because a comparison of the Balinese landscape with the Mayan seemed at first quite unpromising. Hydrologists have mapped 162 small rivers and streams on Bali, about half of which dry up after the rainy season. The great southern rice bowl was formed by a series of volcanic eruptions that deposited a mineral-rich ignimbrite layer over most of southern Bali. The landscape is especially rugged in the region where chiefdoms and early kingdoms flourished on the southern slopes of Mount Batur. In contrast, Mayan kingdoms developed on a level forested limestone peninsula; from a geological perspective it would be hard to find a tropical environment more unlike the rugged slopes of volcanic Bali. The technology developed by the two societies was also very different: whereas the Balinese built canal irrigation systems to capture the flow from rivers and streams, the Maya constructed reservoirs to store rainfall, using angled terraces and strategically placed tanks. But despite these contrasts, Scarborough suggested that from an ecological point of view, the two systems shared important similarities. The problem in both cases was how to capture small quantities of dispersed water resources: rainfall in the Mayan lowlands, and small fast-flowing streams in Bali. What both the Mayan and the Balinese environments lacked was large rivers. But all the water needed for intensive agriculture was available, if the right engineering techniques could be devised to capture and deliver it to well-situated terraces.

Scarborough's model of the growth of Mayan states describes a gradual progression from passive to active systems of water management. Early Mayan farming communities were located on the seacoast, where they could also take advantage of marine resources. Later, small pioneering settlements followed the rivers into the interior. At first these groups were tethered to the rivers because of the need for water in the long summer dry season. But eventually small communities found a way to survive the dry season in the interior by settling near natural depressions, where swamplike conditions provided water for crops and domestic use. Scarborough describes these natural depressions as "concave microwatersheds." They proved to be ideal for Mayan crops, and over a period of centuries Mayan settlements spread out around the natural depressions across the Yucatan, in a process Scarborough describes as "accretional growth." This period of gradual expansion was followed by an abrupt change to a new method of water control coupled with the emergence of kingship. The new settlements were constructed around "water mountains," which were elevated ceremonial centers built of stone, often including pyramids and level courtyards, that were built atop limestone ridges. Scarborough's surveys show that these monuments were strategically planned to channel rainfall into storage reservoirs and agricultural fields. From an engineering perspective, the Mayan water mountains were "convex microwatersheds." The mastery of water by these combined ceremonial centers and storage tanks enabled the Maya to achieve very high population densities in the interior of the Yucatan. Scarborough suggests that the first order of business at a Mayan construction site was the excavation of a tank system. The great acropolis and pyramid of Tikal, for example, is located far from any natural water source except rainfall. A limestone ridge became the foundation of an acropolis, visible for many miles, in which six paved catchments could capture approximately 900,000 cubic meters of water annually. The Mayan landscape eventually became dotted with innumerable convex microwatersheds, each designed to catch, channel, and store the rain falling on a stone acropolis. From an engineering standpoint, expansion meant intensification: larger and more elaborately sculpted water mountains, which became relatively autonomous productive centers. Scarborough suggests that the Mayan architects designed these structures to dramatize the symbolism of water control by priests and kings. At major Classic sites, "reservoirs rest immediately below the most grand temples and palaces. . . . The thin reflective reservoir surfaces defined the tension between this world and the next, with the mirrored ritual actions strengthening their association to and control over water."[27]

By focusing on the broad ecological context in which the ancient Maya devised their systems of water control, rather than the engineering details, Scarborough's accretional model provided a framework from

[27] Vernon L. Scarborough, "Water Management in the Southern Maya Lowlands: An Accretive Model for the Engineered Landscape," in Vernon L. Scarborough and B. Isaac, eds., *Economic Aspects of Water Management in the Prehistoric New World*, Research in Economic Anthropology, supplement 7, Greenwich, Conn.: JAI Press, 1993: 17–69.

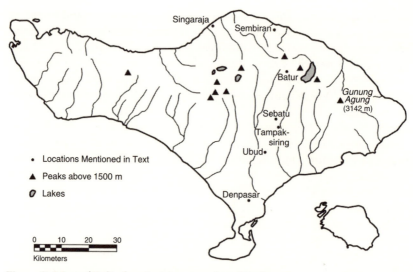

Figure 2. Map of Bali, showing sites mentioned in the text.

which to reconsider the major transitions in Balinese systems of water control. The history of farming that Ardika proposed for Bali resembles Scarborough's account of Mayan expansion: The first sites would have been coastal settlements, followed by pioneering settlements at higher elevations in swampy areas fed by springs. Later, with the appearance of irrigated rice technology, the same sites would have become even more advantageous if springwater could be channeled into simple irrigation canals. One of the earliest Balinese royal inscriptions (A.D. 962) requires villagers to fix the weir at the largest natural spring in Bali, Tirtha Empul, near the village of Tampaksiring (see figure 2). The water from this spring now flows into a large canal that delivers it to three hundred hectares of rice paddies that are located in a valley immediately downstream. In the midst of these terraces are found the largest royal tombs and hermitages ever constructed in Bali, which were completed by the twelfth century (see figure 3). Archaeologist John Schoenfelder has obtained carbon isotope dates from the seventh century A.D. from organic material found at the base of terraces located close to the canal and about two kilometers downstream from the spring. Thus it appears that Tirtha Empul was one of the oldest and most successful water control projects of Balinese kings. The valley forms a concave microwatershed, utilizing a natural spring with very simple technology: the stone weir described in the tenth-century inscription along with a short canal.

But early Balinese kings would soon have encountered a problem. There are only a few large natural springs situated above valleys in Bali;

Figure 3. Twelfth-century royal monuments in the valley of Tampaksiring.

Tirtha Empul is nearly unique. Most rivers and springs are located deep in ravines, and require tunnels and aqueducts to convey their flows to fields downstream where crops can be grown. However, when this became possible, entire hillsides could be flooded with water transported by canals from upstream weirs. Although the water from the spring at Tirtha Empul could easily have irrigated the flanks of a single downstream valley (a concave microwatershed, in Scarborough's terminology), the use of tunnels and aqueducts would have made it possible to flood an entire hillock—a "convex," lens-shaped microwatershed. At first these would have been isolated productive centers, their size dependent on the quantity of available water and the size of the downstream hillocks that could be carved into terraces. But if the water supply was greater than the amount needed for the first available hillock, more canals and tunnels could have been constructed to transport the excess flow from the first terraces to more distant summits downstream. In this way, a sequence of terraced hillocks could have been supported by a single irrigation system, like melons on a vine. Thus, like the Maya, a first phase of engineering using simple canals to bring water to concave depressions or valleys could have been followed by a more elaborate technology enabling the farmers to flood one hillock after the next— Balinese equivalents of the Mayan "water mountains." As in the Mayan case, these would have been small but intensively engineered productive centers.

Figure 4. Rice terraces after flooding, which deprives rice pests of habitat.

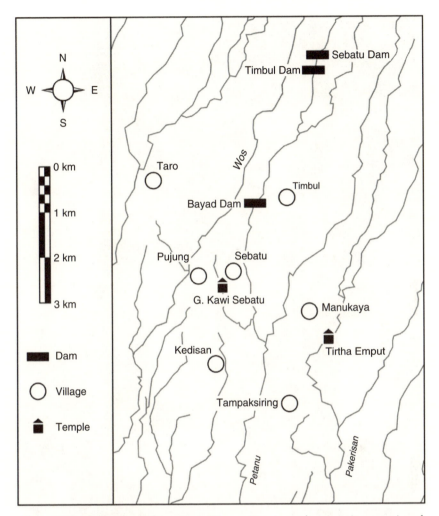

Figure 5. Tampaksiring-Sebatu area, Gianyar Province, showing sites mentioned in the text. *Credit*: John Schoenfelder.

In the summer of 1995 we set out to test these ideas by studying the springs in the little valley south of Sebatu. This site held the promise of reflecting the entire developmental sequence, from earliest cultivation through the creation of both concave and convex systems. Located a few kilometers west of the Tirtha Empul spring, it would have been an attractive site for irrigation development after the first large spring-watered valley had been fully exploited.

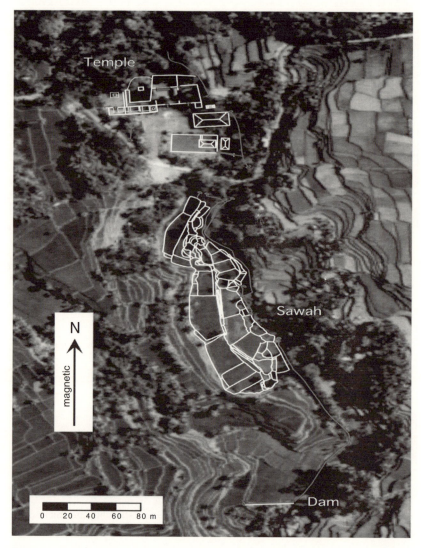

Figure 6. Aerial photograph of the Pura Gunung Kawi (Sebatu) area, with recent map of the water temple and adjacent rice paddies superimposed. *Credit*: John Schoenfelder.

A BALINESE "WATER MOUNTAIN"

The water temple Pura Gunung Kawi (Temple of the Poet's Mountain) is located in a deep natural depression just south of the present village of Sebatu. The temple was built around two natural springs, which it encloses

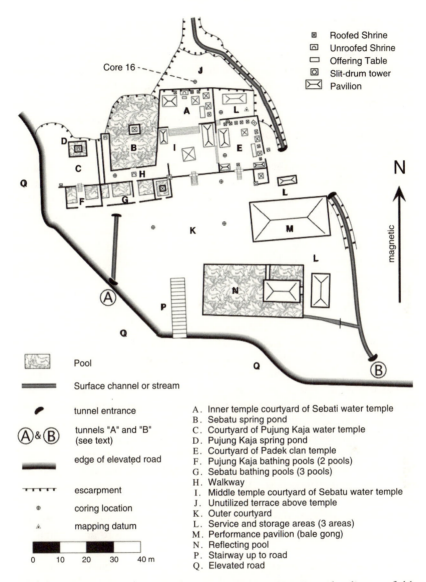

Figure 7. Map of water temple (Pura Gunung Kawi) and adjacent fields showing soil core sample locations. *Credit*: John Schoenfelder.

to create an attractive cascade of pools and fountains. Closest to the springheads are fountains where water can be collected for ritual purifications. Below them the water is led into pools for bathing, and then into a fishpond. The springwater then enters a short tunnel and emerges a few hundred meters downstream, where it irrigates 0.89 hectare of rice terraces. From there the unused water enters a canal that continues for 4 kilometers before emerging atop a terraced hill where it is used to irrigate 31 hectares of paddies. Schoenfelder's measurements show that this system of irrigation canals includes five tunnels, the longest of which is 1.5 kilometers. We speculated that the earliest farmers would have been drawn to this site as an ideal place to grow the crops favored by the Austronesians, including coconuts, taro, bananas, and possibly rice. So it would probably have been one of the first inland sites to be occupied. Later, with the appearance of paddy rice, it would have been one of the most desirable small sites on the island. An abundant source of springwater could easily have been channeled directly into the depression downstream. Digging the first short canals would have been immeasureably easier than carving irrigation tunnels into volcanic rock, so this site would likely have been one of the first to be exploited by farmers who wished to grow paddy rice.

We mapped the temple, the irrigation canals that flow out of it, and the fields that depend on this flow. We also sank eighteen soil cores, to a depth of up to five meters, and carried out sedimentological, pollen, and phytolith analyses on the samples thus extracted. We found that before the advent of irrigated rice cultivation, the valley bottom was a swampy forest dominated by palms and bananas. Sedimentology indicated a very rapid buildup of sediments after the appearance of irrigation systems. For example, a radiocarbon date from core 16, taken from a currently unutilized terrace surface north of the temple, showed that nearly three meters of soil were deposited at this location in the past five hundred years. This observation was particularly interesting in light of Scarborough's accretional model. Local farmers showed us how the predictable buildup of sediments could have been managed so as to broaden and flatten the landscape where the canals emptied into the terraces. Over a time scale of decades, directed flows of sediments could have been used to contour the landscape, enlarging the area suitable for terracing and facilitating the flow of water in small canals—a steady accretional expansion of convex surfaces.

Analysis of the sediment cores also confirmed our predictions about the history of the site. The area around the springs was originally a swamp. Later, it became a managed forest with fruit trees. Taro was probably also grown, but because it does not produce pollen, this could not be directly confirmed. Later, irrigated rice was grown in the small concave depression immediately downstream from the water temple. This little basin widened as a result of sediment buildup, but even today it is much too small to use more than a small fraction of the water that flows from the springs. So at some point the farmers began to construct a series of little tunnels, aqueducts, and canals, which now transport most of the flow four kilometers downstream to the top of the terraced "water mountain" of Delod Blungbang. Three of our sixteen cores struck defunct irrigation tunnels, evidence for the frequency with which landscape changes including the accumulation of sediment compelled the farmers to modify their irrigation systems. We spoke with older farmers who recalled participating in the demolition of a weir and the construction of new tunnels and canals leading out of the topmost fields about forty years ago. Altogether, these results suggested that small teams of farmers were continuously engaged in carefully planned microengineering to maintain control of the flows of water and sediment.[28]

Mayan water mountains were elevated ceremonial centers built of stone, surrounded by storage ponds, pools, and agricultural land. From an engineering perspective they were quite unlike the terraced hillocks built by Balinese farmers, so it may seem odd to call these structures by the same term. Three aspects of the Balinese microwatersheds argue for the adoption of this term. First, the physical structure of Balinese rice terraces is quite unusual: they are not merely flooded plains or valleys, but hillocks or ridgetops that are flooded at their summits. Of course, the scale is wrong; they are not mountains but merely hills and ridges. But this leads to the second point: these lens-shaped terraces are adorned with water temples and field shrines, and the agricultural rituals performed in these temples identify each hillock as a miniature replica of the central volcano, which in turn is identified with the cosmic mountain. The cult of Balinese water temples embellishes the cosmic-mountain symbolism by emphasizing the role of the volcanic crater lakes as the symbolic origin of water, with its life-giving and purificatory powers. Images of the sacred mountain are the central element of the water temple cult, and the supreme deity worshipped in these shrines is the Goddess who lives in the crater lake and "makes the rivers flow." Finally, the "water mountain" metaphor suggests that these systems were quasi-autonomous productive centers, again unlike irrigated valleys or plains.

However, there is also an important difference between Mayan and Balinese "water mountains." Each Mayan water mountain was self-sufficient, and could grow as the population grew by the addition of more terraces and tanks. But in Bali, the expansion of water mountains was limited by the accessibility of water and the topography of downstream hillocks and ridges. These environmental differences had sociological consequences. The creation of water mountains in Bali offered no

---

[28] Vernon L. Scarborough, John W. Schoenfelder, and J. Stephen Lansing, "Ancient Water Management and Landscape Transformation at Sebatu, Bali," *Bulletin of the Indo-Pacific Prehistory Association* 20: 79–92.

scope for large-scale labor inputs. Instead, as we learned by observing the construction of several new irrigation tunnels, such projects require small, highly skilled teams of at most a dozen men, who can move water with great accuracy through kilometers of volcanic rock to flood distant hilltops. Similarly, most hillocks could be cleared and terraced within a few years by a hamlet's worth of manpower. And once the tunnels and terraces are functioning, the rapid rate of sediment transport requires almost continuous reengineering to maintain and rebuild check dams, weirs, canals, and tunnels. These systems of water control become more complex as new hillocks are added downstream. While a single water mountain is typically managed by farmers from one or two villages, several water mountains are often tethered to one or more irrigation systems, creating a need for water management at a larger scale.

Thus the archaeological evidence suggests that the first phase of irrigation development in Bali was based on the expansion of simple "concave" irrigation systems exploiting a few natural springs. This expansion occurred during the Early State period in the first millennium A.D., and was linked to the formation of the first kingdoms. But the areas that could be exploited with this technology were very limited, and the next stage of expansion was based on the creation of "water mountains." Skilled engineers could have tunneled through the flanks of the sacred mountains, enabling prosperous rice-growing villages to bud off daughter settlements. This shift from "concave" to "convex" irrigation systems in Bali could have strengthened the autonomy of village communities with respect to the royal courts, creating a need for effective cooperation among villages sharing a common irrigation system. These developments can be brought into focus by comparing the later evolution of kingship, villages, and temples in Bali with parallel events in Java, Bali's large neighbor to the west. Kingship appeared on the two islands at about the same time, and the administrative structure of early kingdoms was nearly identical. But unlike Bali, Java offered broad plains and large rivers suitable for irrigated rice. Because Javanese kings issued copper-plate inscriptions like those of Bali, it is possible to make a detailed comparison of the developmental trajectories of these kingdoms. As we shall see, Javanese kingdoms grew stronger by weakening the legal powers of villages and appropriating their resources, while in Bali this process was eventually reversed.

A COMPARISON WITH JAVA

The first Javanese royal inscriptions were issued nearly a century before the oldest Balinese inscriptions, in the early eighth century A.D., and were composed in Sanskrit. In contrast, the first Balinese royal edicts were written in the Old Balinese language. But in less than a hundred years Old Balinese was replaced by the language of the Javanese royal inscriptions, now called "Old Javanese." The similarity between early Balinese and Javanese kingdoms extended well beyond the language of the royal edicts: from the early ninth century to the end of the tenth century, their administrative structure was nearly identical. The first Javanese kingdoms appeared in central Java, an upland region with gentle slopes and many small streams and rivers, where small-scale irrigation systems existed before the beginning of kingship.[29] As in Bali, ancient Javanese kings supported their administration by a system of tax farming, and used sima grants to encourage the construction of temples and monasteries. Initially there was only one major structural difference in the two polities: in Bali, rulers interacted directly with village councils, whereas in Java there was an intermediate administrative level, the *watek*. The heads of wateks were called "*rakarayan*," a term that originally meant chief but later referred to a court official. Wisseman Christie traces the origins of the watek to the chiefdoms that existed before the appearance of states:

> The original, major *watek*s appear to have evolved out of the old independent chiefdoms and minor states from which the first major Javanese state was assembled, apparently early in the eighth century. . . . Once a small polity had been absorbed, although it may have maintained some degree of administrative integrity for a time, an irreversible process of absorption and territorial erosion appears to have begun. . . . By the mid ninth century it was unusual for a settlement belonging to a *watek* to be contiguous to any other settlement of the same *watek*. . . . This increasing dispersal of *watek* holdings appears to have been, at least in part, a deliberate policy of successive Javanese rulers.[30]

By the middle of the tenth century, the developmental paths of Balinese and Javanese kingdoms had begun to diverge. In A.D. 928–929 violent eruptions of Mount Merapi, near the center of the early Javanese kingdoms, encouraged the rulers to relocate to East Java, where the fertile plains of the Brantas and Solo rivers offered attractive opportunities for

---

[29] "The Javanese landscape in the upland regions of population growth is generally gentle." Jan Wisseman Christie, "Water from the Ancestors: Irrigation in Early Java and Bali," in Jonathan Rigg, ed., *The Gift of Water: Water Management, Cosmology and the State in Early Southeast Asia*, London: School of Oriental and African Studies, 1992: 12.

[30] Jan Wisseman Christie, "Negara, Mandala, and Despotic State: Images of Early Java," in David G. Marr and A. C. Milner, eds., *Southeast Asia in the 9th to 14th Centuries*, Canberra: Research School of Pacific Studies, Australian National University, 1986: 70–71.

the expansion of rice cultivation.[31] Here the Javanese kings were able to consolidate their power to the point that "they were less reluctant to concentrate more power in the hands of local chiefs."[32] By the eleventh century, these kingdoms had entered an imperial phase.

Recent archaeological surveys in the eastern district of Trowulan, thought to have been the capital of the Majapahit empire, uncovered a huge number of ruins, still incompletely mapped, spread over an area of at least one hundred square kilometers. Kulke comments that the inscriptions "leave no doubt that these temples were directly linked with the imperial policy of unification of the extended core area."[33] The site of Trowulan includes a grid of canals[34] and many large *chandi* (temples in the shape of the cosmic mountain). The East Javanese kingdoms are known from literary sources as well as royal edicts. An important theme in the literature of the era is the king's support for religious institutions, which are linked explicitly to the cult of kingship. For example a passage describing the organization of funeral ceremonies for a queen at her funeral temple includes this commentary: "The reason for it to be fashioned as an eminent religious domain (dharma) was: in order that again the land of Java might become one, that it might have one king (raja), that as one country it would be known in the world in future, not going to deviate. It [the temple] was to be a token of the Illustrious Prince's being a vanquisher of all countries on the earth, a universe-swaying Prabu (cakrawartti prabhu)."[35]

In both Java and Bali, early royal edicts referred to villages with the ancient Austonesian term *wanua*. At first, both Balinese and Javanese kings treated the villages as semiautonomous republics, addressing their inscriptions to the council of married villagers that was the decision-making body. But in Java the relationship of villages to the courts soon began to change. By the end of the ninth century the phrase "all resident in the wanua" (*sapasuk wanua*) was being added to some inscriptions, particularly in East Java. Wisseman Christie interprets this change as

[31] Jan Wisseman Christie, "*Wanua*, thani, paraduwan: The "Disintegrating" Village in early Java?" Bern: *Ethnologica Bernensia* 4 (1994): 36–37.

[32] J. G. de Casparis, "Some Notes on Relations between Central and Local Government in ancient Java," in David G. Marr and A. C. Milner, eds., *Southeast Asia in the 9th to 14th Centuries*, Canberra: Research School of Pacific Studies, Australian National University, 1986: 58–59.

[33] Hermann Kulke, "The Early and the Imperial Kingdom in Southeast Asian History," in David G. Marr and A. C. Milner, eds., *Southeast Asia in the 9th to 14th Centuries*, Canberra: Research School of Pacific Studies, Australian National University, 1986: 16.

[34] Soejatmi Satari, "Some Data on a Former City of Majapahit," in John N. Miksic, ed., *The Legacy of Majapahit*, Singapore: National Heritage Board, 1995: 36–37.

[35] Quoted in Kulke 1986: 16–17.

reflecting the desire of the tax authorities to distinguish between villages as physical sites and as social communities, thus diluting the status of the village as a quasi republic. As the rural population of East Java grew in the tenth and eleventh centuries, the legal fragmentation of the wanua continued. Around A.D. 992 the term for the taxpaying community changed from wanua to *thani*, a term denoting the physical location of the village, and in the eleventh century another term appeared for sub-units of thani. Subsquently communities were referred to as mere collections of these units. By the beginning of the twelfth century, the *karaman*, or village council of the wanua, disappears from the inscriptions; by this point "the community had become the sum of its parts."[36] The loss of power in the villages is also evident from changes in the system of taxation. At first, entire villages were assessed taxes collectively on large areas of land. But as the importance of the village councils declined, landholdings fragmented and the taxable units of land shrank, even though the size of the rural population grew. By the fourteenth century, the large-denomination gold and silver coins formerly used by villages to pay taxes on their communal land were no longer being minted in Java, and the measurement of taxable land was recalculated using smaller units. Meanwhile, the growth of the royal administration led to an ever-increasing horde of tax collectors, so that "as the population grew, they were approached in smaller units by a lengthening chain of intermediaries."[37]

The transformation of villages from wanua governed by a council of married villagers to mere collections of hamlets was a gradual process in Java, but it affected all the villages that are known from the inscriptions, and was apparently complete by the twelfth century. In contrast, many Balinese villages have retained the ancient wanua structure to the present day; indeed many of the surviving inscriptions have been preserved as precious heirlooms in the villages to which they were originally addressed, between seven hundred and eleven hundred years ago. Most of these villages, locally known as "Old Balinese" or "Original Balinese" (*Bali Aga/Mula*), are situated in the highlands above the elevation where paddy rice can be grown, which may have made them less attractive to tax collectors. They continue to be governed by a council of married villagers, and both legal authority and ritual authority are vested in the oldest married couples. The retention of ancient Austronesian patterns is also evident in the architecture of these villages, which bears a strong re-

---

[36] Using data from the inscriptions, she calculates that "amounts of sawah land in a single *wanua* in the ninth century appear to have ranged [to] . . . between 120 and 180 hectares at the upper end of the scale." Wisseman Christie 1994: 38.

[37] Wisseman Christie 1994: 39.

semblance to the common Austronesian longhouse pattern found elsewhere in the archipelago, consisting of a long row of compartments under a single roof, each housing a married couple and their children.[38]
The most senior couple are supposed to reside in the apartment that is
physically closest to an ancestral shrine associated with each longhouse
row. These villages also preserve an ancient type of temple, the *bale lantang*, which is still used for the monthly meetings of married villagers. Bale
lantang consist of a long raised wooden seating platform, with a roof but
no walls, oriented in the same uphill direction as the longhouses. Here
married men are seated in order of seniority facing a row of shrines resembling Austronesian god-stones, dedicated to the deified village founders and gods of local importance.[39] These villages jealously guard their independence, and the council of married villagers often disposes of rights
to cultivate communal land. The survival of these "village republics" in
appreciable numbers suggests that Balinese kings failed to achieve the
breakdown of the autonomy of the wanua that was accomplished in
Java by the first large kingdoms.[40]

THE SIGNIFICANCE OF WATER

In the steep, dissected landscape of Bali, the expansion of rice cultivation meant the proliferation of water mountains, shaped to fit the local
topography and to take advantage of upstream sources of water. Building and maintaining the many small tunnels and canals, and enforcing
equitable rules for irrigation cycles, would have required cooperation at
two levels: among the farmers on each water mountain, and between

---

[38] On the architecture of Bali Aga villages, see Thomas Reuter, "Houses and Compounds
in the Mountains of Bali," in Gunawan Tjahjono, ed., *Indonesian Heritage: Architecture*,
Singapore: Archipelago Press and Editions Didier Millet, 1998: 38–40. The architecture of
typical Balinese houses is described in an article by Robi Sularto in the same volume. For
comparative descriptions of Austronesian longhouse architecture, see James J. Fox, ed., *Inside Austronesian Houses: Perspectives on Domestic Designs for Living*, Canberra: Com-
paraive Austronesia Project, Research School of Pacific Studies, Australian National University, 1993.

[39] Such villages no longer call themselves wanua, reserving this term for a collection of villages that support a single origin temple. The villages within a wanua usually regard themselves as daughter settlements spun from an original mother village, which was thus the
original wanua.

[40] My point is not that these villages escaped royal control or influence, but rather that
they managed to retain their status as quasi-autonomous village republics ruled by the
council of married elders, which was the pattern in Javanese villages before 922 A.D. and in
Balinese villages for as long as royal inscriptions continued to be issued.

communities sharing the same water sources. References to a specialized institution for this purpose begin to appear in Balinese inscriptions by the eleventh century. This institution, called *subak*, was not identical to the village or wanua. Instead its membership consisted of all the farmers who owned land watered by a common source, such as a spring or tertiary canal.[41] Subaks never developed in Java, where irrigation systems were built on gently sloping terrain and managed by the wanua, which appear to have controlled sufficient territory to encompass most of their water sources. More than 80 percent of the Javanese settlements dating to the later first millennium A.D. lie within five hundred meters of at least one river, at elevations between about one hundred and four hundred meters.[42] Although the royal edicts occasionally mention officials who had some connection with water, the Javanese kings did not take an active role in the creation of irrigation systems. Instead, as in Bali, rulers encouraged the spread of rice production by offering tax incentives for settlers to clear land or build irrigation systems.

Later on, only a few Javanese royal edicts refer to irrigation dams: the Harinjing inscriptions from East Java (A.D. 804, 921, and 927) and two later inscriptions from the era of one of the most famous Javanese rulers, Airlangga (A.D. 1021 and 1037). The A.D. 1037 inscription is the most detailed and, from a comparative perspective, the most interesting. It appears that the Brantas River had burst its banks near the hamlet of Waringin Sapta, inundating a number of local communities and destroy-

[41] Cf. the Baturan inscription, A.D. 1022, no. 352 in Goris 1954, also in M. M. Soekarto K. Atmodjo, "Some Short Notes on Agricultural Data from Ancient Balinese Inscriptions," in Sartono Kartodirdjo, ed., *Papers of the Fourth Indonesian-Dutch History Conference, Yogyakarta 24–29 July 1983*, vol. 1: *Agrarian History*, Yogyakarta: Gadjah Mada University Press, 1986: 60; Udayapatya A.D. 1181, Soekarto 1986: 41–42; Er Rara, A.D. 1072, Soekarto 1986: 34–35; and an incomplete inscription probably dating to the late eleventh or early twelfth century housed in the Museum Mpu Tantular in Surabaya (Machi Suhadi and K. Richadiana, *Laporan Penelitian Epigrafi di Wilayah Provinsi Jawa Timur* [Berita Penelitian Arkeologi no. 47], Jakarta: Departemen Pendidikan dan Kebudayaan, 1996: 12–23). The Er Rara inscription mentions fields located in at least twenty-seven named hamlets, belonging to eighteen different communities, in connection with the *kasuwakan* of Rawas. Similarly, Udayapatya refers to nineteen kasuwakan. Soekarto locates these kasuwakan in a region stretching from Lake Batur south into Gianyar. Wisseman Christie comments that "the number of kasuwakan involved suggests a local irrigation network of considerable complexity and more than one water source, used by a community spread over a somewhat awkward landscape." Wisseman Christie, "Irrigation in Java and Bali before 1500," unpublished ms.

[42] Mundardjito, "Pertimbangan Ekologi dalam Penempatan Situs Masa Hindu-Buda di Daerah Yogyakarta: Kajian Arkeologi-ruang Skala Makro," doctoral dissertation, Universitas Indonesia, 1993: 14.

ing their rice fields. The local people tried repeatedly to solve the problem themselves (there is no mention of involvement by any religious or state officials). When their own efforts failed they petitioned King Airlangga to exercise his right to command corvée labor to carry out a large earth-moving project. This he did, and the breach was sealed with a dam, deflecting the river back to the north. But now the king was faced with the problem of assuring continuing upkeep for the dam, since apparently there was no administrative system for this purpose. Airlangga solved the problem by granting a sima charter to the community of Kamalagyan, to which the hamlet of Waringin Sapta belonged, and placed the sima in the hands of a religious foundation attached to the community. As Wisseman Christie comments, it is interesting that the king apparently considered the circumstances to be unusual enough to call for an extended explanation in the charter: "The contents of the charter imply that the ruler's involvement in even major water works was not automatic. Indeed, no reference is made to royal involvement in the building of the original dam."[43] She concludes that Javanese farmers were never placed in the position of needing to create institutions to coordinate intercommunity irrigation systems.

In Bali, however, as tunnels and canals proliferated on the slopes of the volcanoes, the problem of sharing water among subaks would become acute. Conceivably it could have been handled as a purely practical matter. Instead, the solution devised by the farmers involved the creation of a new class of temples, managed by the subaks and dedicated to a prestigious assembly of deities including the Rice Goddess and the gods of the mountains and crater lakes. The subak temples provided an institutional framework for the cooperative management of irrigation, which was accomplished by integrating aspects of the Indian religions promoted by the kings with existing religious practices and beliefs in the villages. The appearance of these temples set in motion profound changes, not only in the relationship of villages to one another, but also in the villages' internal organization and their relationship to the royal courts.

The subak temples of Bali were a relatively late development in the long history of attempts to reconcile ancient Austronesian beliefs with the religions of India. This history can be traced back to the oldest temples built by Javanese kings on the volcanoes of central Java. Physically these monuments would not look out of place in India, but in their written charters they are not described as sites for the worship of Indian

---

[43] Wisseman Christie, "Irrigation in Java and Bali before 1500," 12.

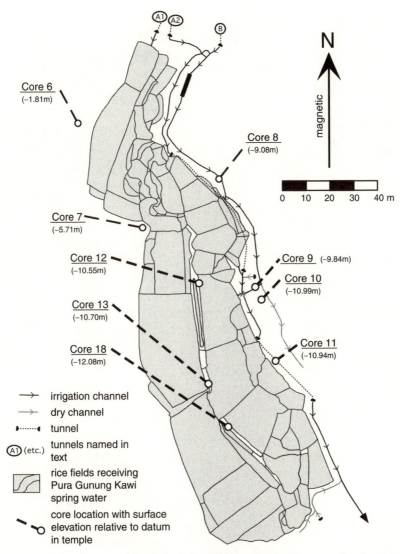

Figure 8. Map of rice paddies below the Gunung Kawi water temple, showing core sample locations. *Credit*: John Schoenfelder.

gods or boddhisattvas. Rather, following the older Austronesian tradition, they are depicted as ancestor temples—burial places for Javanese kings whose spirits were invoked, along with the spirits of the gods who dwelled on the volcanoes, to protect the royal palace and if necessary to

Figure 9. Bathing pools at the Gunung Kawi Sebatu water temple.

act on a curse.[44] Syncretism is also apparent in the association of many mountain temples with springs. From the ninth century onward, most temples were located beside natural springs in order to create sacred bathing pools (*tirtha, patirthan*).[45] Later Javanese temples incorporated symbolic references associating the holy springs (*patirthan*) of the mountain temples with *amrta*, the water of immortality described in Hindu myths, and with the goddesses of fertility. Later on, when kings began to fill the plains and valleys of East Java with temples, wherever possible temples enclosed sacred springs and bathing pools.

In Bali, the term *tirtha* came to refer not to the spring itself but to the holy water that flowed from it. A ritual performed inside the temple could transform ordinary water into tirtha, imbued with the essence of the temple's god. Eventually, the primary sacrament of Balinese religion became an exchange in which worshippers offered the fruits of their labors to a temple's god in return for a blessing of tirtha that could be sprinkled on them and also on their offerings, children, houses, fields, tools, and livestock. By obtaining tirtha from several temples, one could combine the blessings of several gods. Particular temples came to be associated with specific functions or purposes, and also with the human congregations that supported them. Tirtha from these temples could be used to express not only the functional blessings of the gods but also relationships between the human groups that comprised each temple's congregation. For example, since ancient times Balinese households have contained shrines to the family's ancestors. By placing a bowl of water on the shrine and pronouncing a prayer, family members can request tirtha from their immediate ancestors. But to address more distant ancestors requires a bit more ceremony. As in other Austronesian societies, Balinese families can gain status by invoking their relationship to their

[44] Personal communication, Jan Wisseman Christie.

[45] In Sanskrit, *tirtha* is "a passage, way, road, ford, stairs for landing or for descent into a river, bathing place, place of pilgrimage on the banks of sacred streams; also "one of the ten orders of ascetics founded by Samkaracarya," and in a more general sense, a sacred preceptor or Guru (Monier Monier-Williams, *A Sanskrit-English Dictionary*, Delhi: Motilal Banarsidass Publishers, 1993 [1899]: 449). In Old Javanese, these primary meanings are retained, but to them is added a secondary meaning: holy water in general (P. J. Zoetmulder, *Old Javanese–English Dictionary, Part II*, 's-Gravenhage: Martinus Nijhoff, 1982: 2019). In modern Balinese, only the meaning of *tirtha* as holy water is retained (*Kamus Bali-Indonesia*, Dinas Pendidikan Dasar Propopinsi DATI I Bali, 1990: 732). Van der Tuuk's *Kawi-Balineesch-Nederlandsch Woordenboek* offers tentative translations of several compounds derived from *tirtha*, including holy river, possibly pilgrimage, and the performance of a religious purification consisting of bathing for a month and seven days, but does not clearly distinguish between the Old Javanese and modern Balinese meanings. Somewhat mysteriously, he proposes "washing water" for the nominalized *patirthan* (Batavia: Landsdrukkerij, 1899: vol. 3, 599).

earliest founding ancestor.[46] Elsewhere in Indonesia and the Pacific, this idea is often expressed by origin myths, which justify the rank order of descent groups by the order in which they appeared. Tirtha gave the Balinese a way to give this idea a more concrete expression. The origin of descent groups is commemorated in origin temples, where the founding ancestor can bestow tirtha on his descendants. A vial of tirtha can be carried home to dignify rites of passage such as births or weddings. Origin temples became a permanent part of the landscape; to visit one and request tirtha is to express a claim to membership in the descent group that originated with the founder.

In a similar way, the metaphor of water flowing from a sacred origin was used to define relationships among subaks. Subak temples are built to commemorate the sites where water originates, such as springs, lakes, and the weirs where irrigation systems begin. All the farmers who benefit from a particular flow of water share an obligation to provide offerings in return for tirtha at the temple where their water originates. If six subaks obtain water from a given weir, all six belong to the congregation of the water temple associated with that weir. Thus the larger the water source, the larger the congregation of the water temple.

Eventually, the religion of Bali came to be known as the religion of tirtha. The metaphor of water flowing from a sacred source was joined to the ancient Austronesian concept of descent from a sacred origin. When this symbolism was applied to the physical landscape of Bali, the summits of the volcanoes became doubly sacred. Already populated by both Hindu gods and the deified ancestors of kings and lineage founders, the summits with their crater lakes became the ultimate source of tirtha. In this way, the island itself became a metonym for a concept of the sacred that drew from both Indic and Austronesian sources. The logical principle that completed this synthesis and made it possible eventually to cover the flanks of the volcanoes with temples for subaks and descent groups was to relativize the concept of origin. Looking at an irrigation system from the bottom up (see figure 10), there is an origin point for the water that enters a farmer's field. Higher up, there is another origin for the waters of his subak, another for the entire irrigation system (which may include several subaks), and finally an ultimate point of origin at the

---

[46] As James Fox observes of Austronesian cultures generally, "conceptions of ancestry are invariably important but rarely is ancestry alone a sufficient and exclusive criterion for defining origins. Recourse to notions of place is also critical in identifying persons and groups, and thus in tracing origins." James J. Fox, "Introduction," in James J. Fox and Clifford Sather, eds., *Origins, Ancestry and Alliance: Explorations in Austronesian Ethnography*, Canberra: Research School of Pacific Studies, 1996: 5. See also Peter Bellwood, "Hierarchy, Founder Ideology and Austronesian Expansion," in the same volume, 18–40.

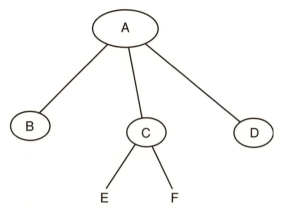

Figure 10. The concept of sacred origins as a basis for constructing hierarchical networks. Here E and F are subordinate to C, which is subordinate to A. Applied to water temples, A could be a volcanic crater lake, and B–D springs or weirs on the slopes of a mountain that are the local origin of irrigation water for subaks (E, F). Analogously, if A is the origin temple (*kawitan*) for a descent group, B–D are branch temples located in different regions, and E and F, village temples of origin for this group.

crater lake. In the same way, there can be origin temples for a single family, a collection of related families, and an entire descent group. Each temple becomes a node in a branching network, its rank dependent on its position relative to the highest point of origin. Tirtha from temples closer to the ultimate origin can be used to sanctify rites performed "downstream," in lower-ranking temples.

To assess the historical significance of these developments, it is illuminating to continue the comparison of Balinese and Javanese kingdoms. From the eleventh century onward, the histories of Balinese kingdoms and those of East Java are closely intertwined. Royal dynasties on the two islands alternately attacked one another and intermarried.[47] Meanwhile, the expansion of royal power by the construction of Hindu temples was reaching its zenith in Javanese kingdoms. But in Bali it was coming to an end. In earlier times, the kings of Bali showed as much

---

[47] Literary sources claim that Airlangga, the king who fixed the problem with the dam on the Brantas River, was born in Bali and married a Javanese princess, becoming a king of Java in 1037. According to this tradition, Airlangga's dynasty ruled in Bali; his grandson was Anak Wungcu, who is known from thirty-eight Balinese inscriptions and is thought to have been the builder of the royal tombs in the Tirtha Empul Valley.

enthusiasm for temple building as their Javanese counterparts. The first Balinese royal edicts are devoted mostly to detailed lists of contributions that villagers are instructed to provide for the support of the king's temples. Archaeological remains from early Balinese kingdoms include sculptural representations of the Hindu and Buddhist pantheons, and rock-cut sanctuaries for the class of professional priests who cared for them. As in Java, these images of the gods are faithful to Indian iconography. But later on the Balinese royal edicts show a reversal of roles, as villagers became the hosts and patrons of royal functionaries. In accordance with the tax-farming system of revenue, villagers were told what they should pay to artists and performers who were under royal patronage but were obliged to support themselves by also performing at village temple festivals. References to village temples include a village temple of origin (*pura puseh*), where the farmers could bypass the royal temples and enjoy direct access to all the gods.[48] By the fourteenth century, the monastic retreats in Bali had been abandoned, artists had stopped creating sculptural representations of the Hindu gods, and the construction of monumental royal tombs and temples had come to an end.

FEUDALISM, CASTE, AND THE LATER KINGDOMS

The gradual replacement of royal temples with branching networks of temples controlled by villagers may reflect a diminution of the powers of the kings. But it did not lead to a corresponding increase in the power of the villages. As we have seen, in ancient Balinese villages the council of married citizens controlled access to agricultural land. This system was well suited to a mode of production based on shifting cultivation, because the council could periodically reallocate land in order to preserve its fertility and make efficient use of the available labor. But wherever irrigation systems were built in Bali, rice terraces became private property. The spread of irrigation thus diminished the importance of the village councils, which lost control of productive land (although they retained control of the land beneath houses and temples). The management of irrigation shifted to the subak temples, which transcended the boundaries of individual villages.

The powers of the village councils were further diluted by the spread of origin temples for descent groups. Like the subak temples, these networks

[48] Korn writes, "The village temples went from places of worship of the village gods and the ancestors who had gone up to the gods, to the place of descent for the Hindu high gods, to whom the village gods could pay attendance on special occasions." V. E. Korn, *Het Adatrecht van Bali* (2nd ed.), The Hague: Naeff, 1932: 229–30 (first edition 1924).

extended social ties beyond the borders of individual villages. More importantly, at some point descent groups began to associate their origin temples with the Hindu concept of caste. At first, caste was restricted to members of the royal courts. In their royal edicts, the kings depicted themselves as belonging to the royal Satriya caste, and Hindu priests were described as Brahmins. The invention of permanent origin temples for descent groups provided a vehicle to extend the ideology of caste to the rest of society. There is no evidence that this notion was encouraged by the kings, but it was probably inevitable given the prestige associated with caste rank by the aristocracy. Once the "caste" of a founding ancestor was agreed on, it would automatically become attached to anyone allowed to request tirtha at his origin temple. In this way, one aspect of the Hindu concept of caste—the principle that social rank is inherited at birth—was joined to the ancient Austronesian system of ranked descent groups. Differences in caste implied differences in social rank, which could be publicly signaled in rites of passage, and eventually by honorific titles and language registers. Hindu ideas about reincarnation also dovetailed nicely with existing traditions of ancestor worship. If the rites were properly performed, ancestors could be given the opportunity for rebirth into their own descent groups. Funeral rites could thus combine veneration for the ancestors with competitive displays of caste status. When seventeenth-century Europeans began to visit Bali, they observed that the funeral rites for aristocrats could go on for months and consume vast fortunes.

Eventually, having lost control of agricultural land, most Balinese village councils became purely ceremonial institutions or disappeared completely. Where village councils managed to survive, the use of caste symbolism for rites of passage was usually banned, perhaps because it conflicted with the principle of equality among citizens. But evidence for the historical spread of ideas of caste into village society is mostly indirect. In the fourteenth century, the best source of historical evidence for Balinese kingdoms, the royal edicts, came to an end. Javanese sources from that time mention the reconquest of Bali by the Majapahit empire, and the installation of a Javanese administration in Gelgel, which became the capital of Bali.[49] The court chronicles of Bali, thought to have been composed centuries after the events they describe, also state that the Majapahit empire established a royal dynasty in Bali in the middle of the fourteenth century.[50] The same texts describe an exodus of

---

[49] Thoedore G. Pigeaud, *Java in the Fourteenth Century: A Study in Cultural History*, 5 vols., The Hague: Martinus Nijhoff, 1960.

[50] Helen Creese, "Balinese Babad as Historical Sources: A Reinterpretation of the Fall of Gelgel," *BKI* 147 (1991): 236–60.

Majapahit courtiers to Bali after the fall of the empire in 1520. But the accuracy of these texts is problematic; the kings of Majapahit were prone to extravagant claims. If Javanese kings attempted to restructure the Balinese systems of land tenure and taxation to bring them into conformity with Javanese methods of administration, the effort left no historical trace. Whoever the rulers of Bali may have been, they stopped issuing sima grants and edicts to villages. We may infer that the disappearance of these documents signaled a major change in the governance of the island. The royal inscriptions were the legal foundation for the system of revenue that supported the kings, their courts, and the class of professional clergy. When kings stopped issuing and revising these documents, the ancient system of centralized governance based on tax farming could not have long survived.

A more impressionistic source of evidence concerning Balinese kingdoms appeared in the following century, with the arrival of European observers. In the seventeenth century, several Europeans wrote accounts of their visits to the court of the king of Bali. Among them was Jan Oosterwijck, a chief merchant in the service of the Dutch East India Company who was sent to Bali in 1633 to attempt to persuade the king to join the Dutch in an attack on the Javanese kingdom of Mataram. Arriving on the north coast, he was instructed to sail to the royal capital of Gelgel, where he was escorted to the palace. Oosterwijck spent weeks waiting but never did see the king, who sent word that he desired only peace with Mataram and was occupied with the funeral of his mother and two of his sons. While waiting to see the king, Oosterwijck witnessed an example of a new element in the royal cult: human sacrifice. At the cremation of the queen mother, twenty-two female slaves were stabbed and burned in the funeral pyre. The Dutch visitors were told that "on the death of the reigning King no less than 120, 130 to 140 women devote themselves to the flames. None of them are previously stabbed to death; irrespective of rank, they all jump into the fire of their own free will."[51]

In all there are five extended accounts of human sacrifice at royal funerals attended by Euopean observers: those by Oosterwijck (1633), Dubois (1829), Zollinger (1846), Helms (1847), and Friederich (1847). From the descriptions it is apparent that these events were spectacles to which an appreciable fraction of the island's population was invited to attend; Helms estimates "not less" than forty thousand to fifty thousand spectators in 1846. Smaller sacrifices also took place at the death of lesser princes. The addition of human sacrifice to the rituals of the royal

---

[51] Alfons van der Kraan, "Human Sacrifice in Bali: Sources, Notes and Commentary," *Indonesia* (1985): 91–95.

cult suggests a parallel with ancient Austronesian patterns, although there was no direct historical connection to human sacrifice in Polynesian societies. But elaborate funerary rites are common to Austronesian cultures, serving to transform the deceased into a deified ancestor. The performance of human sacrifice in the context of grand state funerals may have served to dramatize the transformation of a living human king into an ancestor-god, whose intercession could be sought on behalf of the entire kingdom, as well as for his personal descendants. This association was made explicit by identifying the ancestor temples of the royal dynasty with temples to the mountain gods, thus adding an Austronesian dimension to the royal cult of kingship.

Following Geertz, it is also possible to interpret these rites as grand spectacles organized by rulers whose real powers were waning. Shortly after Oosterwijck's visit, in 1650 the Gelgel dynasty fell. In 1651 a report to the Dutch East India Company in Batavia observed that "all the land is in revolt, everyone alike seeking mastery and wanting to be king."[52] In 1687 a Balinese king sent a letter to the Dutch announcing that he had defeated his enemies and reestablished the Gelgel dynasty in the neighboring village of Klungkung, where he ruled as king of Bali.[53] But despite this claim, in 1693 and again in 1695 he wrote more letters to Batavia requesting weapons and assistance to force his vassals into submission.[54] Thereafter, both Dutch and Balinese sources indicate that the kings of Klungkung never exercised administrative control of the whole island. The most useful Balinese sources for this period are written treaties, some dating to the early eighteenth century, from which it is apparent that henceforth the island was fragmented into several rival kingdoms, with constantly shifting borders. While each little kingdom had a nominal rajah, treaties and alliances between them required the signature of many lesser princes as well as the ruling king.[55]

These princes were constantly at war. The main arena for conflict was the southern rice bowl of Bali, where by the eighteenth century little kingdoms appeared and disappeared on a time scale of decades. Parts of East Java and most of the island of Lombok were conquered and reconquered by Balinese rajahs. Wars of conquest could expand the tax base of kingdoms and also offered the opportunity to capture trading ports

[52] J.K.J. de Jonge and M. L. van Deventer, eds., *De opkomst van het Nederlandsch gezag in Oost-Indie*, 15 vols., 's-Gravengahe: Nijhoff; Amsterdam: Muller, 1862–1909, vol. 4, 24.

[53] Leiden, KITLV, Coll. De Graaf: 8a. For an analysis, see Creese 1991.

[54] Leiden, KITLV, Coll. De Graaf: 8a.

[55] R. van Eck, "Schetsen van het eiland Bali," *Tijdschrift voor Nederlandsch Indie* 7 (1878–80). E. Utrecht: Sedjarah Hukum Internasional di Bali dan Lombok; Bandung: Sumur Bandung, 1962.

and slaves. But according to Dutch reports, most battles were seldom very bloody. Accompanied by a platoon of "screamers" to frighten the enemy, the attackers typically concentrated on capturing people from the borderlands of neighboring kingdoms who could be sold to the European powers as slaves.[56] Seventeenth-century Batavian registers record an average of twenty to one hundred slaves imported from Bali per month.[57] Van der Kraan argues convincingly that slaves became an important source of revenue for Balinese kings but notes that the capacity of slave plantations in Bali to absorb them was not great; most farmland remained in the hands of villagers. The Balinese legal codes provided several sources for new slaves besides war captives: slavery became a punishment for criminals and persons unable to buy their way out of debt. Criminals condemned to death could regain their freedom by headhunting in enemy territory, according to one report.[58]

In 1811 Sir Stamford Raffles visited Bali, and was surprised to discover that the Balinese rajahs were merely one group of landowners among many others: "The sovereign [that is, the rajah of Buleleng] is not here considered the universal landlord; on the contrary, the soil is almost invariably considered as the private property of the subject, in whatever manner it is cultivated or divided."[59] This impression was confirmed a few decades later, when Dutch colonial forces conquered the Balinese kingdom of Buleleng.[60] After the king's surrender, the commander of the Dutch forces, Colonel van Swietan, contemplated the question of whether the colonial government should assume direct rule of the conquered kingdom. The key question was whether by appropriating the defeated king's lands and other sources of income "by right of conquest," sufficient funds would become available to pay for the cost of a colonial administration. The colonel concluded that this would not be the case, because "the most accurate information we have been able to obtain about the Raja's income puts this income at a maximum of 50,000 guilders per year," which was far less than would be required. Moreover,

[56] See Korn 1932: 441, 656.

[57] Alfons van der Kraan, "Bali: Slavery and Slave Trade," in Anthony Reid, ed., *Slavery, Bondage and Dependency in Southeast Asia*, New York: St. Martin's Press, 1983: 315–340.

[58] See Korn 1932: 441; F. A. Liefrinck, *De landsverordeningen der Balische vorsten van Lombok*, Deel 1, 's-Gravenhage: Martinus Nijhoff, 1915: 79.

[59] T. S. Raffles, *The History of Java*, vol. 2, London: Black, Parbury and Allen, 1817: 234.

[60] For historical accounts of this war, see Alfons van der Kraan, *Bali at War: A History of the Dutch-Balinese Conflict*, Victoria, Australia: Monash paper no. 34, Centre for Southeast Asian Studies, Monash University, 1995; Ida Anak Agung Gde Agung, *Bali pada Abad XIX*, Jogyakarta: Gajah Mada University Press, 1989: 499–655; and P. J. Worsley, *Babad Buleleng: A Balinese Dynastic Geneaology*, The Hague: Martinus Nijhoff, 1972.

"there is little prospect of a significant increase in government revenue. The land in Bali is owned by the cultivator and is not, as is the case elsewhere in the archipelago, the property of the sovereign."[61] A few decades later, a senior Dutch administrator, F. A. Liefrinck, carried out a detailed survey of land tenure in the kingdom, confirming that most agricultural land was owned by farmers and managed by subaks, with minimal royal interference. "The explanation of the amazingly high standard of rice cultivation in Bali," he wrote, "is to be found in Montesquieu's conclusion that 'the yield of the soil depends less on its richness than on the degree of freedom enjoyed by those who till it.' "[62]

Having gained a foothold in northern Bali by 1855, the Dutch became increasingly involved with Balinese kingdoms, and by means of treaties and military expeditions gained control of the entire island by 1908.[63] Colonial authority in the conquered Balinese kingdoms was legally based on appropriation of the rights and prerogatives of the defeated kings, invoking the Balinese "war justice."[64] This required the colonial administration to conduct surveys of land ownership and analysis of the legal obligations of villagers to their lords in each little kingdom. Additional surveys were undertaken on the subject of Balinese law, including both internal Brahmanical courts and international treaties, and the "customary law" of the villages. These tasks were faithfully performed, but the results were bewildering. Enormous variation existed in systems of land tenure, law, and the customary obligations of farmers.[65] As Liefrinck observed, a good deal of agricultural land was held as freehold by farmers. But communal land ownership was also common in Bali Aga (old Balinese) villages, and two other patterns of land tenure also existed. The first was direct ownership of scattered tracts of land by kings and noblemen or chiefs (punggawa), which was usually worked by slaves. For example, in the village of Kedisan just south of the water temple that we excavated, a local lord owned about a dozen slaves at the time of the Dutch conquest. These slaves worked his fields and lived in the territory of the village but were not permitted to become members of the village or the subak. They did not participate in village temple festivals, and owed no labor or taxes to the village. Their livelihood was provided by the prince, who also saw to the performance of their religious

[61] Nota Politieke Toestand Van Swieten, Juni 24, 1849, Algemeene Rijksarchief Kol. 1966, The Hague. Quoted and translated in Van der Kraan 1995: 166.

[62] F. A. Liefrinck, "Rice Cultivation in Northern Bali," in J. Swellengrebel, ed., *Bali: Further Studies in Life, Thought, and Ritual*, The Hague: [1886–87] 1969: 3.

[63] See, i.e., I.A.A.G. Agung 1989: 499–655; Geertz 1980; Nordholt 1996.

[64] Korn 1932: 442.

[65] For a summary, see Korn 1932.

rites of passage. But nowhere in Bali did slave plantations become the dominant system of agricultural production.

The second form of land tenure was called *pecatu*, a word deriving from the term for "provision" (*catu*) with the affix *pa-*, meaning a person; thus *pecatu* is a "provisioner." Farmlands conquered in war normally became pecatu, given by the victors to their noble followers. While the farmers thus lost freehold rights to their lands, they retained the right to whatever they could grow from the soil, in return for two types of obligations: a portion of the harvest, and the performance of well-defined duties such as military service and perhaps the delivery of spices, construction materials, or fighting cocks for major festivals at the lord's palace. The nature of these obligations and the extent of agricultural land held as pecatu varied from one village to the next. For example, in the kingdom of Gianyar groups of pecatu holders had very specific duties: some were players of the royal gamelan, others woodworkers, servants, and carriers of lances, guns, or ammunition in battle.[66] Frequently pecatu holders owed various duties to both the lord who owned the pecatu and the king of the realm. Pecatu holders could ordinarily pass these lands on to their sons as an inheritance, but in most cases could not sell or pawn them. Dutch civil servants in the aftermath of the conquest of Bali observed that villagers did their best to "keep the king as much as possible from interfering with the pecatu fields," if necessary taking a lazy farmer in hand and reassigning his land to another villager who would fulfill all the necessary duties. The largest concentrations of pecatu lands were located in the southern rice bowl, where competition among rival rajahs was most intense and land rights were frequently reallocated "by right of conquest." The duties of the pecatu holders were not abolished by the Dutch, but on the contrary were regularized and appropriated by the colonial administration in a series of regulations beginning in 1908. The content of these regulations varied from one kingdom to the next, as did the proportion of land held as pecatu. For example, pecatu holders in the former kingdom of Klungkung were offered the opportunity to buy out their feudal obligations by paying one-third the value of their lands to the Dutch government. But in neighboring Gianyar, the Dutch preferred to retain the right to call up the pecatu farmers for labor services. Thus in 1935 when "His Excellency the Governor General" visited the district, farmers in possession of pecatu lands were called out to guard the road on which the Dutch procession traveled,

---

[66] W. F. van der Kaaden, *Nota van toelichtingen betreffende het in te Stellen Zelfbesturende Landschap Gianyar/Badoeng/Klungkung* (Notes concerning the self-government to be instituted in Gianyar/Badoeng/Klungkung), The Hague: Rijksarchief, 1938.

"for which purpose each had to bring their own little flag that they had paid for themselves." Two years later, when the governor-general made a second visit, the Dutch added a further embellishment: this time eight hundred pecatu holders were called out to guard the road in full ceremonial dress, the cost of their costumes having been paid by another group of pecatu holders. Thus the colonial Dutch struck much the same bargain as the later Balinese kings, allowing the villagers to keep their farms provided they could be counted on act the part of loyal feudal subjects.[67]

The bewildering diversity of Balinese patterns of landholding led to a debate by colonial civil servants on the question of the royal role with regard to irrigation, motivated by the need to determine which revenues could be regarded as fair game for the colonial tax collectors. This debate was summarized by V. E. Korn, a senior offical of the colonial government in Bali, who published a compendious 732-page ethnography of Bali in 1932.[68] Under the heading "Irrigation societies" Korn considers the historical evidence, beginning with the writings of J. Jacobs, who visited Bali in the 1880s: "Even an author like Dr. Julius Jacobs, who has hardly any good words for Bali, feels obliged to express his admiration for the functioning of irrigation on the island. He writes: 'the irrigation works are excellent and the manner for sharing the water among different owners of the sawahs is organized in an exemplary way; each subdivision of these works is under the immediate supervision of the *klijan soebak* [subak head], who cares for the regular sharing of the water, while a *sedahan* takes in the taxes on the water.'" Korn continues: "The care for these excellent irrigation works and the exemplary regular sharing of the water across the sawahs of the various parties who are entitled to it, is almost entirely in the hands of the irrigation societies."[69] Later Korn states, "All water works, with the exception of those built by kings, belonged to the irrigation societies;"[70] also "there is no doubt that the water in the lakes belongs to the gods, and filling the irrigation canals is up to them."[71] But what was the role of the kings? Korn considers the views of the colonial engineer P.L.E. Happé, who saw irrigation as controlled by kings through their *sedahans* (tax collectors), and F. L. Liefrinck, who claimed that the kings gradually increased their role in irrigation by mediating the claims of rival villages.[72] Korn dismisses

[67] A version of this bargain lives on in the World Bank's master plan for tourist development in Bali.

[68] Cf. Korn 1932: 442.

[69] Korn 1932: 251.

[70] Korn 1932: 612.

[71] Korn 1932: 604.

[72] Korn 1932: 252.

Happé's thesis as a "historical fantasy."[73] He sees more merit in Liefrinck's ideas but remarks that "it is clear that here we are dealing with an hypothesis. . . . It seems impossible to us to want to indicate at this point how this development occurred."[74]

CONCLUSION: DISINTEGRATION AND REINTEGRATION

Korn emphasized the breadth of variation in Balinese *adat*, a term that covered everything from the organization of kingdoms and systems of land tenure to the rules governing caste, kinship, religion, economics, and law. He did not attempt to explain the absence of uniformity in Balinese adat, merely observing that the lack of a powerful centralized kingdom over the whole realm was the "great failing" of Balinese kingdoms.[75] Other Dutch scholar-administrators were not so reticent, tailoring colonial policy to fit a historical narrative that depicted nineteenth-century Balinese kingdoms as disintegrating into decadent feudalism. From this perspective the Dutch conquest could be cast in an attractive light as the restoration of a strong centralized government, placing a "protective roofing" over the island, as the senior Dutch official in Bali wrote in 1929.[76] But Korn was too good a scholar to accept these speculations[77] as an explanation for his observations, preferring to set out the pieces of the puzzle with their jagged edges intact.

The explanation I have offered here begins in the distant past, with the remarkable coincidence that, in ancient Bali, the symbolism of Hindu and Buddhist royal cults happened to match the physical landscape. Mythical imagery of a cosmic mountain at the center of the world, and of water with the power to bring forth life, became an empirical reality when the farmers began to construct irrigation systems on real Balinese volcanoes. Whereas in Java the center of state power gravitated to the great rivers and broad plains of the east, the rugged topography of Bali precluded the construction of large-scale irrigation systems like those of Java and the other large wet-rice kingdoms of Southeast Asia. Instead the Balinese perfected a new kind of intensive microengineering. The first Balinese irrigation systems were probably simple canals channeling water from natural springs into adjacent valleys. But as our archaeological investigations at the Gunung Kawi spring showed, the farmers soon

---

[73] Korn 1932: 272–73; see also 111.
[74] Korn 1932: 604–5.
[75] Korn 1932: 307.
[76] ARA MvO Resident L.J.J. Caron 1929.
[77] Korn 1932: 273.

began to transport excess water to distant sites by building tunnels, canals, and aqueducts. Their techniques could deliver small quantities of water with astonishing accuracy to terraces located several kilometers from a water source. Rice cultivation spread as small teams of skilled workers drew the water out in long spidery threads that crisscrossed the slopes of the sacred mountains, creating new, vital connections between villages.

Rice paddies are artificial ponds, which must be kept flooded while the plants are growing and then dried out for harvest. This imposes strict requirements for the management of irrigation water, and puts downstream communities at the mercy of upstream neighbors who are in a position to control the flow. Yet the majority of Balinese rice-farming communities are located downstream from others—often at a great distance from their water source—so a workable solution to this problem must have been discovered fairly quickly. Conceivably the solution could have been control by court officials. Instead, farmers organized themselves into self-governing groups and created a new type of temple network to coordinate irrigation. The sheer number of these small-scale irrigation systems and the need for continuous, intensive management would have made it difficult for state functionaries to control them. Instead, the rulers sensibly chose to leave the farmers in control, while taxing the fruits of their labors.

By the twelfth century, at a time when the neighboring kingdoms of Java were entering an imperial phase, the powers of Balinese kings had begun to wane. In Java, the centralization of power was facilitated by depriving the local chiefs of their tax base, and by royal patronage for a burgeoning class of professional clergy who owed allegiance to the king. The growth of the rural population and the expansion of irrigated rice production generated revenues that were funneled into support for the enterprises of the royal court, including the construction of roads, canals, temples, and monastic retreats. Twelfth-century Javanese tax collectors no longer had to contend with the councils of the *wanua* (ancient villages); those councils had ceased to exist. After their deaths, the later Javanese kings were immortalized as incarnations of Hindu and Buddhist gods in towering stone temples that imitated the shape of the cosmic mountain.[78]

In Bali, events took a different course. There is no evidence that early Balinese kings saw a need to weaken either the wanua or local chiefs.

---

[78] By the fourteenth century, Javanese kings were covering the slopes of a nearby mountain (Mount Penanggunang), whose conical shape resembled Mount Meru, with more than eighty sacred monuments. Nigel Bullough, *Historic East Java: Remains in Stone*, Singapore: East Java Tourism Promotion Foundation, 1995: 99.

Instead, the kings interacted directly with the governing councils of the wanua, which channeled taxes to royal functionaries. Later on, the success of the subak system enlarged the tax base but weakened the village councils, as agricultural land was privatized and its management taken out of their hands. The councils of the wanua were dealt a further blow by the spread of the ideology of caste, which was antithetical to a republican system of governance. The spread of both subaks and caste involved ambitious programs of temple construction, but these were carried out by the villagers, not the kings, and bore little resemblance to the imposing stone monuments of an earlier era.

Yet the end of the era of royal temples in Bali was merely a sign of the weakening of Balinese kingship. The immediate cause was the appearance of a new class of feudal gentry, who took advantage of the decline of the wanua to create their own base of support in the countryside. I suggest that the seeds of this development can be traced to the ancient system of tax farming, which empowered local officials to collect taxes directly from the villages. When the wanua councils lost control of productive land, they could no longer be held to account by the kings. The disintegration of the old centralized system of tax farming created an opportunity for local chiefs or officials to collect taxes directly from individual farmers. With the development of the *pecatu* system of quasi-feudal relationships, the gentry class acquired permanent rights to parcels of land. Thenceforth, kings no longer asserted their rights to a stream of taxes from the wanua. Instead, they bestowed pecatu rights to specific land parcels on their followers. Having lost command of a centralized system of taxation, the kings themselves became members of the gentry class, supported by pecatu lands as well as small latifundia that they owned outright. But as these plantations never grew very large, it appears that the large-scale replacement of peasants by slaves was found to be unworkable.

Eventually the pecatu system produced a baroque complexity of rights to land and labor in the Balinese countryside. Conquest or successful rebellion enabled a victorious lord to reallocate pecatu rights to his followers, and also produced war captives who could be sold as slaves. From the late seventeenth century, the rulers of Bali were almost continuously at war, if not with one another then with rebellious lords in their own domains. The pecatu system enabled the spoils of war to be divided into tiny fragments, which could be doled out to reward coalitions of followers. This produced a welter of claims on the lands and labor of the farmers. Writing about Balinese kingdoms of the nineteenth century, Clifford Geertz observes that "one of the more exotic results of this was that it was possible for a man to be a *kawula* (subject) of one lord, to be a land tenant of a second, and to pay taxes to a third . . . there was no unitary government, weak or powerful, over the whole realm at all."[79] The most valuable pecatu lands were those in close proximity to the larger palaces in the rice-growing regions of the south, where competition was keenest. Mountain villages located above the elevation where rice could be grown were often simply ignored.

Competition among the gentry was fueled by the productivity of the pecatu lands, which produced the most abundant harvests in the archipelago. Claims on the surplus harvests and labor of the farmers could be reallocated as the fortunes of the gentry rose and fell. But the farmers and subaks were left in control of the fields and irrigation systems. The villages became theaters for a different sort of contest, between the egalitarian ethos of the subaks and the hierarchical ideals of the caste system. The penetration of caste into the villages was given additional impetus by the gentry, who chose particular descent groups to provide agents for mobilizing the pecatu holders to fulfill their obligations. These agents were awarded titles and privileges signifying their elevated status, which became hereditary. In this way members of some descent groups in the villages achieved the lower ranks of gentry status. The effects of this stimulus for status competition can be seen in the proliferation of gradations in rites of passage signaling differences in rank, and also in the popularization of registers for the core vocabulary of the Balinese language. This was not a matter of creating a distinct dialect to be spoken in the courts (as for example in Japanese). Instead, to speak ordinary Balinese one must constantly indicate status differences with respect to speaker, hearers, and those of whom one speaks.

Differences in inherited rank or "caste" are anchored in membership in the ranked origin temple networks. These "caste" or origin temples resemble the water temples of the subaks in that the organizational principle is the same for both: descent from a sacred origin. The similarity between the two types of branching temple networks extends even into the fine details of their rituals, because the rites of the agricultural cult are based on a metaphor equating the growth of the rice plant with that of a person. The two types of temples are so similar that a Balinese farmer visiting a neighboring village could have difficulty distinguishing a water temple from that of a descent group. Given this degree of similarity, it is perhaps ironic that the two temple networks enshrine opposite principles of social order: social equality and shared responsibility in water temples, versus hierarchy in caste temples.[80] The irony deepens when we recall that water temples, caste temples, and village temples were all offspring of

---

[79] Geertz 1980: 68.

[80] This contrast, which as we have seen was a major theme in Geertz 1980, is further investigated by Carol Warren in *Adat and Dinas: Balinese Communities in the Indonesian*

the ancient royal cult, because it was precisely these institutions that gradually marginalized kingship while at the same time accomplishing most of its goals. Thanks to the development of these village-based temple networks, irrigation systems spread across the landscape and achieved a very high level of functional integration, perhaps surpassing that of ancient Java or Cambodia. Similarly, beliefs and practices associated with the Hindu caste system, complete with a rich panoply of Brahmanic ritual, took root in the countryside. All the core projects of the ancient royal cult of kingship succeeded—except kingship itself.

State (Kuala Lumpur: Oxford University Press, 1993). More recently, Arlette Ottino has emphasized the competition among commoner kinsmen to convert symbolic and material resources into the sort of status that is indexed by temples, rites of passage, titles, and other honorifics: "the egalitarian discourse of high-ranking commoner groups is contradicted by their own matrimonial practices which recall those of the gentry." Ottino, "Revisiting Kinship in Bali: Core-lines and the emergence of elites in commoner groups." *Asia Pacific Journal of Anthropology* 4, nos. 1 and 2, (2003): 25–53.

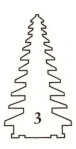

The Emergence of Cooperation on
Water Mountains

THE IRRIGATION SYSTEM that provides the water to flood the Sebatu water mountain begins at a dam several kilometers upstream, deep in a valley carved by the Petanu River. The dam allows a third of the river to flow downstream, where it is captured by other subaks, and shunts the rest into a tunnel. The tunnel parallels the river but gains a little elevation, so that when it emerges a few kilometers downstream, it is at the top of the Sebatu water mountain. The flow from the tunnel is immediately divided in two: one canal floods the Sebatu rice terraces; the other begins a circuitous journey across the landscape, dipping into forested ravines and sometimes tunneling for as much as half a kilometer through the soft volcanic rock. From time to time a portion of the flow is diverted to downstream subaks, strung along the irrigation line like melons on a vine. The canals and wooden flow dividers are physically fragile. Merely by tossing an innocent-looking rock or a log into the water above a divider, an unscrupulous farmer could steal water by blocking the flow into a neighbor's fields. Yet farmers on distant downstream water mountains can apparently rely on a steady supply of irrigation water, and so could their grandfathers. In a dry year, the farmers in the upper subaks admit that they are often tempted to take a little more water. But such cheating is rare, and usually occurs only in the tiny canals that feed individual plots. So the strength of the social bonds between farmers and subaks must compensate for the fragility of the canals, tunnels, aqueducts, and dividers. One could say that the very existence of the downstream water mountains is a tribute to the generosity of their upstream neighbors.

Might these farmers possess an extra gene for altruism? If so, its effects are most conspicuously on display at the subak meetings. Everyone who owns paddy fields on a water mountain must belong to the local subak. This group has responsibility for maintaining the local irrigation works and for choosing an irrigation schedule. Decisions are made by consensus; anyone who fails to attend subak meetings or work assignments is subject to fines and penalties levied by the collective. The most severe sanction is to cut off someone's water supply or expel the offender from the subak. The subak also elects a leader who attends monthly meetings of fourteen subak heads, which together form the congregation of a regional water temple called Pura Masceti Pamos Apuh, which I will call the Pamos water temple. This group also makes decisions by consensus; it has the power to levy fines and can cut off the water supply for an entire subak if its members do not keep up with their responsibilities. The system works well enough that several thousand people on fourteen water mountains depend on it for their livelihood.

But if an engineer working for a development organization such as the World Bank were to propose building an irrigation system based on this design, the project would certainly be vetoed by the social scientists, who would probably recommend that the engineer read Garret Hardin's classic paper on the "tragedy of the commons." As the reader may recall, in Hardin's original formulation of this problem, some medieval English villages possessed a shared pasture, or "commons." Because the commons belonged to everyone, anyone could bring an animal there to graze. If a farmer added an extra sheep, the advantage was all on his side, since the disadvantages of overgrazing were shared by the whole community. The only way for the other villagers to make up their loss would be to add more animals of their own. But then, as a result of overgrazing, the commons would disappear. In the Balinese version of this predicament, the common resource is irrigation water. Nearly everyone could grow more rice if they took a little extra water, but should they yield to this temptation, the resulting chaos would disrupt the water supply for everyone except the farmers whose paddies lay closest to the main canals. During the Green Revolution, this actually occurred in many villages. The same dynamics are apparent in the shifting fortunes of the communal coffeepot in our lab: from one semester to the next, whether there is a reliable supply of coffee depends on the relative proportion of altruists and free riders in the group.

The "tragedy of the commons" has been extensively studied by social scientists, and has had an immense impact on public policy. Economists have seized on it as an argument for privatization: the problem with the commons, they say, is precisely that it is held in common, so the solution is to divide it into individually owned parcels. In cases where this is not possible, there are two other possible solutions: either an external coercive authority that enforces the rules governing shared access, or a system based on reciprocity (I fill the coffeepot today, and it's your turn tomorrow). But direct reciprocity will not work for the subaks, because the downstream subaks can never reciprocate. Since it appears that there is no external coercive authority to protect the water rights of the downstream subaks, their very existence becomes rather puzzling; all the more so since irrigation water is an extremely valuable commodity that is often in scarce supply.

This chapter describes our search for an explanation for the existence of the downstream subaks (that is to say, for the patterns of cooperation that enable the water mountains to function). If neither external authority nor reciprocity provide the solution, what does?

LIVE AND LET LIVE

A useful starting place is Robert Axelrod's famous analysis of the emergence of cooperation between groups of frontline soldiers who faced each other across the trenches of the Western Front in World War One. Axelrod wondered how cooperation could have developed between groups of men who could not converse and were in fact trying to kill each other. His approach was to try to identify the strategic choices each group faced in dealing with its opponents across No Man's Land. Thus a vigorous assault at an unexpected time might lead to a victory, with many enemy dead. But the same option was also available to the enemy. Alternatively, if each group only pretended to attack, and made its artillery fire completely predictable, its opponents would have time to take cover. If both sides adopted this strategy, neither side would suffer casualties. In terms of the available options, while a successful attack is the best possible outcome, to be a victim of such an attack is clearly the worst, and "live and let live" falls somewhere in between. For a "live and let live" strategy to work, each side must trust the other. Such informal truces broke out repeatedly along the trenches, and became a major headache for the high command on both sides.

Axelrod suggested that the underlying dynamics of the "live and let live" system could be represented as a game. The advantage to such formalization is that it becomes possible to compare the World War One case with other unlikely instances of spontaneous cooperation, to see if similar processes are involved. It turns out that if one represents the problem in this way, it is logically identical to the "tragedy of the commons." This game is called the Prisoner's Dilemma. As the story goes, two prisoners are each given the choice of giving evidence against the other and so reducing their own sentence. The dilemma arises because if they cooperate with each other, the police can convict them both only on a lesser

TABLE 1
The Prisoner's Dilemma

	Player 2: Cooperate	Player 2: Defect
Player 1: Cooperate	3, 3	0, 5
Player 1: Defect	5, 0	1, 1

charge. But if one defects (by giving evidence to the police), he goes free while the other goes to jail. If both defect, both will receive slightly less than the maximum penalty. These choices and their respective payoffs are represented in table 1. Here the rewards are scaled from zero (maximum sentence, the worst) to five (going free, the best). Mathematician Karl Sigmund suggests that the game becomes more interesting if we think of these payoffs as gold bars, not "measly little numbers." In table 1, the paired numbers refer to the payoffs: the first number is the payoff for Player 1, and the second for Player 2. So if Player 1 cooperates and so does Player 2, the payoff for each is three, as shown in the top left. But if Player 1 cooperates and Player 2 defects (top right), Player 1 receives the "sucker's payoff" of zero, while the unscrupulous Player 2 reaps the maximum reward: five gold bars (or a ticket out of jail in the original anecdote).

The problem is that the optimal strategies for each player create the worst possible joint outcome. Thus if the other player defects, you are better off defecting (you get one bar instead of none). If the other player cooperates, you are still better off defecting (you get five bars, he gets none). So, cold logic indicates that the best strategy is always to defect. But because the same logic holds for the other player, the likely outcome is mutual defection, and everyone loses. The chief advantage to defining the problem in this way (as a simple game) is that can help to reveal the essence of the problem. Indeed one can see that the "tragedy of the commons" is another instance of exactly the same game. All fishermen would be better off if they exercised voluntary restraint and did not take too many fish. But in such a situation, an unscrupulous fisherman who decides to take more fish will reap greater rewards than the "suckers" who take only their share.

Game theorists suggest that the tragedy of mutual defection can be avoided only if players understand themselves to be in a situation where continuing cooperation can pay off, because the circumstances of the game will recur. In other words, it is worthwhile to cooperate with me today provided I am in a position to repay you by cooperating tomorrow. In the trenches of World War One, according to an anecdote Axelrod relates, artillery from the German side opened up at an unexpected time and killed some British soldiers, thus violating the implicit agreement. Some Germans came out under a flag of truce to apologize and promise that the mistake would not happen again. Subsequent studies have emphasized the wide applicability of the Prisoner's Dilemma. For example, sociologists have compared the behavior of drivers in large cities versus small towns and villages. Shaking one's fist at other drivers, honking the horn, and other acts of rudeness are more frequent in big-city traffic, perhaps because drivers in cities can assume that they are anonymous.[1]

But cooperation between groups of farmers on Balinese water mountains is not a Prisoner's Dilemma, for several reasons. First, the downstream farmers are never in a position to reciprocate. Second, the payoff is different. In Axelrod's example, the reward for cooperation is cooperation itself: a truce between soldiers. But in the Balinese case, the reward comes from nature in the form of better harvests. Cooperation is only a means to that end. And finally, cooperation occurs not only between farmers in a subak but among clusters of subaks; otherwise the downstream water mountains could not exist. In other words, there is a hierachical structure of cooperating groups: farmers cooperate with farmers, and subaks with subaks. If the farmers behaved as if they were in a Prisoner's Dilemma, the upstream farmers would take all the water they wanted, and their downstream neighbors would have to make do with whatever was left. But in reality, the downstream farmers can apparently rely on receiving their fair share. What prevents these systems from falling victim to the tragedy of the commons?

A Game Played with Nature

In the past, most anthropologists have tended to give formal models from game theory a wide berth. Such models represent a kind of drastic reductionism that runs against the grain of our preferred methods of interpretive cultural analysis. Since many of my readers may share this view, let me suggest some reasons why this argument may be worthy of their attention. First, on a conceptual level, it can be helpful to consider the ways in which cooperation among Balinese farmers is unlike a Prisoner's Dilemma. In this sense the model is merely an heuristic device, a way to disentangle the social aspects of cooperation from the environmental and historical context. Second, as will become clear as the argument proceeds, analyzing the problem of cooperation at this level of abstraction suggests a possible explanation for the emergence of higher-level social

---

[1] Karl Sigmund, *Games of Life: Explorations in Ecology, Evolution and Behavior*, New York and London: Penguin Books, 1993, chap. 8.

Figure 11. Flooded rice terraces. Synchronized flooding after harvests deprives rice pests of habitat and food.

institutions from small-scale, local interactions. Bear with the formalism, and rewards may come in the form of a richer understanding of cultural processes.

We need a simple model that will predict the circumstances in which cooperation among farmers will be rewarded, and when it will fail. A colleague at the Santa Fe Institute, economist John Miller, suggested that the simplest case involves two players: an upstream farmer, who by virtue of his location controls water flow, and a downstream farmer, who needs some of this water. To simplify the problem, let's assume that these players can adopt one of two possible cropping patterns, A and B (for example, A could mean planting in January and May, while B means planting in February and June). Further assume that the water supply is adequate for both players only if they stagger their cropping pattern. If both plant at the same time, the downstream farmer will experience water shortages, and his harvests will be somewhat reduced. So far, the model would seem to leave the upstream farmer in a position to control the game. But as noted earlier, Balinese farmers also use their control over water to reduce the populations of rice pests, such as insects and rats. When the farmers can schedule simultaneous harvests over large areas, pests are deprived of their habitat and their numbers will be reduced (figure 11). To capture this effect in the model, assume that pest damage

TABLE 2
A game of cooperation between rice farmers

	Downstream A	Downstream B
Upstream A	$1, 1 - w$	$1 - p, 1 - p$
Upstream B	$1 - p, 1 - p$	$1, 1 - w$

will be higher if plantings are staggered (because the pests can migrate from one field to another), and lower if plantings are synchronized (more pests will go hungry). Let p $(0 < p < 1)$ represent the damage caused by pests, and w $(0 < w < 1)$ represent the damage caused by water shortage. Given these assumptions, the payoffs are as shown in Table 2.

Here the first number in each quadrant is the payoff (harvest) for the upstream farmer, and the second is the harvest for the downstream farmer. Thus, if both farmers plant on the same schedule (either A or B), the harvest for the upstream farmer is 1, but it is $1 - w$ for the downstream farmer because of insufficient irrigation water. If the two farmers choose different schedules (upstream choosing A and downstream choosing B, or vice versa), then each farmer achieves a harvest of $1 - p$. Staggered schedules will eliminate water stress but allow the pests to survive by migrating between the upstream and downstream fields.

We can immediately draw several conclusions about the payoffs for alternative strategies. The upstream farmers are never affected by water stress, but their downstream neighbors may be. (This is known to planners as the "tail-ender" problem: the farmers at the tail end of an irrigation system are at the mercy of their neighbors upstream, who control the irrigation flow.) However, the upstream farmers *do* care about pest damage, because pests, unlike water, can move upstream. So a strategy of synchronized cropping patterns to control pests will always produce higher yields for the upstream subaks. When $p > w$, the downstream farmers will also achieve higher yields by synchronizing. Note that if they do so the aggregate harvest is higher (i.e., the total harvest for both farmers goes up). If $p < w$, the upstream farmers do better by staggered planting, which eliminates their water shortage. Interestingly, when $w > p > w/2$, adding more pests to the fields until $p > w$ actually increases the aggregate harvest for the pair of subaks, because it encourages the upstream farmer to cooperate in a synchronized schedule (even though he must give up some water). But if the farmers are not worried about pests, the upstream player has no incentive to give up some of his water.

Based on this logic, behavior in accordance with the model may be predicted. In general, the downstreamers should prefer greater offsets in irrigation schedules, and be willing to accept higher losses from pests as a result, up to the point where pest damage becomes worse than water stress ($p > w$). The upstreamers, at that point, should be willing to give up some of their water to enable the downstreamers to synchronize their irrigation schedule. Both then benefit from a coordinated fallow period, and consequently fewer pests. Put another way, the presence of pests in the ecosystem gives the downstream farmers a bargaining lever to persuade their upstream neighbors to give them the water they need to avoid shortages.[2]

How well does this simple model capture the actual basis for decision making by the farmers? In the summer of 1998, we carried out a survey of farmers in ten subaks that belonged to the congregation of the Pamos water temple. In each of the ten subaks, we chose a random sample of fifteen farmers. Of these fifteen, five were selected whose fields were located in the upstream part of their subak; five more from the middle of the subak, and the last five from the downstream section of the subak. To test the predictions of the game, we simply asked, "Which problem is worse, damage from pests or irrigation water shortages?" The results, shown in figure 12, show that the upstream farmers worried more about pests, while the downstream farmers were more concerned about water shortages.

The same dynamics can occur at the next higher level of organization. Not only individual farmers but whole subaks must decide whether or not to cooperate. In our sample, six of the ten subaks were situated in upstream/downstream pairs, in which the downstream subak obtained most of its water from its upstream neighbor. Thus it was also possible to compare the aggregate response of all the farmers in each downstream subak to the response of their upstream neighbors. Figure 13 shows this result.

Here also, the upstream farmers were more concerned with potential damage from pests than from water shortages, and so had a reason to cooperate with downstream neighbors. By adjusting their own irrigation flows to help achieve $w < p$ for their downstream neighbors, the upstream subaks had the power to promote a solution that was beneficial for everyone. In the real world, losses from pest outbreaks can quickly approach 100 percent after a few seasons of unsynchronized cropping schedules. In contrast, reducing one's irrigation flow by 5 or 10 percent (or using one's labor to reduce seepage losses in an irrigation system and so improve its efficiency) imposes lesser costs on the farmers, unless water is very scarce indeed. These results are also supported by our video-

---

[2] For a fuller analysis of these dynamics, see J. Stephen Lansing and John H. Miller, "Cooperation Games and Ecological Feedback: Some Insights from Bali," *Current Anthropology*, in press (February 2005).

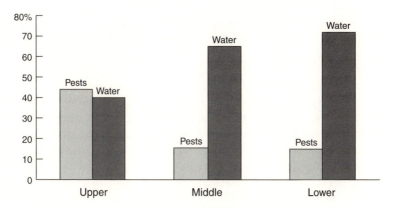

Figure 12. Which is worse, pests or water shortages? (individuals).
Relationship of the location of a farmer's fields to his views on the relative importance of losses from pests or water shortages, based on a sample survey of 150 farmers in 10 subaks in the Sebatu region.

taped records of monthly meetings in which the heads of all ten subaks (plus four others not included in the survey) discuss intersubak affairs. The willingness of upstream subaks to synchronize cropping patterns appears to be clearly related to the perceived threat of pest invasions. It

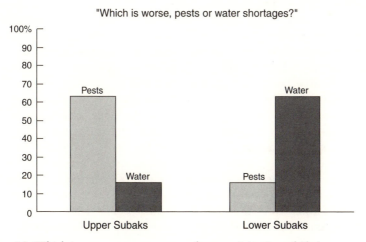

Figure 13. Which is worse, pests or water shortages? (entire subaks).
Aggregate responses of 90 farmers in 3 upstream subaks and 3 downstream subaks.

is important to note that which subaks synchronize cropping plans with their neighbors varies from year to year. An increased threat of pest damage, such as has occured recently in several cycles of pest infestations (brown leafhoppers, rice tungro virus) quickly leads to larger sychronized groups, whereas a period of light rains encourages greater fragmentation.

We drew two conclusions from this study. First, a very simple model appears to capture the essence of the trade-offs involved in decisions about cooperation among the farmers. Thus the model suggests an ecological basis for long-term patterns of cooperation. Second, the same dynamics recur at the group level, which provides a possible explanation for the aggregation of farmers into subaks, and subaks into multi-subak groups. In computer simulations of the game with multiple players and realistic ecology, this is exactly what occurs. Groups of subaks begin by experimentally cooperating with a neighbor or two, which helps to control the pests and stabilize irrigation flows. Within a few years, clusters of subaks form that interact with other clusters. Soon pest outbreaks and water shortages are minimized for the entire watershed. In other words, by iterating the model we can watch the formation of clusters of subaks. As these clusters appear and adjust their borders, average harvests steadily improve. Observing this process, we noticed one more phenomenon that might have a bearing on the persistence of cooperation among real farmers. The simulation models show how average rice harvests increase throughout the watershed as cooperation spreads, bringing pests and water under effective control. But such a process might contain the seeds for conflict. One of the threats to cooperation is envy, stemming from a disparity in benefits. It may not matter that you and I will both benefit from cooperation, if I believe that your share of the benefits will be greater than mine. Thus it was necessary to ask whether the emergence of cooperation was associated with a perceptible variation in harvests that could produce feelings of envy among the less fortunate.

In the simulation model, the answer is clear. As cooperation spreads, differences between harvests dwindle. Soon everyone obtains nearly identical yields, which average out to be nearly twice as good as they were before cooperation began (figure 14). As for the real world, in the same survey we asked the farmers to compare their own harvests with those of their neighbors. The results are quite clear: 97 percent of the farmers responded that their own harvest was about the same as the harvests of the other farmers in their subak. This is also confirmed by our measurements of actual harvest yields, which were typically uniform in cooperative subaks. In the region where we conducted this survey, variance in yields from test plots seldom exceeded 5 percent. But when asked how

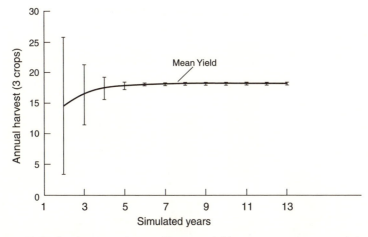

Figure 14. Reduction in variance of harvest yields as cooperation spreads in the simulation model of the Oos and Petanu subaks. Rainfall, rice, and pest parameters based on data collected by Lansing and Kremer in 1988.

their harvests compared with those of farmers elswhere in Bali, opinions were randomly distributed (figure 15). This suggests that the farmers were merely guessing about other subaks. But within each subak, farmers perceived harvests to be equal.

Thus, with the aid of the model, we appear to have captured the trade-offs that are involved when farmers and subaks decide whether or not to synchronize cropping patterns with their neighbors. But how do the decisions made by interacting pairs of subaks lead to regionwide cropping patterns that apparently optimize conditions for everyone? To answer this question we need to shift our attention from the interaction of pairs of autonomous agents (the upstream and downstream subaks in the two-player game) to the entire dynamical system; in this case all the subaks in a watershed. Intuitively, this is reasonable because the actual flow of water in the rivers and irrigation systems will depend on the cropping schedules set by all the subaks, not just pairs of subaks. We speculated that the patterns of cooperation (synchronization of cropping patterns) among the subaks could be the outcome of a historical process in which the subaks sought to find the best balance between water sharing and pest control. Using empirical data on the location, size, and field conditions of 172 subaks in the watershed of the Oos and Petanu rivers in southern Bali in 1987–88, we modeled changes in the flow of irrigation water and the growth of rice and pests as subaks decided whether to cooperate with their neighbors. Here each subak

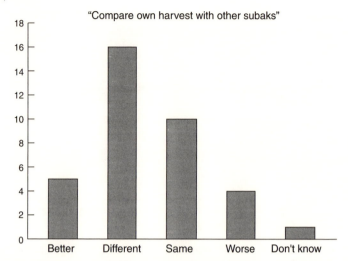

Figure 15. Farmers' views on their own yields relative to other subaks. "How does your rice harvest compare to harvests in other subaks?"
Responses from 150 farmers belonging to 10 subaks in the Sebatu area.

behaves as an "adaptive agent" that seeks to improve its harvest by imitating the cropping pattern of more successful neighbors.[3]

In this model, we simulate the flow of water from the headwaters of the two rivers to the sea, at monthly intervals. The amount of water available for any given subak depends on seasonal patterns of rainfall and groundwater flow, and on the amount of water diverted by upstream subaks for their own needs. As a new year begins, each of the 172 subaks is given a planting schedule that determines which crops it will grow and when they will be planted. As the months go by, water flows, crops grow, and pests migrate across the landscape. When a subak harvests its crop, the model tabulates losses due to water shortages or pests. At the end of the year, aggregate harvest yields are calculated for the subaks. Subsequently, each subak checks to see whether any of its closest neighbors got higher yields. If so, the target subak copies the cropping schedule of its (best) neighbor. If none of the neighbors got better yields, the target subak retains its existing schedule. When all the subaks have made their decisions, the model cycles through another year. These simulations begin with a random distribution of cropping

[3] J. S. Lansing and J. N. Kremer, "Emergent Properties of Balinese Water Temples," in Christopher Langton, ed., *Artificial Life III*, vol 10, 201–25, Redwood City, Calif.: Addison-Wesley and the Santa Fe Institute Studies in the Sciences of Complexity, 1994: 212.

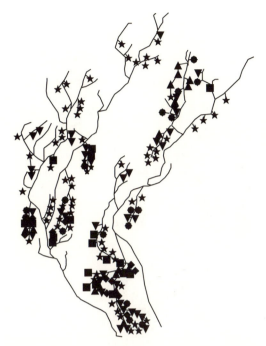

Figure 16. Initial conditions for a simulation model of irrigation flows and rice and pest growth for 172 subaks. Differences in cropping patterns are indicated by different symbols (subaks with the same symbols have identical cropping patterns).

patterns (a typical example is shown in figure 16). After a year the subaks in the model begin to aggregate into patches following identical cropping patterns, which helps to reduce pest losses. As time goes on, these patches grow until their simultaneous needs for water cause shortages. Soon patch sizes become smaller. Yields fluctuate but gradually rise. The program continues until most subaks have discovered an optimal cropping pattern, meaning that they cannot do better by imitating one of their neighbors.

Experiments with this model indicate that the entire collection of subaks quickly settles down into a stable pattern of synchronized cropping schedules that optimizes both pest control and water sharing (figure 17). The close similarity between this pattern as calculated in the model (figure 17) and the actual pattern of synchronized planting units (figure 18) is apparent. In the model, as patterns of coordination resembling the water temple networks emerge, both the mean harvest yield and the highest

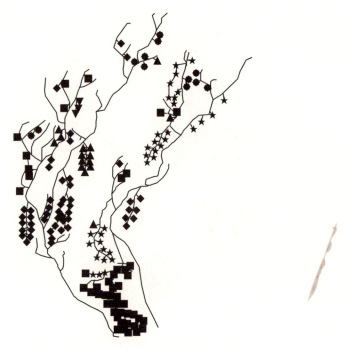

Figure 17. Model cropping patterns after 11 simulated years.

yield increase (figure 19), while variance in yield across subaks declines (see figure 14). In other words, after just a few years of local experimentation, yields rise for everyone and variation in yields declines. Subsequent simulations showed that if the environment is perturbed, either by decreasing rainfall or by increasing the virulence of pests, a few subaks change their cropping patterns, but within a few years a new equilibrium is achieved.[4]

In summary, although the "tail-ender problem" leads to a tragedy of the commons, making the model a little more realistic by considering pests as well as water creates a different game, in which both cooperation and mutual defection may occur. In this game, decisions about cooperation are influenced by the relative magnitude of the two relevant ecological factors, and these in turn are affected by where one's fields are located. This creates a coupled system in which the players' decisions influence local ecological conditions, which in turn affect the payoff for cooperation in the next planting season. Survey data suggest that the farmers' perceptions are in accord with this model. Moreover, a more re-

[4] Lansing and Kremer 1994: 215–16.

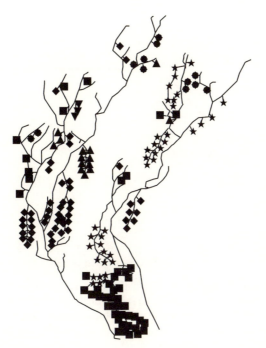

Figure 18. Actual observed cropping patterns (1987).

alistic simulation model based on this logic shows that if all the subaks in a watershed play this game with their immediate neighbors, cooperation will quickly spread, to their mutual benefit, and generate a pattern of synchronized cropping that closely resembles actual historical patterns of cooperation. We have moved from the world of the Prisoner's Dilemma, which is concerned only with people, to one in which the physical and social environments form a single coupled system, with dynamics that unfold over time.

What should we conclude from these results? (After all, a skeptic might point out that it is not difficult to coax computers to create realistic-looking simulations!) Perhaps a brief digression on the "real world" is appropriate here. On the advice of consultants from the Asian Development Bank, in the 1970s the Indonesian government performed an experiment on the subaks of Bali, in which the traditional patterns of synchronized planting were deliberately disrupted in the interests of boosting rice production. All farmers were instructed to plant rice as often as they could, preferably three times a year. In other words, the initial chaotic conditions for our computer model (see figure 16) were deliberately imposed. The Bank now acknowledges that the results were catastrophic:

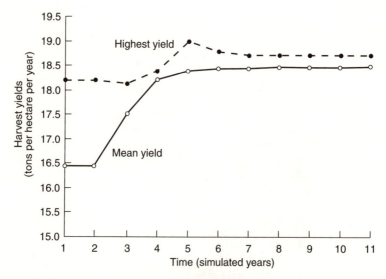

Figure 19. Increase in harvest yields in the Bali irrigation model. Variance in yields also declines, as the yields converge toward the (rising) mean. In further experiments we varied the virulence of the pests. Highly virulent pests produce large blocks of coordinated cropping. But if pests are not very damaging, there is little coordination between subaks.

pest populations exploded and caused losses of up to 100 percent, while irrigation flows became chaotic. Balinese farmers remember this episode today as a time of harvest failures and hunger. It was only when the farmers spontaneously returned to cooperative synchronized planting schemes that harvests recovered, and the government ended the campaigns of aerial pesticide spraying. Downstream subaks naturally suffered the heaviest losses from water stress, but their upstream neighbors often found that even heavy doses of pesticide could not save their harvests. At the time, consultants interpeted these events as unfortunate but unpredictable acts of God.[5] The model suggests a different explanation. It is as if the Bank had persuaded the farmers to run our simulations backward, from figures 17 and 18 back toward the initial conditions of figure 16, disrupting the patterns of cooperation among subaks and making the environment more chaotic. In fact, from an analytical standpoint this policy might be considered as a real-world test of our conceptual model, which strengthens our confidence that we have captured the essential

[5] See the correspondence and reports from the Asian Development Bank summarized in chapters 1 and 5 of my book *Priests and Programmers: Technologies of Power in the Engineered Landscape of Bali*, Princeton, N.J.: Princeton University Press, 1991.

dynamics of the cooperation among farmers thats permit water mountains to exist.

But the very fact of such close agreement between the model and reality raises a deeper question. Why should the actual patterns of cooperative planting observed on the landscape bear such a close resemblance to computer simulations of optimal solutions? It is as if the Balinese gods had agreed to balance their respective powers over pests and water in such a way as to promote cooperation by the farmers. But did they have any choice in the matter? If we could rewind the tape of history and begin again a few centuries ago, how likely is it that similar networks of subaks and water temples would develop?

Answers to such historical questions might appear to be forever out of reach. But recent work in the mathematical theory of dynamical systems offers some insights. In the model, each subak is treated as an autonomous agent that reacts to information from its immediate neighborhood (which of my closest neighbors got the best harvest?). The whole network of subaks can be viewed as a "complex adaptive system": a group of actors or agents engaged in a process of coadaptation, in which adaptive moves by individuals have consequences for their neighbors. The concept of complex adaptive systems (CAS) was developed by John Holland, who proposes as examples such disparate phenomena as automobile traffic in a city, species in an ecosystem, investors in stock markets, and even immune systems. Clearly, the concept of a CAS is at a very high level of abstraction. But Holland and others have shown that viewing these diverse examples as instances of a class of CAS permits us to ask some penetrating questions about their expected patterns of behavior.[6] This idea was mentioned briefly in the introduction; now it is time to fill in the details. What one hopes to gain from this type of analysis is an understanding of typical patterns of behavior: what should we *expect* the subak model to do? How sensitive is the overall behavior of the model to the fine details of watershed ecology or the choices made by farmers?

As before, we begin by simplifying the problem. In the model of the Oos and Petanu rivers, every subak has a physical location that determines who will be its neighbors. After each harvest, subaks check with their four closest neighbors to find out whether any of them have a better cropping plan. If so, the subak copies its (best) neighbor's plan. But what if each subak compares itself with only one neighbor, or with twelve neighbors, or fifty-seven? Does the richness of the local connections among the subaks affect the ability of the entire network to minimize

---

[6] Simon A. Levin, "Complex Adaptive Systems: Exploring the Known, the Unknown and the Unknowable," *Bull. Amer. Math. Soc.* 40, no. 1 (2002): 3–19.

losses from pests and water shortages? This question—the connectedness of the subaks in the model—can be considered apart from the question of the ecological problem they are trying to solve. It turns out that
the behavior of the network—whether it is capable of solving problems
like pest control—is critically dependent on the structure of connections
between the subaks. In other words, the structure of the network matters. In his book *The Origins of Order* (1993), biologist Stuart Kauffman provides an elegant example to explain why this should be the case.
Imagine a collection of N Christmas tree lights. Each bulb has one of
two possible states, on or off, and is wired to k other bulbs. A simple
rule tells each bulb what to do. For example, set $k = 3$, meaning that
each bulb is wired to three other bulbs. From one moment to the next,
each bulb decides whether to turn itself on or off in accordance with the
state of these neighbors. A typical rule is "majority wins," meaning that
if two or three of its neighbors are on, the bulb will itself turn on; otherwise it will turn off. How will such a system behave when the electricity
goes on? There are three possible patterns of behavior:

1. Chaotic: if k is large, the bulbs keep twinkling chaotically as they switch
   each other on and off.
2. Frozen: if k is small ($k = 1$), some flip on and off few times, but very soon
   the whole array of lights stops twinkling.
3. Complex (the "edge of chaos"): if k is around 2, complex patterns will
   emerge in which twinkling islands appear, slowly changing shape at their
   borders but never freezing into a fixed pattern or becoming chaotic.

A system that is either frozen solid or chaotic cannot transmit information or adapt. But a complex network—one that is near the "edge of
chaos"—can do both. As it happens, the subak model provides an unusually clear illustration of this point. Let's say that the subaks in our
model are responding to an unusually dry period lasting for a decade.
Some of the subaks in the mountains adopt staggered cropping plans, to
use the available water more efficiently. Downstream clusters of subaks
respond to a cascade of these small changes, perceived along their borders, and within a few years the whole network has adapted to the
changed environment. But now suppose that the network has a different
configuration: instead of basing their response on the four closest neighbors ($k = 4$), each subak is connected to all the others ($k = N$). Then the
network cannot adapt; instead it merely flips randomly from one state
to another. At the opposite extreme, if each subak acts independently
($k = 0$), then no learning is possible and the network is frozen. Similarly
if $k = 1$ the network may become trapped in a configuration far from optimal, unable to find its way to a better solution.

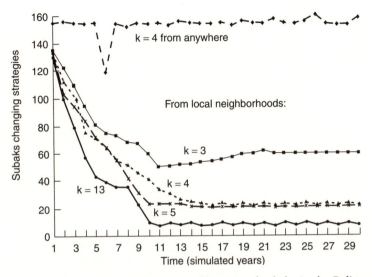

Figure 20. Effects of varying *k* on the coadaptation of subaks in the Bali watershed model. Each subak compares its recent harvest to the harvests of *k* neighbors, and adopts the cropping schedule of the most successful neighbor. Increasing *k* from 3 to 4, 5, and 13 progressively enlarges the search space and increases the speed at which most of the subaks arrive at a Nash equilibrium, with high mean yields. But if subaks compare their harvests to those of distant neighbors (*k* = 4 from anywhere in the watershed of 172 subaks), the system becomes chaotic and mean yields do not improve.

As Kauffman has shown, for a network of this kind to be capable of solving problems (such as irrigation schedules), it must be configured to exist in the region intermediate between frozen order and chaos, not far from the edge of chaos. This configuration depends on the richness of connections among the agents, governed by the *k* parameter. In the real world, subaks collect information about irrigation schedules, harvests, and pests from a subset of their neighbors. In effect, they are tuning the *k* parameter, finding the right degree of connectedness to enable them to adapt to their local environments. Unbeknown to the farmers (or government planners), the effect of all these local adjustments is to define the global structure of the network of subaks and temples for entire watersheds. Figure 20 shows the results of varying *k* from 3 to 13 in our simulation model. As long as the subaks connect only with their closest neighbors, expanding the search space increases the speed with which networks form and harvests improve. But if *k* includes very distant neighbors, networks cannot form, because distant neighbors are not responding to the same environmental signals as one's immediate neighbors. Similarly, when $k = 4$ subaks from anywhere in the watershed (rather than close neighbors), the result is chaos.

This may seem like much ado about a simple result, but consider the implications. Most agricultural extension plans are based on the results from experimental plots located at research stations. Farmers are encouraged to imitate these distant models. But if the farmers react to these signals, rather than those emanating from their immediate neighborhoods, the process of coadaptation will cease. In the Oos-Petanu simulation model, each subak decides whether or not to cooperate with each of its neighbors using a simple myopic strategy ("imitate a neighbor who is doing better") that ignores the real and formidable complexity of their problem. Luckily for the subaks, this ill-informed collection of strategies is all that is needed for them to rapidly climb the foothills of their local adaptive landscapes. Within a short time, a collection of autonomous agents (the subaks) becomes a network, forming islands of cooperation where all the farmers enjoy nearly identical, relatively bountiful harvests. The structure of these networks bears a remarkable resemblance to the lattice configurations of spatial games, for the excellent reason that both solutions are driven by the same coevolutionary dynamics.[7] The entire network has a structure, in which the value of both cooperation and noncooperation varies according to spatial location. This structure is itself adaptive: perturbations that change local payoffs trigger small cascades of change that allow the entire network to respond effectively to events such as the addition of a new irrigation system or a new rice pest.

• • •

Suppose a nineteenth-century Balinese king or a modern planner decided to take over direct management of the irrigation systems in the Oos-Petanu watershed. If the officials charged with implementing this plan were equipped with flow meters, rainfall gauges, computers, and a knowledge of differential equations, they could set about their task by gathering data and writing down equations to express the water balance for each and every subak, as a function of natural precipitation and upstream water demand. The real headaches would begin if the planners also hoped to minimize the damage caused by rice pests, which would require another batch of coupled partial differential equations. When a master plan for irrigation schedules finally emerged from these calculations, it

[7] K. Lindgren, "Evolutionary Dynamics of Simple Games," *Physica D* 75 (1994): 292–309.

would represent a terrible temptation to the spirits of the rivers and fields, who are known to be mischievous. Small deviations in rainfall, planting dates, or pest dynamics, especially in the upper regions of the watershed, would trigger a cascade of effects downstream, disrupting the plan. Doubtless the frustrated planners would dream of a simpler ecology, with fields and rivers large enough to minimize the interdependence that is so fundamental to the ecology of the Balinese subaks.

But by honoring the local gods in their branching networks of water temples, the farmers discovered a much more powerful solution, one better suited to a highly interdependent watershed ecology. Water temple networks provide a framework for neighbors to share information about harvests and pests, to agree on schedules for planting and irrigation, and to organize these schedules at the appropriate scales. In this way the temples become a coordination device, enabling subaks to behave like agents in a complex adaptive system. For the subaks to solve the problem of optimizing irrigation for an entire watershed, the temples must possess a certain authority, so that from year to year the farmers stick to the plans they agree on. But as our models show, there is no need for an external authority to enforce these agreements. The water temples derive all the authority they need from their practical success in managing the ecology of the rice terraces, and their symbolic association with the gods.

The first work on the mathematics of complex adaptive systems began in the 1970s, at about the same time that planners were instructing the farmers of Bali to set aside the water temple schedules and plant rice as fast as they could. One can hardly fault the consultants for wanting to boost rice production, or for failing to anticipate the mathematics of complex systems. But it is a little sobering to realize that the subak system was very nearly demolished before its ecological role was recognized. One wonders whether institutions like water temples exist elsewhere in the world, and if so what form they might take. Perhaps, like the water temples, they are regarded as religious institutions that can be safely ignored by planners and engineers.

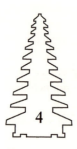

Tyrants, Sorcerers, and Democrats

ONE AFTERNOON ABOUT fifteen years ago, a group of farmers stormed angrily out of a meeting in the village of Kedisan and declared that they would no longer participate in subak affairs. The reason for their anger was the refusal of their neighbors to agree to call them by an honorific title. This title had recently been adopted by some of their relatives in other villages, as a prerogative based on the hierarchical rank or "caste" of their descent group. Their neighbors, however, were inclined to view the title not as the restoration of an ancient prerogative but rather as a pretentious innovation. This dispute soon began to unravel the social fabric of the village. To avoid having their names called out without the coveted title in subak meetings, some farmers began renting their rice fields to sharecroppers from neighboring villages, thus foregoing much of their income. Meanwhile, another descent group in the village began putting forth the claim that they, too, should be addressed by an honorific title appropriate to the rank of their descent group. For the duration of one growing season, the subak barely functioned, though when the time came for the next planting the claims and counterclaims for honorific titles were quietly dropped.

Incidents like this are not infrequent among the fourteen subaks of the Pamos water temple. When cooperation breaks down in a subak, the precipitating quarrel is far more likely to be about social status than about agriculture. In the previous chapter we saw that a balance of ecological forces rewards the farmers for cooperation. But because this purely ecological model predicts that some level of cooperation is always the best choice, it cannot account for the occasions when cooperation fails. Perhaps, then, we need two theories, one to explain cooperation and another for conflict; the first having to do with ecological processes in the rice paddies and the second, social processes in the villages. But are these truly independent phenomena? In other words, do the farmers cooperate because they must, for the sake of their harvests, and otherwise quarrel for all the usual reasons that people find to fight about?

For three years my colleagues and I studied the causes of conflicts among the subaks of the Pamos temple. Our strategy involved a double-blind investigation, carried out by two independent teams of Balinese researchers. One group observed ecological conditions in the rice paddies. Every two weeks this team measured irrigation flows and tracked the growth of the crops in each subak. Pest infestations were carefully monitored, and at the end of each growing season, harvests were tallied so that they could be compared. The second team studied decision making and conflict resolution in the subaks. Subak meetings were videotaped, and when disputes arose the protagonists were interviewed. Conflicts were followed over periods of months or even years, and a series of questionnaires was administered to subak members to test our interpretations. Because the two teams of researchers were independent, we could correlate objective ecological conditions with the subjective perceptions of the farmers. This chapter describes what we found.

Several things became clear almost immediately. First, we saw that there was considerable variation in the ways that subaks governed themselves. Each subak was free to construct its own institutions, and there was no external pressure to conform to a standard model. But while the subaks were supposed to function within a circumscribed domain—managing the rice terraces—in practice it was not possible to keep the egalitarian ethos of the subak from coming into conflict with the principle of hierarchy based on caste. For example, should the head of a subak be the person of highest rank, or someone who embodies the values of an egalitarian assembly? Several subaks were perceived as weak by their own members because they allowed powerful men to achieve dominance, though their control had to be discreetly hidden behind a democratic veneer. In these subaks, the ordinary members were said to "*mebebek*," to quack like ducks, which make a lot of noise but will go wherever they are led. In strong subaks, on the other hand, it was said that "the voice of the meeting is the voice of God," a voice strong enough to subdue the powerful. In general, for a subak to function effectively as a cooperative and self-governing unit, it must restrain the tensions associated with status rivalries that are always simmering in the background. All this makes real subaks different from the artificial ones in our model. For the artificial subaks invariably act as a unit, and can always strike an advantageous bargain with their neighbors. But real subaks are sites where people's livelihood and social standing are at stake, and cooperation can never be taken for granted.

For these reasons, we came to see the subaks not as purely pragmatic instruments for managing water but rather as ongoing experiments in self-governance. For example, in one village the democratic ideals of the subak proved to be so attractive that the community decided to abolish all caste distinctions and broaden the scope of democratic rule to include the whole of village life. For them it had become evident, as Herodotus said of the Athenians, "that equality is an excellent thing not in one respect only, but in all respects."[1] Yet their immediate neighbors to the east were ruled by a petty tyrant; our videotapes show him quelling a democratic rebellion that began just before the start of our study. As the stacks of videotapes accumulated, we saw that the extent to which the egalitarian ethos of the subaks permeated the rest of village affairs varied widely. Some tapes recorded meetings where every speaker paid the closest attention to democratic etiquette, addressing the members of the subak as if they were honored elder kinsmen, while others captured scenes of powerful men issuing peremptory commands. The breadth of this contrast surprised us, and the question of how the subaks govern themselves began to nudge aside ecology as the central focus of our investigations.

• • •

We began this phase of the research with Marx's simple question: who benefits? Do the downstream subaks usually receive their fair share of irrigation water without any difficulty? Or is there a need for powerful leaders to enforce the claims of those who might otherwise be dispossessed? While the question is easy to ask, obtaining an answer proved to be a difficult matter because it is hard to measure irrigation flows in Bali. The physical structure of these centuries-old irrigation systems is formidably complex, with many small weirs and springs, and flows that vary with the seasons and the weather. Most of the water used by the Pamos subaks comes from three weirs located on a branch of the Petanu River (figure 21). These diversionary dams shunt water into tunnels that emerge downstream as much as two kilometers away, at the summits of water mountains. Surface canals continue downstream, flooding one hillock after the next until the water is used up. Most subaks obtain additional water from springs, seeps, and surplus flows from upstream subaks; these flows are especially hard to measure. Moreover, the amount of water that is required to grow paddy rice is not constant but varies over the growing season. The maximum quantity is needed just before planting, to saturate the soil and create a shallow pond. Later, when the rice is nearly ready for harvesting, the paddy is drained. On average, over an entire growing season a continuous flow of at least two liters per hectare

[1] Herodotus V. 78, in G. R. Stanton, *Athenian Politics c. 800–500 B.C.: A Source Book*, London: Routledge, 1990: 187.

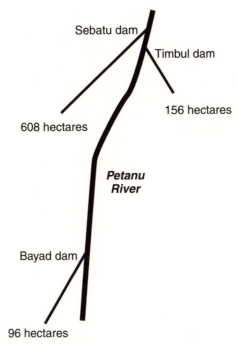

Figure 21. Water diversions for the 14 subaks of the Pamos water temple (not to scale).

is required for paddy rice; actual flows often dip below this level during the dry season.

Water rights are considered immutable and are based on religious obligations to the gods enshrined at the Pamos water temple. Anyone who obtains water for a field in the vicinity of this water temple incurs an obligation to assist with its annual cycle of rituals. The more water one receives, the greater the obligation. Water is allocated in units called *tektek*, with one tektek roughly equivalent to 25 ± 6 liters per second at high flow volumes during the rainy season. Because the farmers have no way to calculate flows directly, tektek are measured as fractional divisions of the total flow, using proportional dividers. For example, the two largest irrigation systems in the Pamos system begin at a couple of diversionary dams in the Petanu river. The Sebatu weir is located farthest upriver, at the bottom of a steep forested ravine about one hundred meters below the elevation of the surrounding countryside. This little dam divides the river into two channels. One disappears into a tunnel headed southeast, where it irrigates Sebatu and six other subaks, while the other channel continues downstream to the next weir. The diameter of the tunnel determines the maximum flow. With a maximum measured flow of 2,332 liters per second, the tunnel can accomodate up to 3.8 liters of water per hectare for 608 hectares of rice paddies. But the farmers calculate the capacity of the tunnel as seventy-four tektek of irrigation water, even if the tunnel is half empty. For them, the key question is not the total flow volume, which is out of their control, but rather how it is divided.

The water that is not diverted into the Sebatu tunnel is guided into the middle of the riverbed, where a rectangular slot has been cut into the dam. The dimensions of this slot are such that at low flows a quantity of water equal to one-quarter of the flow into the tunnel will pass through it. When flows exceed the capacity of the tunnel, the extra water overflows the weir and continues downstream. About sixty meters downstream, there is another weir and another tunnel, this one headed west. This weir belongs to the subaks of Timbul and Calo, which comprise 156 hectares of rice paddies, one-quarter the area of the paddies watered by the Sebatu tunnel. The slot in the Sebatu dam ensures that they receive precisely one-quarter as much water. Farther downstream, a third dam captures water for Subak Bayad (96 hectares). At this elevation, rivers recharge rapidly in the wet and porous landscape.

Where the tunnels emerge downstream, the water encounters a series of proportional dividers. For example, there are six major dividers on the Sebatu canal. We measured the flows at these dividers, paying particular attention during the dry season when water scarcity may occur (in the rainy season the problem is usually too much water). Table 3 shows average flows for the month of July in 1997 and 1998, at the height of the dry season. It is evident that Sebatu and Jasan, the subaks located farthest upstream, had a slight advantage over their downstream neighbors. However, this appears to be a consequence of the way that flows were measured, not a deliberate attempt to cheat. The tektek system is based on proportional division at the points where the flow is divided, which does not take into account downstream losses from percolation and evaporation. Our measurements confirmed that the flows were indeed proportional to the agreed-on division by tektek (table 4). It is also apparent from table 3 that the subaks farthest downstream (Kebon, Kedisan Kelod, and Pakudui) were not at a disadvantage compared to the middle subaks. From year to year, flows varied with the weather, but the proportional divisions did not change, except when downstream subaks arranged to borrow surplus water from their neighbors. We concluded that the division of water was equitable, though the subaks farthest upstream had a slight advantage. A survey of 150 farmers from ten subaks agreed with this conclusion: in answer to the question "Is the division of water by the Pamos water temple equitable?" all said yes. We

TABLE 3
Average measured irrigation flows in the Pamos system during the dry seasons of 1997 and 1998

Subak	Flow	Sawah	Flow/Sawah
Jasan & Sebatu	368	117	3.15
Timbul & Calo	460	156	2.95
Pujung Kaja	207	97	2.19
Kedisan Kaja	214	29	3.44
Bayad	198	97	2.04
Pujung Kelod	111	50	2.22
Kebon, Kedisan Kelod, Pakudui	337	145	2.32

Jasan, Sebatu, and Timbul are located farthest upstream; Kebon, Kedisan Kelod, and Pakudui are farthest downstream. "Sawah" means rice paddies. Flow units are liters per second; land units are hectares.

also found a very high ($r = .96$) correlation between flow volumes measured by tektek and by flowmeter.

Our next question had to do with the distribution of landholdings. Perhaps the weak subaks would turn out to be dominated by a few rich farmers. Figure 22 shows average landholdings per farmer in the same survey of 150 farmers in ten subaks. The average farm size was 32.75 are, or about a third of a hectare. But while the average farm size was

TABLE 4
Water rights of the Pamos subaks

Subak	Tekteks
Pujung Kelod	5.5
Pujung Kaja	11.5
Pakudui	9.0
Kebon	8.0
Kedisan	16.0
Jasan	4.0
Sebatu	12.0
Tegal Suci	7.5
Calo	7.0
Timbul	14.0
Bayad	7.0
Bonjaka	2.5
Jati	1.5

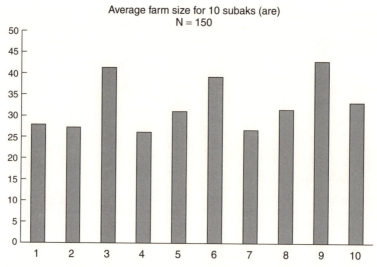

Figure 22. Mean farm size (in are, or hundredths of a hectare) among 10 subaks in the Pamos system.

remarkably uniform across subaks, the survey also showed that within each subak there were typically several farms of a hectare or more, and others that were tiny (the average standard deviation in farm size for all subaks was 19.3 are). This result led us to undertake another survey. We wondered whether the pattern of variation in landholdings reflected the purchase of land by ambitious farmers. Alternatively, the variation in farm sizes could be the result of simple demographic variation in inheritance: only males inherit land, and an only son will inherit more than will men who must share with their brothers. In a detailed survey of thirty-seven farmers focused on land ownership, we found that nearly all the farms (96 percent) were acquired by inheritance. With regard to the size of landholdings, the results of this second survey were nearly identical to those of the first: the average farm size was 33 are, with a standard deviation of 17.68 are. Interestingly, in no instance were the largest farms owned by the elected heads of subaks. Instead, all these men owned middle-size farms inherited from their fathers.

Most villages also contain a population of laborers who sometimes work as sharecroppers. These men are typically employed by households that inherited rice paddies but choose not to work them. In such cases, the subak customarily allows the landowner to buy himself out of subak obligations. These arrangements can become quite complex, since the landowner owes numerous obligations to the subak.[2] He is required to attend subak meetings and to participate in the repair and maintenance of the subak's irrigation works. He is also obliged to contribute to the annual cycle of subak rituals, which involves labor, financial contributions, and the preparation of gorgeous ceremonial offerings made of rice flour, fruit, and flowers that may take days to construct (more about these anon). In a typical arrangement, a sharecropper provides half the harvest to the farm owner and must also fulfill the labor obligations to the subak, while the landowner is responsible for the financial and ritual obligations of subak membership. In general, only landowners may become subak members and attend subak meetings. Consequently, the voices of the poorest and the richest villagers are seldom heard in subak meetings; the active subak consists of landowning farmers. The proportion of sharecroppers varies from village to village. In the Pamos system during our period of research, the largest proportion of inactive landowners was in the village of Bayad, where 82 active subak members were outnumbered by 106 absentee landowners whose land was worked by sharecroppers. The Bayad subak also rewarded 12 priests and elected village leaders with full exemption from subak duties, even though they were landowners, because it was considered that they performed other valuable services to the community. Among the 82 active subak members, about half also worked as sharecroppers on their neighbors' farms. In this way, a man who owned only a third of a hectare of rice fields could make a living as a full-time farmer.

According to census records from the Dutch occupation of Bali in the first half of the twentieth century, most villagers were full-time farmers, so the increase in both sharecroppers and absentee landlords is evidently a recent phenomenon. At the time of the Dutch land surveys, a large proportion of the farmers in this region were pecatu holders, not landowners. In the past half century, the rural population has roughly doubled, but at the same time, new occupations for villagers have appeared. The apparently insatiable appetite of Western consumers for brightly colored Balinese handicrafts has made it possible for most farm families to diversify their incomes, and the Pamos area is a center for handicraft production, annually shipping containerloads of polychrome wood carvings to the world's gift shops. Most households include one subak member who

---

[2] The significance of the distinction between the respective roles of landowners and sharecroppers is pursued by Nitish Jha in his doctoral dissertation at Brandeis, in which he also distinguishes between the "ritual" and "water" subak in a village near Sebatu. Members of the "ritual subak" are owners of sawah, whereas the "water subak" includes sharecroppers who till the fields. Nitish Jha, "The Bifurcate Subak: The Social Organization of a Balinese Irrigation Community," Ann Arbor Mich.: UMI Dissertation Services, 2002.

TABLE 5
Who should inherit a farm?

All male children, in equal shares	68
The youngest son	20
The oldest son	3
Can't say	9

$N = 100$, ten Pamos subaks

is usually a full-time farmer, while other adults and older children produce wood carvings (unless they can find a better job). For example, the administrative district of greater Kedisan includes seven villages: Kedisan Kaja, Kedisan Kelod, Kebon, Pakudui, Bayad, Cebok, and Tangkup. In the year 2000 a census counted 1,031 households and 933 active farmers.

However, in the more distant past, when nearly every household head was a farmer, over a period of generations average farm sizes would gradually diminish as a result of inheritance. While carrying out this survey we began to wonder what happens when the amount of heritable land in a subak falls below what is needed to sustain an average household. The answer to this question depends partly on the rules of inheritance. In the rice-growing regions of China, since time immemorial the law has ensured that all male children inherit equal portions. But Balinese customs with regard to inheritance are more flexible, and one often hears of conflicts over inheritance. We asked one hundred farmers in ten subaks who should inherit agricultural land. Their response is shown in table 5.

Which of these patterns is followed will obviously have an effect on the rate of fragmentation of landholdings, and the fact that opinions differ opens the door to conflict between brothers. But in the long run, the only solution is to develop new farmland. Three of the subaks in the Pamos system were created in the past half century, as daughter settlements founded by inhabitants of several of the more ancient villages. We speculated that this process probably began much earlier. Perhaps the earliest villages were the ones nearest the dams, which later spun off daughter settlements when they grew too large (this question is still being investigated). For the moment, the answer to our original question (who benefits?) seems clear: both the physical evidence and the farmers' responses to our questions suggest that the patterns of both land and water rights in the subaks of Pamos are broadly egalitarian. Farms are roughly equal in size and so are water allocations. In the modern era, a smaller proportion of adult men are full-time farmers than in the past. There are probably more sharecroppers and more rich men. But the subaks continue to function as egalitarian assemblies, despite these social and demographic changes.

Overall these results were puzzling. On the one hand, it appeared that egalitarianism in the subaks had a solid economic foundation. With equal division of land and water, there was little sign of economic dominance by the rich and powerful. But this made the frequency of conflicts within subaks all the more mysterious. Fully a third of the fourteen Pamos subaks appeared to be weak: prone to conflicts, and poorly organized. Why should this be so? We sought to answer this question by intensifying our observations of the weaker subaks, and also by means of comparative surveys of farmers' attitudes and opinions. Anthropologists are usually suspicious of questionnaires, but we were interested in discovering the breadth of farmers' opinions on a wide range of topics, and in any case there was no other way to keep an eye on fourteen subaks at once. In the end, we carried out five surveys. The first one was directed mostly toward the ecological issues described in the previous chapter (testing the predictions of the game-theoretical model). But we also included a few rather naive questions about subak affairs, including one about the trustworthiness of the subak leadership. Naturally nearly all the farmers prudently refrained from criticizing their leaders. But in two subaks, several farmers were sufficiently discontented that they chose to tell us plainly, if incautiously, that their leaders were untrustworthy. In subsequent surveys we tried to explore the reasons for this dissatisfaction, replacing direct questions about the honesty of subak heads with a series of hypothetical cases. This strategy worked quite well, and in the end we were able to learn quite a lot about the kinds of tensions that exist in subaks, and the reasons why some allow themselves to fail.

• • •

In our first survey of 150 farmers, only a handful (3 percent) were willing to question the right of the subak to assess fines. But this proved to be an accurate indicator of deep conflicts in the subaks where farmers were bold enough to complain (figure 23). The highest level of dissatisfaction came from the members of a subak whose leader was widely suspected of open dishonesty. The other dissenters belonged to a subak in which two factions based on descent groups were engaged in a bitter struggle for power, and seized every opportunity to put their rivals at a disadvantage.

In a follow-up survey we asked 37 farmers from eight subaks a direct question about the incidence of water theft. Most responded by implausibly denying that it ever occurs (table 6). More candid responses

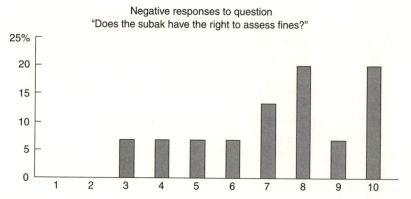

Figure 23. Negative responses to question, Does the subak have the right to assess fines? $N = 150$ male farmers, from 10 Pamos subaks.

were obtained by posing similar issues in terms of hypothetical situations (table 7). Here the proportion of farmers who advocated an active response was 22 to 14. But this balance shifted when we asked what one should do in the face of an apparent theft by the head of the subak, rather than a neighbor (table 8). The most popular response, "leave it to palakarma," requires a little explanation. The doctrine of karma holds that one's evil deeds in this life must be expiated in future lives. This is often associated with an idea that the burden of a person's accumulated sins may be visited on their immediate descendants. Such beliefs are reflected in an oath that people sometimes offer to swear: "If I speak falsely, may a curse fall upon my family for seven generations." If the matter is sufficiently important, a person may be asked to swear such an oath in a temple. Given these beliefs, it is ethically defensible to take no action against an evil deed, instead leaving the punishment to the working out of karma. On the other hand, leaving matters to karma (or the miscreant's fear of karmic punishment) offers no immediate solution. So, how does one decide when to take action, and when to leave things to karma?

TABLE 6
How often does water theft occur in your subak?

Seldom	9
Sometimes	1
Never	27

TABLE 7
Suppose a farmer sees that a neighbor (a person he knows well, from the same subak) stealing water. What's the best thing for him to do?

Approach him directly	6
Report to the subak head	14
Ask a question in the meeting	2
Do nothing	10
Depends on the amount stolen	4

This relates to the responses to another hypothetical question (table 9). By conventional Balinese standards, there is no doubt that Ketut is the superior candidate. Subak heads are supposed to serve only reluctantly, and to disavow any personal ambition. But as everyone also knows, it can be dangerous to thwart the desires of an ambitious colleague. The psychological considerations are perhaps not dissimilar from those involved in the election of heads of academic departments in American universities. And some respondents pointed out that an ambitious leader may be more energetic in promoting the group's interests than someone who is concerned only to assure the success of majority rule. This trade-off is evident in the answers to two more questions (tables 10 and 11). Another question was based on a well-known recent incident (table 12). Perhaps because the question dealt with a real case, most respondents chose the safe answer.

Finally, we asked the farmers to offer open-ended comments on which aspects of the subak meetings were truly democratic, and which merely offered a democratic "decoration" or veneer (*hiasan*). The responses were surprisingly bold (table 13). The suggestion from ten farmers that "fertilizer usage" was an example of a democratic veneer covering the exercise of power may seem a little odd, and merits a word of explanation. For the past several decades, uniformed agents from the Department of

TABLE 8
Say that there is a subak head who has collected money from the members for repairing the main canal. Afterward he returns most of the unspent funds, but keeps some for himself. What should one do?

Ask a question in the meeting	12
Question him in private	0
Leave it to palakarma	25
Depends on the amount	0
Report to the village head	0

TABLE 9

Suppose that there are two candidates for subak head. Wayan is very keen to become the head, and according to general opinion it is because he is ambitious. Ketut is the second candidate. Ketut is willing to serve but doesn't care whether he is elected or not. Who would you choose?

Wayan, because otherwise the subak will become "hot" (contentious)	12
Ketut, because he would be more trustworthy	23
Not sure	2

Agriculture had visited the subaks annually to offer recommendations for the selection of "technology packets," which consisted of seeds for a particular hybrid rice variety, bundled with fertilizer and sometimes pesticides. In the 1990s the choice of packet was mandatory, but more recently the farmers have supposedly been allowed to decide for themselves. The response to this question suggests some skepticism on this point.

Overall, our first surveys revealed a pattern in which two-thirds of the subak members usually advocated taking an active role in democratic governance, while the other one-third were more inclined to let ambitious men have their way and leave justice to karma. Since the balance was fairly close, one might wonder what would happen if the passive participants suddenly found themselves in the majority. In June 1998, the members of Subak Calo found out.

We began to take a special interest in Calo soon after the videotaping project began. Along with the head of the subak, most subaks also elect a treasurer and secretary. It is considered desirable to replace the entire leadership of a subak from time to time, and it is taken as a sign of honesty and good faith for the leadership to offer to resign en masse. This is of course most desireable when it is least likely to occur: when corrupt leaders hope to hang on to their positions. "Corruption" (korupsi) is an English word that has recently come into common parlance in Balinese, apparently borrowed from newspaper accounts of dishonest politicians. In the context of the subaks, it generally means dishonest accounting by the leadership. Subak heads routinely collect money from the membership for a variety of purposes, such as the purchase of materials for repairs to irrigation systems and temples, as well as expenses connected

TABLE 10
Who is the best choice for subak head?

Rich man	11
Average wealth	27
Poor man	0

TABLE 11
What's the most important quality for a subak head?
(*open-ended question*)

A peacemaker	21
Rich	7
High caste	4
Decisive	3
To be fairly elected	1

with the rituals at water temples. Unspent funds are supposed to be returned to the members at the next meeting, and the collection, dispersal, and refunding of money is part of the routine business of subak meetings. The subak head and treasurer thus handle money all the time, and there is ample opportunity to cook the books if one is so inclined. The standard remedy for this temptation is for the leaders to go through the subak's books in painstaking detail at every meeting, producing receipts and settling all accounts. When this does not occur, the farmers say, it is not a good sign.

The head of Subak Calo was a man named Maling,[3] who had served for about ten years and was widely suspected of petty corruption. In 1997 a faction in the village led by the village head came up with a stratagem to replace Maling. Like most water mountain villages, Calo maintains a separate subak for agricultural lands that are not irrigated, called a *subak abian* (dry-fields subak). Ordinarily these organizations have very little to do, because there is no need for collective management of garden plots. As dry-fields agriculture is unimportant in Calo, the village head suggested that it would be efficient to merge the two subaks; the new joint subak would elect a single leader. In order to accomplish this administrative reform, the village head proposed that all village officials

TABLE 12
After a temple festival at Pamos, the contributions from the subaks amount to about 1.5 million rupiah a year. Each subak head is required to be at the temple for 3 days to help with the festival. Suppose that afterward the 14 subak heads decided to divide 500,000 rupiah among themselves as an honorarium. Do you think that they would be entitled to do so?

Yes	84%
No	12%

---

[3] This is not, of course, his real name.

TABLE 13
Assessment of decisions by my Subak: which are truly democratic, and which are merely a democratic veneer?

Decisions by My Subak	Real Democracy	Democratic Veneer
All decisions	5	3
Choice of subak head	17	14
Water division	28	0
Fines	20	9
Sharing ritual duties	17	0
Choice of cropping pattern	10	0
Pest control	4	0
Fertilizer usage	1	10
Finances	0	4
Don't know	0	1

join him in a mass resignation, and Maling had little choice but to go along. In a subsequent meeting, the newly constituted joint subak chose as its leader a man called Nyoman Rata. Rata's chief attraction was that he had no interest in the job and begged to be excused. But the subak was adamant, and the members' insistence raised the stakes: to refuse a second time would mean that Rata must resign his membership in the subak and also risk incurring divine wrath, since "the voice of the assembly is the voice of God." Reluctantly, Rata agreed. Shortly after his election Rata called his first subak meeting. At the appointed time, the slit drum was sounded to summon the members, and Rata and his two lieutenants (the treasurer and scribe) seated themselves to wait for their arrival in the subak meeting pavilion. But after an hour only three farmers had appeared, so the meeting was rescheduled for the following week.

We were alerted that something interesting might be afoot in Calo, so on the appointed day one of our researchers joined Rata as he waited for the subak to appear. But once again, only a few farmers showed up. Rata grew annoyed and had the slit drum beaten vigorously every quarter hour, but the meeting hall remained empty. The house of Maling happens to be located across the street from the subak meeting place, and around one o'clock the man himself appeared walking up the street, evidently on his way home. Rata hailed him and courteously invited him to join the meeting, but Maling shook his head, mumbling "what's this for? There's no need," and disappeared into his house. Half an hour later Rata gave up. At the next village meeting ten days later, Rata addressed the community. He reminded them that he never asked to become subak head and had agreed to do so only because they had insisted. Yet having compelled him to take this post, nearly all of them had chosen not to appear at the subak meetings. Had he misunderstood their wishes? Perhaps someone could explain this mystery to him.

As everyone knew, Maling had "played the secret puppeteer," quietly letting it be known that he would look favorably on anyone who failed to attend Rata's meetings. But evidently no one had anticipated that virtually the entire membership of the subak would lose their nerve.[4] As Rata sat and waited for a response, our video camera panned the sheepish expressions of the villagers, most of them staring at the floor as they contemplated how they had allowed themselves to be manipulated by the petty thief they had hoped to retire. The stifled chuckles of our researcher are audible on the video as Rata waited a few beats for a response and then, with admirable timing, asked demurely if there would be any objection now to his resignation as subak head. This time no one said a word, and a few months later a new leader was chosen. In a subsequent interview Rata commented on his moral victory over Maling: he said that while waiting for the farmers to come to the meetings, he had felt like a fool, but by behaving properly he had foiled the plot, because the villagers now blamed Maling for making them all look like fools.

After this episode, for several months the farmers of Calo had to endure an occasional witticism from their neighbors. But they were spared excessive merriment from their closest neighbors downstream, in the village of Bayad, which had problems of its own. The head of the Bayad subak was an old man called Mulyadi, who had served as subak head for forty-one years when we began visiting his subak in 1997, and had recently defeated a serious challenge to his rule. The challenge came from his own treasurer, Made Irihati. Irihati objected to two aspects of Mulyadi's rule. First, Mulyadi habitually bypassed Irihati to collect contributions from the members directly, and seemed to feel no need to open these books for the treasurer's inspection. Irihati strongly suspected that Mulyadi frequently failed to return funds collected in excess of necessary expenditures. Indeed he was more open about his peculations than Maling, giving the impression that the appropriation of unspent funds was his prerogative, whereas Maling was thought to have fiddled the books in secret. Second, the treasurer objected to Mulyadi's lordly style: in subak meetings the old man invariably sat on a raised platform facing the subak, in the manner of a great man dealing with underlings. Over the years there had been several attempts to challenge Mulyadi's power. But it was said that in the past, whenever would-be challengers came into Mulyadi's presence, they would lose their nerve and become confused and inarticulate.

---

[4] A game theorist might suggest that the choice as to attending the meeting had become a Prisoner's Dilemma, in which nearly all the players chose to defect.

When our interviewers pressed for an explanation for this odd behavior, several subak members confessed that Mulyadi was suspected of wearing a magical belt, which helped him to sustain his power. Such devices actually exist; I have myself been offered several to purchase. There are various types of magical belts and amulets: one kind endows the wearer with eloquence, another makes one irresistible to beautiful women, while the type said to be worn by Mulyadi creates awe and confusion in the minds of anyone who tries to oppose the wearer's wishes. I confess that I was at first tempted to acquire a small collection of these items for ethnographic study. But I was advised to reconsider, because the acquisition of a magical belt involves a Faustian bargain: the powers of the belts are thought to come from living spirits that are always hungry, and must be fed on living, preferably human flesh. In the end, the belts are said to corrupt both the spirits and the bodies of their owners, unless the debt is postponed to be paid by their descendants. The market for such magic is thought to come from persons of warped spiritual development, in whom short-sighted ambition has gained ascendancy. When normal people come into contact with such power-mad sorcerers, it is of course to be expected that they will be easily daunted; people who are forced to interact with sorcerers are entitled to console themselves with the thought of the karmic price that the belt wearer will someday have to pay. Consequently, as several members of the subak explained, there is no particular shame attached to deferring to someone like Mulyadi.

But Irihati, the treasurer of subak Bayad, had other ideas. As he explained on tape, he was tired of Mulyadi's peculations, and even more tired of being treated like an underling. So Irihati began to talk about holding an election, and put himself forward as a candidate for the headship. Shortly after this notion began to circulate among the subak members, but before it was brought up as a formal proposal, Mulyadi left on a month-long trip to Jakarta to visit one of his children. Mulyadi's absence coincided with the most important subak rituals of the year, which take place over a period of several days at two temples and also at a shrine at the weir. These rituals are elaborate affairs that require a great deal of careful planning. Responsibility for constructing, assembling, transporting, and praying over an impressive variety of offerings must be delegated, so that the rituals occur on time and in the correct order. The treasurer did his best, but in the end the ceremonies failed to come off like clockwork, and it was said that the treasurer was not quite up to the job. Whatever his faults, Mulyadi was acknowledged to be a master at organizing temple rituals. So when Mulyadi returned a week later, the embarassed treasurer yielded to the inevitable, abandoning his plan to propose an election and resigning from the subak in favor of his younger brother.

We pieced this story together from interviews with the treasurer and other farmers after the events had taken place. But while the treasurer ridiculed the cowardice of the subak, other farmers pointed out that Mulyadi was not only much better at organizing complicated rituals; over the years he had also been successful in obtaining benefits for the subak from government officials, such as the rehabilitation of several canals. With regard to the magical belt, the treasurer opined that no one could be certain that Mulyadi really wore one, but on the other hand, the rumor was widespread, and Mulyadi had never denied it. However, other subak members observed that if Mulyadi was really using magic, the entire subak would share in the benefits derived from these powers, while he alone would someday pay the price.

Both of these cases, the one in Calo and the other in Bayad, involved the internal governance of individual subaks. But not all of the problems that arise within the subaks can be handled internally; sometimes they affect relations with other subaks. In such cases they become a matter for discussion at the monthly meetings of the "Greater Subak"(*Subak Gde*), to which each of the fourteen subaks of Pamos sends a representative, who is normally the subak head. This organization functions like a higher-level subak: the members elect a leader and hold meetings in much the same style as the strong (i.e., democratic) subaks. The main responsibilities of the Greater Subak are coordination of irrigation and cropping patterns at the regional scale; maintenance of shared irrigation works; performance of the annual ritual cycle at the Pamos water temple; and coordination with the supreme water temple at Batur (see chapter 6). In 1998, for example, three hundred meters of irrigation tunnel from the Sebatu weir collapsed, and the Greater Subak decided to assess the seven subaks that receive water from this tunnel to pay for the repairs. An engineering contractor was hired for seventeen million rupiah, and this cost was assessed by tektek. We followed the progress of this project by means of our videotapes, beginning with the decision to hire the contractor to oversee the repair of the tunnel and ending, six months later, with refunds of unspent funds to the subak heads. In this case, everything went smoothly, but a few months later a new case came up that required a decision to take punitive action against one subak.

This case began with the decision of the priests of the supreme water temple of Batur to go on a purificatory pilgrimage to the sea, carrying sacred images of the Goddess and her retinue of lesser deities. The procession would travel by truck, accompanied by three orchestras and at least one hundred people. The priests of Batur sent word of this decision to major water temples located on the route to the sea, among them the Pamos temple. The Greater Subak of Pamos responded by inviting the Goddess to stop for a visit on her way back from the sea. A few weeks later the procession arrived for a three-day sojourn. The Pamos subaks brought offerings for the Goddess, hired dancers and shadow puppeteers to provide almost continuous performances in the temples, and organized themselves to provide food for over a hundred visitors from Batur for the duration of their visit. While this was going on, not a few visitors remarked that the chief water temple of Pamos seemed sadly in need of repairs. In a burst of religious enthusiasm, the Greater Subak representatives decided to assess themselves half a million rupiah per tektek to pay for these repairs as well as the costs incurred by hosting the Goddess and her retinue. Once this decision had been taken, it became the responsibility of each subak head to collect contributions from the members of his subak. These were assessed according to how much water each person received, measured in units called "small tekteks."

Most subaks came up with their contributions in time for the next monthly meeting of the Greater Subak, but the head of Subak Kedisan Kelod missed this meeting and did not send a delegate. At the next meeting he claimed that he had not been aware of this financial obligation. No one really believed this story, but he was given another month to collect the two million rupiah owed by his subak. At the next meeting, he again failed to appear, and the other subak heads discussed what steps to take. The head of the closest neighboring subak said that he had the impression that the money had already been collected from the subak members, so the group decided to wait and see whether the missing funds would be delivered to the treasurer. But another month went by, and at the next meeting a new face appeared: a young farmer from Kedisan Kelod who said that he was there to represent his subak at the request of the subak head, who had urgent business elsewhere. This announcement was greeted with broad smiles by the other subak heads, and the head of the group asked the newcomer if he was aware that his subak was four months late with its contribution. The young man looked surprised, and said that the funds had long since been collected by the missing subak head. Surely they had been paid. The older men assured him that they had not, and a merry little discussion ensued: Hadn't the subak head been seen riding a new motorcycle? And wasn't he known to be fond of gambling at cockfights? But presently the meeting sobered up, as the head of the Greater Subak reminded everyone that if the money was not paid, they would have to share the burden among themselves. Did they not realize that he himself (their elected leader) had made up the difference so that he could pay the full amount owed to the various contractors on time? This little speech brought immediate results: in a matter of minutes the subak heads decided to give Subak Kedisan Kelod two weeks to pay its debt; otherwise their water would be cut off. How the subak came up with the money was of no concern of the Greater Subak; the responsibility lay with the members of Subak Kedisan Kelod. At this the young man looked so miserable that the older men in the group told him not to worry; it was certainly not his fault, and responsible people in Kedisan Kelod would undoubtedly take care of the matter. And indeed, at the next meeting of the Greater Subak, a newly elected head of Subak Kedisan Kelod appeared with two million rupiah and an apology from the old subak leader, who confessed to having spent some of the money—on a family ritual, he said. His village saw to it that he could borrow enough money to pay the subak's debt, but he was required to step down as subak head. Later we spoke to some farmers from Kedisan Kelod, who expressed their desire to have this incident forgotten as soon as possible. They said that the delinquent subak head would suffer no further punishment, but the fact that he had brought this shame on the village would not be forgotten, all the more so because the funds he had taken had been meant for the gods.

• • •

The videotaping, interviews, and surveys of the subaks went on continuously for two years, and occasionally thereafter. At first, our minimal goal was to record the moments when the Greater Subak and its member subaks made decisions relating to the management of the rice terraces. We videotaped nearly every meeting of the Greater Subak, and one or two regular subak meetings each month. Because we had a second team of researchers recording ecological conditions in the fields belonging to these subaks, we hoped to find out what kinds of information about field conditions were actually discussed in the meetings. We expected to record discussions in which farmers reacted to problems such as rice pests, and weighed the consequences of changes to their irrigation schedules. But it turned out that this sort of discussion was quite rare. Typically, once a year the Greater Subak has a brief conversation about the choice of crops and irrigation schedules for the upcoming year. Probably because the cropping patterns of these subaks are already close to optimal, the proposals usually amount to no more than minor tinkering, so an agreement is typically reached within half an hour. Later in the year, as the dry season approaches, subak heads often negotiate informally among themselves to borrow water. If an upstream subak has more water than it needs, it is expected to relinquish the extra water to downstream neighbors who ask for it. Because the water belongs to the Goddess, the upstream subak cannot charge for it, but it will certainly win the gratitude of its neighbors.

Overall, during the course of our research, ecological topics were seldom discussed in subak meetings, with a single exception. As mentioned earlier, not long after the project began we became concerned about the high levels of chemical fertilizer that the farmers were applying to their fields. We began to measure nutrient loads, and to talk informally about our findings with interested farmers. After we determined that the rivers and irrigation canals carried high levels of mineral nutrients, colleagues from the Ministry of Agriculture research center carried out field trials with us, testing the relationship between fertilizer and rice yields. One day when I was attending the monthly meeting of the Greater Subak, a subak head asked if I could summarize for the representatives what we had learned. I said that we had only preliminary data on nitrogen, but that we were pretty confident that there was no need to apply any potassium fertilizer, and that phosphate could be reduced by at least 75 percent. This of course would mean a large savings for the farmers. The subak heads carried our suggestions back to their members, and many farmers chose to follow our advice. The results were satisfactory, and after the next harvest, whenever members of our research team appeared to tape subak meetings, they were often asked to comment on the progress of our research on nutrient levels and rice pests. Perhaps this made our presence a little more conspicuous, but it certainly increased the warmth of our welcome at subak meetings.

As time went on, and we gained confidence in our understanding of the ecological dynamics of the rice paddies, the focus of our interest gradually shifted, at first toward the governance of the subaks, and then toward the background of religious and cultural ideas that shaped the farmers' attitudes. Perhaps the most important conclusion we drew from the videotaping and interviews was that similar tensions existed in all subaks, and the balance could easily shift from "strong" to "weak," democratic to authoritarian governance, for reasons that had little to do with ecology. So we began to focus on the question of how a balance of power was achieved within subaks, and what could cause this balance to tip. This called for more intensive case studies of decision making in the subaks. Two incidents will be briefly related here. The first consists of a brief verbal exchange that lasted less than half an hour in one of the strongest subaks; the second is drawn from an interview that proved to be the key to understanding a process that lasted for decades and led to the complete collapse of another subak. Viewed in tandem, these cases bracket the range of behavior that we observed, illustrating the circumstances under which some problems could be quickly resolved, whereas others could grow until they spiraled out of control.

The first case occurred at a meeting of Pakudui, the subak that is located farthest downstream on the irrigation system that originates at the Sebatu weir. The meeting began with routine business: a roll call of the members and an assessment of minor fines on members who had failed to show up to help clean the canals a few days earlier. These fines are typically paid in cash, on the spot. (Inflation has weakened the value of fines as a deterrent, but the shame attached to being fined is still meaningful). Then the subak head began to speak to the group informally, at first in deferential High Balinese, but soon in very colloquial language. He said that he needed to tell them that he had lost some money belonging to the subak. Someone asked "how much?" and he mentioned an insignificant amount, the equivalent in rupiah of less than three dollars. These were unspent funds from a ritual at the weir, representing contributions from all the members, that should have been returned at this meeting. Many people probably began to wonder, as I did, how such a small amount of money could be divided among thirty men, assuming that it could be found or replaced. But before someone could ask this question, the subak head continued with his story. He said that a few days earlier, after paying all the expenses for the ritual, he had put the remaining funds in a little packet and hung it for safekeeping in a basket above his bed. Perhaps he had had a premonition that something might go wrong. . . . The next morning the money was gone. He questioned his wife and children, who answered that they knew the money belonged to the subak and would never have dared to touch it. The family looked everywhere, but the money simply could not be found. He was prepared to swear an oath about the money: "in fact, maybe I should take an oath in the temple." Looking up at the ceiling, he uttered one of the conventional formulas that Balinese sometimes use when their honesty is in question: "my intentions were pure like a child's." He paused, and as the silence lengthened, the treasurer began to talk about a different matter while the subak head sat back, apparently lost in thought. A little while later, when the business of the treasurer was finished and there was another pause, the subak head began to speak again. He said in the same quiet voice, as though confiding to a friend, that he had served as subak head for over a decade. "Older people start to forget things. . . . And people don't realize how much a subak head has to remember and attend to." Anyway, he had certainly served a long time and now would like to "ask leave," or in other words to resign as subak head. At this there was a loud murmur from the whole group, who were straining to hear every word: "No, no, *Jero Kli*.[5] This could happen to anyone. Such things happen all the time, all the time!" Then one of the most outspoken members of the group made a short impromptu speech in High Balinese, and the subak fell silent: "You have been our trusted guide for many years. This matter of the money is nothing, it means nothing at all,

---

[5] "Jero Kli" is short for "Jero Klihan." "Jero" is an honorific title like monsieur; "klihan" is the head of an organization such as a subak or hamlet (banjar).

do not allow yourself to be disturbed. We want you to continue; do not think any more about this."

I was able to attend this meeting, and immediately afterward I asked my Balinese colleague who had videotaped it why such a trivial matter had assumed such importance. Surely the subak head could simply have replaced the missing money with his own funds. My colleague said that he also found it puzzling, but offered an interpretation that turned out to be correct. In Bali there is a widespread belief in magical spirits that can be sent to steal money. Someone who wishes to get money in this way must go to a practicing sorcerer or witch, confess this desire, and ask to become an apprentice. If the sorcerer agrees, after a short period of study the apprentice will be asked to use magic to kill a particular animal—one for which he feels some affection. The spirit of this creature is captured in a magical amulet, and thenceforth it can be summoned to travel secretly at night and steal money. Every retail shop owned by a Balinese has some magical defenses against these spirits, called Blerong. But there is a secret associated with the creation of the Blerong: even though the apprentice is told that the magical procedure involves killing an animal (and indeed an animal is actually killed, or so it is said), in fact it also brings about the illness or death of a loved one.[6] In this way, the creation of a Blerong binds the apprentice to the sorcerer and commits him to a new career of evil deeds. Because the money had mysteriously vanished, the subak head apparently concluded that he was probably under attack by some hidden enemy who had employed a Blerong to steal the money. This would be very upsetting; it meant that the magical protections surrounding his house were inadequate (or more ominously, that the attack had come from within his own extended household). Moreover the money itself—the physical paper money—was sacred because it had become the property of the subak; it would not do to replace it with other bills. So the disappearance of the money was alarming. It could mean that both the leader and his subak were vulnerable to a malevolent witch or sorcerer. The subak head later confirmed that this was indeed what was going on in his mind during the meeting; though he said that he could not be sure he had been the victim of a Blerong, the incident had been upsetting, and he had decided on the spot, as he was talking, to resign.

This subak head was one of a handful who received the highest approval ratings in our surveys. The incident passed and was soon forgotten; the offer to resign was not repeated. But as my colleagues and I discussed what had happened, we concluded that it showed the vulnerability

---

[6] Thus an unexpected death from accident or disease may create suspicion: has someone in the extended family decided to study witchcraft?

of even the strongest subak to transitory moments of weakness. A subak head can fail by being too trusting as well as too aggressive, if he loses confidence in his ability to unify and lead the group. The witchcraft beliefs of the Balinese emphasize that sorcery always begins with some weakness of character. Indeed, it is said that it is invariably the weak who are attracted to sorcery and become both its agents and its victims. Because the tensions that produce discord in a subak begin in the desires and ambitions of individuals, the only way to sustain an egalitarian subak is for its leaders to be attentive to the balance of emotional forces in the group. A united subak is powerful; its decisions are nearly always correct, and its collective voice is godlike—a point we will return to. I was told many times that sorcerers find it nearly impossible to harm individuals who have pure intentions and strength of purpose. But if this calm unity is disrupted, weaknesses can be seized and exploited.

On one level this belief can be interpreted in straightforward Durkheimian terms: sorcery beliefs may be viewed as objectifications of emotional problems within these communities, such as the weaknesses of ambitious or greedy men, and the reciprocal weaknesses that take the form of ambivalence or cowardly acquiescence among their neighbors. In other words, the vocabulary of sorcery provides a way to describe the emotional origins of problematic behavior in these democratic assemblies. The ideal leader must combine the attributes of the fictional subak leaders "Ketut" and "Wayan" in our survey: he should be an excellent speaker and an energetic and meticulous organizer—a man of action and ambition, in other words, but also someone who respects his neighbors and seeks to achieve unity. Still, everyone recognizes that the temptation to seize a little extra authority is ever present in a society that is as obsessed with hierarchy as a Balinese water mountain village.

To explain the significance of the last case that will be considered in this chapter, it is necessary to say a few more words about the ways in which the issue of hierarchy become problematic among the subaks. A quarrel over honorific titles in Subak Kedisan was briefly mentioned at the start of this chapter: some years ago, this subak nearly ceased to function over a dispute about how the members should be addressed in the roll call. Although the problem was temporarily resolved, the underlying stresses persisted. Because it proved to be impossible for rival descent groups to persuade others in the village to address them with honorific caste titles, a different way had to be found to assert status claims, one that did not require the active cooperation of one's rivals. So status competition shifted to funeral rites, perhaps the commonest venue for such contests in Bali. The Balinese cremate their dead in ornate biers, and caste status is supposed to determine the type of ornamentation that is permissible. In this way funeral rites proclaim the relative status of each descent group. In the days of the rajahs, it is said, no family would have dared to display greater ostentation than its deceased member was entitled to by birth, but in the modern age no one has the authority to enforce these rules. Instead, the desire to elevate one's status in this way is generally restrained by the widespread belief that if the rites and symbols are inappropriate to the status of the deceased, they will imperil the path of the soul. The greater the disparity between the actual caste of the deceased and that which is indexed by the funeral rites, the more likely that the soul of the dead may be harmed. By the time we began our project in Kedisan, the two rival descent groups had been trying to outdo each other in the grandeur of their annual funeral rites for several years, to the point that both groups were cremating their dead in biers that would not be inappropriate for a minor prince. This did not escape the notice of their neighbors, who joked that Kedisan was filling up with very old people who were terrified to die.

The reader may wonder, as I did, how the democratic customs of the subaks can survive in an atmosphere of such acute rivalry between neighbors. Much depends on the authority of the subak head, who must insist on strict observance of the rules that enforce egalitarian behavior, most importantly the etiquette of speech within the meetings. It is also my impression that strong subaks offer a welcome relief from the anxieties of social status, providing a setting where it is manifestly in everyone's interests to set aside everything to do with "caste." But for the subak to become such a refuge, it is necessary for the members to cede considerable power to their elected leaders.

With this background, we turn to the travails of Subak Cebok. Some years ago, according to our sources in the village, this small subak found itself in need of an effective leader. Cebok is located in the midst of the territory of the Pamos water temple, but it does not belong to the temple's congregation. The reason for this is that the principal source of water for Cebok is the spring at Gunung Kawi. As the reader may recall from an earlier chapter, the water from this spring is channeled downstream to be shared by two small subaks, Dlod Blumbang and Cebok (figure 24). Because the waters from the spring may be regarded as a gift from the deities of the Gunung Kawi temple, these subaks have opted not to acknowledge any obligation to the god of the Pamos water temple, and do not belong to the "Greater Subak" of Pamos. Instead, Dlod Blumbang helps to support the annual cycle of rituals at the Gunung Kawi temple. As the temple is located within the territory of the village of Sebatu, this means that Dlod Blumbang shares these expenses and duties with the citizens of Sebatu. Below the Dlod Blumbang weir, the small subak of Cebok has a second weir, which captures whatever remains in the stream after Dlod Blumbang has taken the main flow. Cebok does not

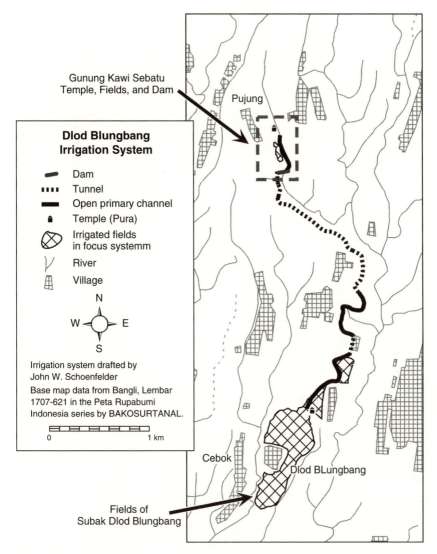

Figure 24. Irrigation systems originating from springs at Gunung Kawi Sebatu. *Credit*: John Schoenfelder.

offer contributions (*suwinih*) to the rituals of the temple of Gunung Kawi; the members explain this by noting that the water they capture at their weir would otherwise belong to the next major village downstream, Manuaba. So, following this reasoning (thought to be a bit sophistical by their neighbors), Cebok makes no contributions to the water temples

of Gunung Kawi or Pamos, contenting itself with occasional offerings to
the principal water temple of Manuaba.

Under these circumstances, it is not surprising that Cebok is chronically
short of water. Long ago—no one is quite sure when—someone came up
with a scheme to increase Cebok's share of the flow from Gunung Kawi.
This temple actually encloses two springs, one large and one small. The
larger spring belongs to Sebatu, and the smaller one is claimed by the village of Pujung. Cebok proposed to take the water from the Pujung
spring, in return for accepting the responsibility to assist Pujung with its
share of the costs of the rituals at the Gunung Kawi temple. There were
two ways Cebok could take this water: its members could build a new irrigation system starting at the Pujung spring, or they could measure the
flow coming out of the spring at Pujung shrine and request that this
amount be released at the Dlod Blungbang weir, from which it would
continue downstream to be captured at the Cebok weir. In that case, Cebok would stop or reduce its suwinih contributions to Manuaba and instead offer suwinih to Pujung. This plan would provide Cebok with
more water, at the expense of Dlod Blumbang; it would also provide Pujung with contributions to the temple festivals, at the expense of Sebatu.

According to our informants, this scheme had been talked about for
decades, but no one took any positive steps until the early nineties, when
two men became prominent in the villages of Cebok and Kedisan Kelod.
The powerful village head of Kedisan Kelod inherited some rice lands in
Subak Cebok, and began to attend subak meetings there. He became interested in the old scheme to capture the water from Pujung, which would
greatly increase the value of his fields. To actually bring off this ambitious
plan, Cebok would need a new leader, a strong and effective subak head.
A young man in the village caught his attention as a possible candidate:
Gde was poor but aggressive and ambitious, and was very willing to become the protégé of the village head. In short order he was elected head
of Subak Cebok and began to negotiate informally with the heads of the
other subaks over the question of the spring. Unfortunately, his aggressive style soon offended the leaders of Pujung, who quietly joined with
Dlod Blumbang to definitively block the plan. Soon thereafter, according
to our sources, Gde began to act capriciously. Funds collected from the
subak were not returned. When questions began to be asked in the meetings, he stopped holding subak meetings altogether. Some farmers told
us that they feared to oppose him openly, because he was a clever man
and still had the backing of the neighboring village head. Meanwhile, our
ecological team reported that harvests were dwindling in this subak because the irrigation schedules were very disorganized. Farmers complained about water theft by their neighbors, and in our first survey, two

farmers implied that Gde himself was not above stealing water. In an interview with one of our researchers, Gde was asked about this rumor. As the camera rolled, he laughed and said, "Why shouldn't anyone take water whenever they want to? As far as I'm concerned, go ahead!" Matters continued in this unsatisfactory state until 1999, when a section of tunnel collapsed and the main water supply for the subak was cut off. This of course put a stop to rice farming, although some farmers began to plant vegetable crops using unused water from their neighbors. Meanwhile, the subak head was taken to court on charges that he had tried to sell land belonging to the village to a buyer from the city.

Gde's behavior had amounted to an open challenge to his neighbors. But rather than unite to remove him, they had quarreled among themselves as their irrigation system fell apart. Interestingly, none of our informants suggested that Gde had practiced sorcery to sustain his control; instead his behavior was interpreted as that of a selfish and immoral man. But the question remained: why didn't the subak members exert themselves to regain control before it was too late?

• • •

Our original decision to videotape subak meetings was made while we were still entranced by the patterns of emergence in the computer simulations, which seemed to explain so much about the basis for cooperation among the subaks. Why not select a small region from the original model, put it under the microscope, and see if the predicted behaviors actually occurred? By videotaping the subak meetings, we could observe the links between signals from the environment and decisions taken by the farmers—in real time, as the computer scientists say. As the reader now knows, the results were not what we anticipated. In retrospect it is not surprising that the subaks of Pamos did not spend much time discussing their irrigation schedules; they had had many years to experiment and find out what works best. The real mystery is why they seemed to find it so difficult to sustain a cooperative and egalitarian system of governance, despite its manifest benefits. Our studies suggest that even the strongest and most democratic subaks were in a state of precarious balance, in constant danger of sliding into authoritarian rule or else into a kind of chaos, where water theft becomes commonplace and the gods do not receive their due at the temples. The surveys show that the farmers were well aware of the benefits of democratic governance; when a subak allowed itself to fall apart, the effects were quickly felt as the harvests fell prey to water shortages and pests. Altogether, the advantages of democratic governance seemed so obvious that I began to wonder whether the still only partly explored libraries of manuscripts in the Balinese language might include the writings of some Balinese Plato, debating the merits of republican versus aristocratic forms of government. After all, many subaks have written constitutions in which the rules of democratic procedures are carefully set out. The existence of these constitutions argues for an implicit theory of democratic governance. Why shouldn't some Balinese writer have attempted to articulate the concept itself, even if only, like Plato, with the aim of disparaging the capriciousness of democratic rule?

Soon after the videotaping began, I persuaded myself to be on the lookout for such a manuscript, and even made a few forays into Balinese libraries. Meanwhile, two of my Balinese colleagues were busy carrying out the second survey of farmers' attitudes. In the village of Pujung Kaja, they reported having difficulty with some of the questions, namely those pertaining to caste. They said that this village had decided some years ago to abolish all caste distinctions, and people were reluctant to state their caste affiliation. Perhaps these questions should be omitted from the questionnaires. On the other hand, to do so could compromise the value of the surveys, because caste had proven to be crucial for understanding questions of governance in the other subaks. While our team was deciding what to do, the head of Subak Pujung sent word that he would like to talk with us about the surveys, because several members of the subak had expressed some concerns to him.

The news that a water mountain village had decided to abolish caste was intriguing. Among the "Bali Aga" villages in the highlands, it is often forbidden to assert caste privileges, but elsewhere, so far as I knew, caste is always a dominant feature of the social landscape. I arranged to meet with the subak head the next afternoon, accompanied by one of the members of our survey team. When we arrived we were surprised to find not only the subak head but the entire leadership of the village, nearly a dozen men, waiting for us. After offering us refreshments, they invited us to explain in detail exactly what we hoped to accomplish with our surveys and videotaping, and what this had to do with our ecological studies, which they said they understood and appreciated. We described our aims as best we could, emphasizing our interest in understanding the reasons for the dramatic variation in styles of governance among the Pamos subaks. Eventually we came to the delicate matter of caste. I said that we realized that many Balinese are reluctant to mention their caste or supposed hierarchical rank, especially to outsiders, but that the topic could not be avoided if we hoped to understand the reasons for conflict within subaks. But before I could finish, a temple priest interrupted me. He said that caste had no meaning in their village, because everyone now had the same caste. When I responded that people must surely remember their ancestral heritage (the origin temples of their forebears), he answered that it was no longer necessary to do so, because holy water for all rituals, including marriages and funerals, was available to everyone from a special village temple. Several other village leaders then entered the discussion, explaining that in their opinion it would be disruptive for us to insist on interviewing people about their caste. Certainly people remembered their ancestry, but it had become the policy of the village to strongly discourage any attempt to assert one's caste, because experience showed that this created discord in the community. In answer to further questions, they said that as long as we refrained from stirring up the subject of caste, we were free to attend their subak meetings and to ask villagers to participate in our surveys. We should know that subak meetings had been merged with those of the village (*desa*); while the two institutions remained discrete, they saw no need for separate meetings, because both groups were governed by the same people.

Pujung became a turning point in our research. It seemed that the hypothetical republic I had been imagining might actually exist, in the very center of our study area. In subsequent conversations with members of this village, we tried to discover whether at some particular point in the past the village had formally decided to become a republic. We sought out older people and asked about the history of the village. How had the abolition of caste come about? Had they (or their forebears) considered the merits of democratic rule, weighed the consequences, and voted to abolish caste? The answer that emerged from numerous conversations was that this was approximately correct; however, this way of summarizing the history did not quite capture their own view of how the decisions had been taken. Where I saw one issue, they saw two: the abolition of caste distinctions, and the strengthening of democratic governance. The two points were admittedly linked, but from their perspective the expansion of democracy was only one of several effects produced by their decisions concerning caste. As an example, nearly everyone we talked to stressed the material benefits derived from prohibiting status competition among descent groups. It is a good deal cheaper to get married, celebrate a child's birthdays, or perform a funeral in Pujung than in any neighboring village, because all these rituals have become standardized and ostentatious displays are strictly forbidden. However, our informants told us that the abolition of caste came about not for political reasons but because of the availability of holy water from a special village temple. Tirtha from this temple had long been accepted by most people in Pujung as appropriate for any and all varieties of ritual that might be performed within the village, including the worship of the gods as well as human rites of passage. Thus there was no need to obtain tirtha from other sources like caste origin temples. And according to the logic of

Balinese beliefs about holy water, if two families use the same tirtha for rites of passage, they are of equal caste status.

It appeared that in the 1970s and 1980s the leadership of the village chose to follow this chain of reasoning to its logical conclusion, and passed resolutions in the village council (to which every household sends a member as representative) that to be a citizen of Pujung, one must accept the holy water of the village temple as sufficient for all one's needs. A fortiori, one must accept the equality of caste status of all citizens of Pujung. Anyone who disagreed with this ruling was free to leave the village (Balinese village councils have legal authority over the land used for dwellings, and so have the power to deny residence to anyone who refuses to obey their rules). But nearly all of the families in the village chose to stay and relinquish their caste titles, in preference to exile.

Several village leaders told us that, at the time, they had not anticipated how dramatically these decisions would strengthen democratic rule in Pujung. Some said that the abolition of caste distinctions was spearheaded by a faction of wealthy Sudra families, as a way to diminish the status of hereditary minor aristocrats in the village. One elder quietly commented that wealth, rather than caste, had become the key to social status in Pujung. And some farmers complained that the affairs of the subak generally took second place to those of the village, because the two assemblies now meet as one body, and topics pertaining to farming generally come last at these meetings. But these caveats aside, it seemed that formal democracy had gained a decisive and seemingly permanent victory over caste hierarchy in Pujung. This brought clear benefits that even the ex-aristocrats acknowledged: the subak is thought to be exceptionally well run, and families are spared the financial and emotional costs of caste competition with their neighbors.

At first, the abolition of caste in Pujung seemed like a marvelous confirmation of everything we had learned about the subaks. Our original ecological analysis and modeling had shown that cooperation within and among subaks could be explained as a self-organizing process driven by ecological dynamics. But the sociological studies of the subaks showed that conflicts emanating from competition in caste status frequently hindered cooperation. In the days of the rajahs, caste was officially sanctioned, but in the modern era caste tends to be viewed by government officials as a troublesome anachronism.[7] Pujung seemed to prove that this problem could be eliminated at a single stroke. With the dawn of democracy, the contradiction (in Marxian terms) between an archaic caste hierarchy and a mode of production based on cooperative

---

[7] Unsurprisingly, officials of high caste are much less troubled by the caste system than everyone else.

subaks could be overcome. We began to congratulate ourselves that we had arrived with our video cameras and questionnaires just in time to catch the fruits of an era of experimentation, as Pujung showed the face of the future to the other communities in the region.

Or at least, such were my own thoughts, enthusiastically communicated to my Balinese colleagues. But as I gloated over our luck in capturing "history on the wing," eventually I began to notice that my colleagues were less certain that Pujung's democracy would soon be imitated by the other communities. It seemed that they took more seriously than I the claim that the key to Pujung's democracy was its special tirtha. When we put this question to our informants in Pujung and also in some other subaks, they pointed out that Pujung alone has access to such omnipotent holy water, thanks to its special temple, and so Pujung is the only community that can choose to abolish caste. I found this unpersuasive. At the risk of impiety, I reminded my colleagues that the will of the Balinese gods is subject to reinterpretation at any temple festival by trance mediums, so that if the gods wished, they could certainly provide the holy water needed for democratic reforms at other village temples. But as we were debating this point and contemplating the next steps in our research, new information came to light, and the picture shifted once again. First came the news that Pujung had formerly been nominally ruled by a *Kebayan*, and expected to be so again in the future. This was very surprising. The most conservative Old Balinese villages of the highlands, which preserve antique forms of governance that are mentioned in thousand-year-old inscriptions, are nominally governed by a pair of elderly priests who are called *Kebayan*. But Kebayan are not found in water mountain villages; their position is based on a gerontocratic principle that has little salience in these villages. Yet alone among the villages of Pamos, Pujung had found a place for a Kebayan in its village hierarchy. Stranger still, we were told that the *Kebayan* of Pujung ruled alone, rather than as half of a pair, the usual custom among Old Balinese villages. But most astonishingly, we were informed that to take up his position, the *Kebayan* must be consecrated by the performance of the ancient Sanskrit rite for the installation of kings, *abiseka ratu*. This notion seemed so outlandish as to verge on the nonsensical. Abiseka ratu is known to have been performed at the installation of Balinese kings in the nineteenth century; one such event was carefully recorded by a colonial scholar, who pronounced the Balinese version of this rite as faithful to the spirit, if not the letter, of the Sanskrit original. But the citizens of the democratic republic of Pujung proposed to carry out this rite for a village priest. They also told us that it had been performed once before in the twentieth century, for a Kebayan who died in the 1960s. As best we could gather without actually witnessing this rite, its purpose in Pujung would be to consecrate the Kebayan as a sacred ruler, but one whose authority would be confined to religious matters. Even after the installation of the Kebayan-king, we were told, the day-to-day governance of the village would remain in the hands of the democratic assembly.[8]

Our faith that we had discovered the path that the subaks were fated to follow could not quite survive these discoveries. A better Marxist than I might still choose to believe in the eventual triumph of secular democratic rule in Pujung, and its spread to the other subaks in the region. But as we continued our interviews with the citizens of Pujung, it became clear that their political passions were focused less on their republican democracy than on the grandeur they hoped to achieve with the installation of their Kebayan-king. As far as the village leaders were concerned, the greatest benefit of the abolition of caste was to unite the village behind this project. Pujung is noted for its lavish village temple festivals; it appears that what the citizens saved on rite-of-passage expenses by the abolition of caste has mostly been redirected toward these communal celebrations. Indeed their strongest motivation for desiring a sacred ruler, a Kebayan-king, was apparently to provide themselves with the most impressive kind of leader to carry out such rites. Thus, rather than marking the historical transformation from feudalism to secular modernity, the adoption of democracy in Pujung appears to have been a means to a different end—part of a strategy meant to help the community pursue more ancient political ambitions.

So in the end, our questionnaires and videotapes did not lead us to a clear solution to the question of the governance of the subaks. Based on the results of the earlier ecological modeling, we expected to find a strong historical current reinforcing cooperative bonds in the subaks,

---

[8] I later learned that Leopold Howe, an English ethnologist, had written a doctoral dissertation about Pujung based on fieldworld carried out in the late 1970s. His study confirms what we were told. Concerning status in the village, he writes as follows: "when I first arrived in Pujung one of the first tasks I put myself was the discovery of all the different titles to be found in the village. I was therefore somewhat surprised when, to my rather ineptly put questions, I received a large proportion of negative replies. Most of my neighbors denied possession of a title and some tried to discourage me from enquiring any further. They said people in Pujung were unaccustomed to confessing to such titles as it would have a debilitating effect on village harmony. . . . Pujung, they said, was based on equality of status. . . . This view of the structure of Pujung society was in large part supported by everyone in the village" (392). Howe also commented on the shared use of holy water (*tirtha*) by high-status groups such as the Pande: "For a place like Bali this is an astonishing state of affairs. Generally speaking no Balinese will pray in, or accept holy water from, a temple which is considered to be of a clearly inferior status. In fact as a rule we may say that in Pujung no one refuses to pray in any temple, whether public or private, or to receive holy water there, as a direct result of status considerations . . . the irrelevance of title to temple membership is largely a function of the egalitarian ideology. . . . I was told that if

and weakening the countercurrents of caste competition now that Bali is no longer ruled by kings. Instead we observed mostly spiraling eddies, as the balance of forces in each subak flowed first in one direction and then the other. When we tried to make sense of specific cases, very often we found ourselves confronted by apparently irrational elements: Blerong spirits, ritual kingship, the arcane practices of the caste system. It seemed that Balinese democracy might be fated to remain entangled with the supernatural for a few more generations; if so, perhaps we had reached the outer limit of what could be explained.

---

the kubayan tried to up his status there would be nothing preventing members of the batuan group from claiming the title of gusti. In such an atmosphere village unity would certainly be lost and the kubayan's power would suffer. Thus some of the more astute villagers feel the kubayan dare not go too far in his manipulation of the village banjar (these days sometimes known as the banjor belog, 'the banjar of fools'), because to do so would undermine his own power base. In conclusion there appears to be a finely balanced conflict between the egalitarian principles, which had always had the upper hand, and the possibility of a status drive by certain powerful members of the village, which would, of course, destroy the old consensus" (393). Leopold E. A. Howe, "Pujung: An Investigation into the Foundations of Balinese Culture," doctoral dissertation, University of Edinburgh, 1980.

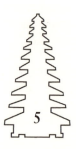

5

Hieroglyphs of Reason

THE KEBAYAN-KINGS OF Pujung were merely the latest in a long list of stray elements that had so far eluded capture in our simulation models, videotapes, and questionnaires. Witches, sorcerers, Blerong spirits, and for that matter the entire panoply of rituals at the water temples had been spared our attentions; it was much easier to catch leafhoppers—or gossip, for that matter. But while supernatural beings are usually left untroubled by scientists, the one exception is anthropologists. While my colleagues were gathering factual data with their flowmeters and surveys, when left to myself I often reverted to old habits, asking questions about temples and witches long after the cameras had been turned off. At first it did not occur to me that these conversations might turn out to be relevant to our project. Instead Balinese religion seemed to be merely part of the unchanging background of village life; our studies were designed to see through it, or past it, to underlying ecological and social processes.

When my perspective changed, it was for reasons that at first had little to do with our activities in Bali. Having returned to California to teach during the academic year, I happened to be asked to review a manuscript by my colleague Valerio Valeri. Valeri was an Italian philosopher-turned-anthropologist whose studies of a tribal society in eastern Indonesia were deeply influenced by Hegelian philosophy. In *The Forest of Taboos*, his last book, Valeri explored the meaning of taboo for the Huaulu, who number fewer than a thousand persons and inhabit one of the most remote corners of Indonesia. In one sense, Valeri argued, the hundreds of taboos that the Huaulu try to follow are rightly seen as fanciful and arbitrary. But on the other hand, it is hardly irrational for them to interpret their world in light of taboo. After all, generations of Huaulu have struggled to bring their society into conformity with its unusual logic. As a result, taboo is deeply embedded in most aspects of their daily life.

On reflection, it seemed to me that the same argument might apply with even greater force to the Balinese. At the core of Balinese religion is the belief that the universe is coherent, and that it has been built up from a finite set of elements including colors, letters, numbers, sounds, and forces (which can also take the form of emotions). From the combination of these elements emerge both the physical universe (the macrocosm, or *bhuana agung*) and the inner world of the self (the microcosm, or *bhuana alit*).[1] The underlying premise is that simple forms give rise to more complex ones in orderly patterns: combine white and red and you get pink; between two full musical tones there must be a half tone. Here Valeri's argument would seem to apply perfectly. Of course these cosmological symbols belong to the realm of magic, not science. Yet everywhere one looks in a water mountain village, they are there to be seen: carved into stone and wood in the houses and temples; shaped into colorful offerings; even played as musical themes on the gamelan orchestras. But are these symbols merely pretty decorations, suitable for holidays, religious festivals, and illustrations in sacred texts? Or, as with the Huaulu and their taboos, have they actually become woven into patterns of thought, and the fabric of social life?

The question is especially pertinent with regard to the management of water mountains, which are one of the focal points of Balinese cosmological symbolism. According to Balinese belief, the order that one sees in the world does not occur naturally or spontaneously. When left to itself the natural world is thought to be in a state of maximum disorder, as for example in uninhabited jungles or along the seacoast. In contrast, water mountains have been shaped to fit the most exacting principles of sacred geometry; they are triumphs of order. I remember when I first learned to see them in this way. One moonlit evening I was driving down the mountainside, accompanied by a subak head. Below us, most of the water mountains that we could see had recently been flooded, so that the moonlight was reflected from the terraces. They shine, my companion remarked, like jewels against the dark surrounding jungle. Jewels are revered as especially powerful cosmological symbols; priests and sorcerers strive to align their own inner worlds into jewel-like perfection, since self-mastery is the foundation of both wisdom and power. The suggestion that water mountains might also resemble jewels helped to clarify, for me, the deeper meaning of the endless rituals that the farmers carry out on them. For example, rice is initially grown in seedbeds and transplanted by hand into the terraces after they are flooded. Usually

---

[1] Similar systems of cosmological classification are found in many Indonesian societies; the close parallel with Javanese ideas is discussed in Stephen C. Headley, *From Cosmology to Exorcism in a Javanese Genesis*, New York: Oxford University Press, 2001: 193–99.

the seedlings are pushed into the mud in orderly rows, but sometimes farmers plant them in complex mandalic patterns, following formulas that take into account the farmer's own birth date. Before World War II, according to colonial scholars, such planting in mandalic patterns was the custom (one that struck some scholars as a particularly mindless example of agricultural magic). But if Valeri's argument is correct, these Western observers missed the point. The inspiration for the mandalic patterns is not simple close-your-eyes-and-wish magic, but a more subtle cosmological dualism. Consider that for a water mountain to function, with water flowing in timely patterns through its complex channels and leveled terraces, its physical geometry must achieve an almost jewel-like perfection. An ordinary jungle ridge or hillock must acquire a faceted, almost crystalline shape, with sheets of water held in place by perishable earthen bunds and simple wooden gates. For this to be achieved, both the water mountain and the desires of the farmers who sustain its artificial shape must be aligned to far more rigorous patterns than they would take if left to themselves. All this is a question of engineering, not magic. The magical idea is that the two problems are really one—that the forces needed to align the water mountain already exist in the inner world of the farmers.

As Valeri saw, what is most Hegelian about these beliefs is the idea that, over time, the human world can be brought into closer and closer approximation to an idealized order as a kind of collective social project. In the *Philosophy of History*, Hegel argued that a society's creative accomplishments—its music, philosophy, architecture, mode of governance, mathematics—inevitably build on the accomplishments of the past. He called these creations "Objectified Reason": ideas that are given physical existence in the world. According to Hegel, from one age to the next they acquire greater coherence, drawing ever nearer to ultimate truth. In this sense, the inhabitants of water mountain villages are faithful to Hegel's vision. They have objectified the Reason of their cosmological vision into innumerable symbolic forms, to the point that it pervades their experience of the world. At birth, the spirit of an infant is invited to compose itself into an orderly mandalic pattern, and the dead are covered with shrouds inscribed with slightly modified versions of the same cosmological symbols. Several times each week, women re-create these images as offerings (*bebanten*) using woven palm fronds, flowers, coins, and rice. The bebanten are placed everywhere: at the entrances to houses and temples, beside stacks of books, atop motorcycles, at every crossroads, so that the village is regularly blanketed with hundreds of colorful images of cosmological perfection. In a deeper sense, everything from the naming of children to the techniques for cooking, healing, and the composition of poetry is supposed to conform to mandalic patterns.

After reading Valeri, it was no longer possible for me to see all this as mere magic.

• • •

Indeed, Valeri's reflections on the Huaulu suggested an explanation for one of the more surprising discoveries from our surveys of the fourteen Pamos subaks. All subaks require their members to perform rituals in the fields and water temples. But the amounts of time and treasure devoted to these religious activities vary widely, and it turns out that the largest expenditures we noted in our study were made by the subaks that scored highest on egalitarianism. Why should the most democratic farmers spend more time fashioning offerings to the gods than their more autocratic neighbors? The conventional, off-the-cuff answer that an anthropologist might reach for is simple Durkheimian functionalism: the rituals help to promote social solidarity. But this explanation will not stand much scrutiny. Durkheim saw rituals as occasions for "collective effervescence," whereas water temple rites are generally sober affairs where the display of elaborate offerings often has a thinly disguised competitive flavor.

Valeri's analysis suggests a different approach, one that focuses on the cognitive rather than the performative aspects of ritual, in particular on the ways that the achievement and maintenance of order can become a collective social project. This view is not too far from the interpretation that the Balinese themselves give to their ritual practices. Like the Huaulu, the Balinese try to follow an ethical code that obliges them to resist disorder by imposing systematic principles of order on the self as well as the world. This religious project is clearly relevant to the questions we have been pursuing in this book. Indeed one could argue—as I intend to do here—that the rites of the water temples manifest a profound analysis of the problem of cooperation on the water mountains. And further, that the attention lavished on these rituals is itself a powerful social and historical force.

The subject of this chapter, then, is the cult of water temples, seen from the perspective of its own inner logic. Earlier chapters have addressed the question of the practical ecological role of the temple networks, and offered an interpretation for their emergence in ancient Balinese kingdoms. But to complete the picture, it is also necessary to convey something of their meaning from the inside, as the historical culmination of the cognitive processes that produced them. To that end, this chapter will offer an interpretation of the water temple cult as a system of beliefs, one that has diverged from Brahmanical traditions to suit the needs of the farmers. By framing these beliefs in a broadly Hegelian context, I mean to convey something more than the idea that the temples and their rites express coherent cosmological ideas. There is also the implication that these ideas aspire to the status of universality—that they represent the culmination of a historical process through which society discovers its own meaning. Hegel believed this to be true of the institutions of his own society. He wrote of the thrill that scientists of the Enlightenment felt when they began to see that their mathematical ideas matched their obervations of the natural world. I have heard Balinese priests express a similar excitement as they contemplated how well their cosmological principles explained the inner workings of the micro and macrocosms. (This particular thrill, by the way, is one that they are surprisingly eager to share with inquisitive anthropologists.) We will return to this theme later on, as the various strands of this analysis of the water temples are brought together.

• • •

A strict doctrine of cosmological dualism has its charms as a philosophical principle, but it presents a rather challenging foundation for the organization of daily life. Assembling the many varieties of offerings needed for the annual round of agricultural rites, to take but one example, imposes a relentless series of obligations on households, and women frequently find themselves working late into the night, sometimes near tears with exhaustion, trying to finish them in time. Yet one hears few complaints; most farm families simply take these tasks for granted. But how did their ancestors come by these beliefs, and why did they choose to adopt them? Why is it thought to be necessary to shape the world—and oneself—into such exacting patterns?

The answer to the first of these questions might seem obvious but for the fact that, since ancient times, farmers have been forbidden to read the religious texts that are the ultimate source of these cosmological ideas. Indeed, most such texts in Balinese contain an explicit warning: *aji wera*, "do not disseminate" (with the implicit meaning "except to persons of suitable caste whose studies are supervised by Brahmins"). Were the farmers to ignore this warning and continue with their reading, in the *Dharmasastra-s* they would learn that their duty as members of the Sudra caste is simply to serve the higher castes. The reason for restricting access to religious texts to persons of high caste is related to the basic purpose of religious instruction. Balinese religious texts draw from three ancient Indian sources: Saivasiddhanta and Samkya Hinduism, and Vajrayana Buddhism. An important theme is karma, the notion that one's station in life is predetermined at birth by one's spiritual progress in past lives. From this belief flows the key distinction between *ekajati* and *dwijati*, once and twiceborn, low caste and high. The goddess Durga determines which souls shall be reborn on the basis of their karma. In my experience, this belief is widespread among contemporary Balinese villagers. For example, when a child dies, families may be consoled by the observation that the good die young because they have fewer sins to expiate. In any case, according to the texts (and their Brahmin guardians) only the twiceborn are eligible to receive religious instruction. Prospective students must undergo ritual purification before beginning a course of study supervised by a Brahmin.[2] The aim of religious study is to guide the individual along a path of heroic spiritual progress, as mastery of the self leads to knowledge and powers beyond those available to ordinary mortals. Such knowledge is vital for rulers and their priestly advisers, because their personal spiritual prowess is the ultimate foundation for a Dharmasastric kingdom. But the dharma of the onceborn farmers requires only that they support and obey their rulers; in return they may enjoy the benefits of life in a peaceful and prosperous society.

The emergence of the water temple cult is thus somewhat puzzling; it has no basis or precedent in the core religious texts available to the Balinese. But perhaps this did not greatly matter since in any case the farmers were forbidden to read them. A more surprising issue has to do with the issue of caste itself. The Indian authors of the religious texts forbidden to the farmers took for granted that society was organized into castes: endogamous social groups based on hereditary occupations that exchange goods and services with other castes. But this assumption did not hold for ancient Bali, as we have seen. Early Balinese rulers whose authority ultimately depended on their status as twiceborn aristocrats were thus obliged to sustain a historical fiction—to pretend that their societies were organized by the principle of caste, as in this passage from an eleventh-century inscription: "including Nayaka, Brahmana, Ksatriya Wesya, Sudra, master slave, old young male female, married celibate. . . ."[3] But when the inscriptions refer to actual social groups in the villages, or issue instructions concerning taxes or regulations, there is no mention of specific Sudra castes. Pigeaud concluded that castes were also absent from contemporary ancient Javanese kingdoms: "Though well-known in Old Javanese literature the Indian system of four castes

---

[2] This restriction has been challenged by religious reformers spearheaded by the Pasek Sanak Pitu, a politico-religious organization promoting the Pasek descent group. It has also become more difficult to enforce as religious texts are published and sold.

[3] Prasasti 410 Serai AII, era of Anak Wungcu (eleventh century), no. 302 in Roelf Goris, *Inscripties voor Anak Wungçu, Prasati Bali I–II*, Bandung: C. V. Masa Baru, 1954. VLLb.1–2 irikanang rrgep buru sanayaka, bramana, ksatriya wesya, sudra, hadyan hulun ma muda, lakilaki wadwan . . . .

seems to have had no validity in actual life."[4] In ancient Balinese king-doms, it appears that only the twiceborn and the metalsmiths were or-ganized into something resembling a South Asian caste. But the fiction of a universal caste system remained indispensable to the twiceborn rulers and was frequently invoked, as in this passage written by a nineteenth-century Balinese king: "Humanity is divided into four; the first is Brah-mins, the second Ksatriya, the third Wesya, these are called tri wangsa, another term is twiceborn, the fourth group is the Sudras, the onceborn, these distinctions are unchangeable, they are called the four Varnas."

The laws and regulations pertaining to caste in the later Balinese king-doms were almost entirely confined to protecting the status of the twice-born, for example by proposing the death penalty for sexual relations between twiceborn women and onceborn men.[5] But as long as the vil-lagers paid due deference to their rulers and priests, they enjoyed some freedom to govern themselves, and most villages not engaged in wet-rice agriculture expressly rejected caste as a principle for their own internal organization. Still, from the perspective of the ruling class all farmers were categorized as Sudras, and as such were barred from the study of Brahmanical expository texts. These texts were often intentionally com-posed in such a way as to make them difficult to read, to ensure that they could be understood only with the guidance of a knowledgeable mentor. Altogether, it seems evident that since ancient times it was not consid-ered to be in the interests of the state to permit farmers to pry into Brah-manical metaphysical doctrines, especially those having to do with the principles of caste.

But this prohibition was not very successful. The rites of the water temples, I suggest, draw deeply from the same metaphysical ideas that are the foundation of Brahmanical religious education. But whereas the twiceborn are encouraged to study the texts in order to emancipate themselves from base emotions and become fit to rule, the water temple cult has little direct connection with the texts, and pursues a different end. The aim is to awaken the powers of the collective, not the individ-ual, by emphasizing not the singular but the universal and stereotypical.

But before trying to clarify these differences, two preliminary points need to be made. The first is to resolve the question of how the farmers came by their knowledge of Indian metaphysics. I suggest that the an-swer is to be found in the ancient inscriptions, which show that the vil-lagers were in close contact with the clergy from the time of the earliest

---

[4] Theodor G. th. Pigeaud, *Java in the Fourteenth Century: A Study in Cultural History*, vol 4, The Hague: Martinus Nijhoff, 1962: 259.

[5] Cf. F. A. Liefrinck, *Landsverordeningen van inlandsche vorsten op Bali*, 's-Gravenhage: Martinus Nijhoff, 1917: 319–23 n.

kingdoms. The second, more problematic point has to do with my suggestion that the rituals and practices of the water temples constitute a distinct cult that has diverged from the Brahmanical textual tradition. This interpretation would certainly be controversial in Bali. I have discussed it with Balinese Brahmins; most are inclined to see the temple rites as integrally related to their own religious practice. Others, however, agree that the aims of these public ritual performances are fundamentally different from the inner journey that is the basis for their own religious practice. Clearly, public ritual performances serve different ends than solitary reading and meditation. Both are concerned with the discovery of universal truths. But the question is, are the universal truths of the water temples the same as those of the aristocratic religion, or are they different? My claim is that they do not overlap very much and are to some degree contradictory, but it should be noted that knowledgeable Balinese disagree with me.[6]

• • •

Cosmological dualism is older than Hinduism in Indonesia. It continues to pervade the tribal religions of the islands to the east of Bali, where myth and ritual divide the cosmos into paired contrasts: Sun and Moon, male and female, elder and junior, wife giver and wife taker. Similar ideas are present in the inscriptions and art of the earliest Balinese kingdoms. When Indian religions came to Bali, they did not contradict this worldview but enriched it by adding a subjective dimension. The philosophical basis for this form of dualism is expressed in three related terms that are among the core concepts of both Saivasiddhanta and Samkya Hinduism. The first of these terms is *bhuta*. In Sanskrit and Old Javanese, *bhUta* has several meanings, but the relevant ones include that which is or exists, any living being (divine, human, animal, and even vegetable); the world; one of the five elements (of which five are reckoned, viz., ether, air, fire, water, earth). The second term, *mahabhuta* (Sanskrit *MahAbhUta*, the great or supreme bhuta), refers specifically to these five irreducible

---

[6] Jean-François Guermonprez suggests another possibility in "La religion balinaise dans le miroir de 'hindouisme," *Bulletin de L'Ecole Française D'Extreme-orient* 88 (2001): 271–93. Here Guermonprez considers the manifold ways in which Balinese religion differs from Hinduism as practiced in South Asia. I will not attempt to summarize those differences here. Instead I suggest that over the centuries what I have called the "temple cult" of Balinese villages gradually reshaped the role of the Brahmin clergy, naturalizing (as Guermonprez observes) the gods that Hinduism humanized. But while Balinese Brahmin priests (*pedanda*) found a new role for themselves as sources of tirtha and sacrifiers for village rites, some of them also retained a traditional role partly based on their knowledge of written texts, as celebrants of the cult of kingship, and advisers (*purohita*) to Balinese rulers.

elements, which are also associated with the five senses; cardinal directions (the fifth direction is the center); musical tones; primary colors; and primary emotions. More complex elements are formed from the recombination of the mahabhuta. The concept of bhuta thus includes not only physical elements but also the subjective qualities that make up the realm of inner experience or mind. In the Saivasiddhanta tradition this subjective aspect of bhuta is termed *bhuta tanmatra* (Sanskrit *bhŪta tanmatra*):

> these gross elements are not the perceptible gross substances found in the outside world, but capacities located in bodily members like eye, ear, & etc, enabling them to become aware of outside objects (as a lens does). The subtle elements (tanmatra) are to be taken as capacities which process the external objects captured by the bhuta, extracting their special features (sound, feel, shape etc.) to convert into ideas . . . then from the five named bhuta derive those elements that inform the bodies of all organic life from plants upwards.[7]

The concepts of bhuta, mahabhuta, and bhuta tanmatra define a dualistic cosmos that posits a perfect correspondence between the constituent elements of the outer universe and the inner world of subjective experience. This philosophical viewpoint is articulated in ancient Balinese inscriptions, as for example in a concluding passage from a twelfth-century text issued by the Balinese king Anak Wungcu: "all beings comprised of Bhuta witness this seeing far and near, day and night."[8] But while all beings are composed of bhuta, only humans and gods have the ability to organize them into complex well-ordered forms; the natural tendency of bhuta is to decompose into raw and unruly combinations such as overgrown landscapes, bad music, or minds in which crude desires have gained ascendency. To comprehend and master the bhuta is a necessity for any constructive human purpose, from the composition of music or poetry to the governance of a kingdom, and such tasks always require an inner journey as well as action in the world. This lesson is frequently expounded in metaphysical texts, but it is also given more engaging expression in myth and ritual.

One such myth, which will be recounted below, tells the story of the birth of the *bhutakala*, the bhuta that are subject to time. To the best of

[7] H. W. Schoterman, *Saiva Siddhanta: An Indian School of Mystical Thought*, New Delhi: Motilal Banarsidass, 2000 (orig. 1912): 126.

[8] 441 Sawan VIIb 5, Icaka 995, transcribed and translated in I Wayan Ardika and Ni Luh Sutjiati Beratha, *Perajin pada masa Bali Kuno Abad IX–XI*. Denpasar: Fakultas Sastra, Universitas Udayana, 1998: 361–62.

Kita masuking sarbwamasarira, sakala saksibhuta tumon angadoh lawang apar rahina wngi.

my knowledge the concept of bhutakala is a Balinese invention that does not exist in the Sanskrit tradition; in Sanskrit *bhUtakAla* means simply past time or the preterit tense. But the association of bhuta with time does relate to the Hindu notion of the four great ages of the world, which mark a gradual decline from divine perfection in the first age to chaos in the last. What we think of as the modern age is located at the end of the last era, named for the destroyer goddess Kali, whom the Balinese identify with Durga. During this period Mind loses its ascendancy over the bhuta. According to my Brahmin sources, the bhutakala of our era, those subject to time, are manifest in troubles and sicknesses like the annual plagues of cholera and smallpox. But they also exist in the five elemental or mahabhuta that make up the transient inner world of each newborn human, and gain ascendancy in the witches and sorcerers who appear in every generation. In this, the final age of the world, retaining some measure of control over the bhutakala becomes the central problem of human existence. The Brahmanical tradition offers a solution in the form of studies designed to heighten a student's faculties of understanding and awareness. A different approach is taken in the rituals of the water temples, which frame the problem of the bhutakala not as desires or evils to be suppressed but as a mélange of personified spirits, natural forces, and internal desires that must be rebalanced and harmonized. While our concern here is primarily with the farmers and their water temples, it is necessary to understand something of the Brahmanical theory of the bhutakala in order to establish a context for the farmers' beliefs. Why should farmers feel it necessary to marshal such an elaborate apparatus of metaphysical concepts to celebrate such mundane events as harvests, the control of rice pests, or the birth of their children? Part of the answer doubtless lies in the philosophical depth of these ideas. But they also lend a seductive grandeur to village affairs through their association with the royal cult. Thus, in water temple rituals, the problem of too many rats in the fields becomes an emblem of the corruption of spirit in the final age of the world, a matter worthy of the attention of Brahmins and princes.

The aristocratic Brahmanical tradition with its many texts and treatises, and the largely unwritten traditions of the water temples, offer contrasting approaches to the problem of social existence as it appears in the context of these metaphysical ideas. An intriguing example of the aristocratic formulation is provided by two poems composed at the time of the Dutch conquest of the kingdom of Badoeng, in the first decade of the twentieth century. A story that already has elements of grandeur, the doomed struggle of the last kings against the colonial empire of the Dutch, is framed in metaphysical terms as the ethical dilemma that faces mortal rulers in the Age of Kali. The fundamental issue at stake is not only the fate of the kingdom but the risks that heroes are forced to take when they struggle with the bhutakala of the outer world.

The first of these poems was composed by the rajah of the southern Balinese kingdom of Badoeng in 1905. The title, *Purwa Senghara*, is not easily translated into English; *Purwa* means origin or beginning, while *Senghara* means disorder or chaos, traditionally associated with the Age of Kali. The poem explores the question of how a ruler should behave when the bhuta become impossible to control, as must happen with increasing frequency in the final age of the world. By 1905 it was clear to the kings of Bali that the Dutch colonial empire had set its sights on the conquest of their island. The northern kingdoms had already fallen to the Dutch after three successive invasions. If the Dutch chose to invade the south, their overwhelming technological advantage assured the defeat of the Balinese kings. How then to prepare for this conflict? The *Purwa Senghara* begins with the story of a hero's anguish as he sees a great kingdom about to be overrun by destructive bhutakala, personified as raging demons:

> Again Lord Arjuna asked the sage Bhagawan Abyasa
> How can the kingdom of Dwarawati fall?
> For it is justly ruled by Krishna
> The god Wisnu himself watches over this land.[9]

The sage Abhasa answers by explaining that nothing on earth can escape the endless cycles of life and death:

> You need not speak again of the sacred powers of Lord Wisnu
> Whose power to care for the realm and bring prosperity is without end
> Birth, life and death rule the world, even the gods cannot escape them.[10]

The sage explains that in the last phase of this cycle of the world, the violent bhuta that are nothing more than embodiments of raw desire must grow ever stronger until their ultimate triumph. This becomes the theme of the poem. The kingdom of Dwarawati is destroyed by thousands of rampaging demons, and a sorrowful Arjuna goes to the forest to meditate. Meanwhile, Wignotsawa, a demonic incarnation of the destroyer god Rudra, attacks the heaven of the divine nymphs, who choose not to resist. The gods attempt to come to the rescue of the nymphs, but

---

[9] Geguritan Purwa Senghara, Pupuh VIII/Pucung, verse 17, original manuscript housed in the library of the Fakultas Sastra, Udayana University, Bali (my translation).

[10] Jati tuhu paragan Sang Hyang Wisnu, tan nyandang parnayang wireh pakumpulan lewih, Sang Hyang Wisnu, prasida sarining jagat. Ne tetelu utpeti, stiti, puniki, tekaning pralina, kawisesa makasami, twara nyandang, cening rahat manyakitang. Purwa Senghara, Pupuh VIII, verse 19.

are vanquished by Wignotsawa's army of demons. On earth, the Buddha is reincarnated as the greatest king of this age, Sutasoma, who seeks by his example to awaken the demons to their higher nature. When Rudra reappears in the body of a gigantic flesh-eating demon, Sutasoma courageously offers his own body as food for the demon. But his sacrifice is not enough to halt the dissolution of his kingdom, and the poem ends inconclusively, with premonitions of a final, cataclysmic war.

The Balinese king who wrote this poem drew several lessons from his survey of the struggles of virtuous rulers in the Age of Kali. The most important is the need to avoid having one's spirit poisoned by lingering too long on earth:

> Because the world has entered the final age
> the best are unwilling to remain in it for long.
> Their duties completed, they quickly depart this earth
> Aiming for the heavens.
> They fear to be corrupted by the poisons of the Age of Kali.[11]

Kali or Durga is the demonic female aspect of the destroyer god Siwa; she is the female counterpart of Rudra. In Balinese thought, she is sometimes incarnated in Rangda, the queen of witches. She is also the mother of the bhutakala, which in this era are manifest as destructive and unreasoning forces like plagues and demons. Elsewhere in the poem, the king explains that it is impossible to fight her demonic armies without losing one's own virtue: not only are the demons far too numerous, but they attack in horrible ways and do not follow the rules of war. They cannot be beaten, and to fight them is to risk contamination by the poisons of the Age of Kali. Better, then, for one's spirit to return quickly to heaven, and await the next age of the world.

Although the kingdoms described in the *Purwa Senghara* belong to the mythical past of epic poetry, the author understood that he was about to face a similar dilemma himself. Less than a year after he finished the poem, a fleet of Dutch warships appeared off his coast. He did not survive to write the history of the destruction of his own kingdom, but the story of how he met his end is told by one of the Brahmin priests who witnessed the war, in a poem called *Bhuwana Winasa*. *Bhuana* is the term for cosmos: bhuana alit, the small realm, is the microcosm, while bhuana agung, great realm, is the macrocosm. In this context *bhuana* refers to the kingdom of Badoeng, or the Balinese world, while *winasa* means destruction or annihilation. This poem introduces us to the real king of Badoeng as he prepared to meet the Dutch invasion:

---

[11] Purwa Senghara Pupuh XXXIII, verses 46–47.

An envoy arrived, from the government of Java
Called the Great Tuan,* a cunning man
Accompanied by four others, all clever ones
Arriving at the palace, all sat in chairs before the king.

The Great Tuan spoke slowly, "my lord King,
Will you pay for the goods from the shipwreck"?
The King answered, "why should this be my wish,
I have not taken these things, nor my people at the seaside
In brief, I shall not do so, for this is against our rights."

The foreigners answered, "our friend, this answer saddens us
Perhaps our lord does not comprehend, this is a command
Direct from the rulers of Batavia.**

[*tuan=master; **Batavia=the Dutch imperial capital]

The "Great Tuan," J. Eschbach, left immediately but sent an ultimatum to the king instructing him to pay the required compensation within two weeks or face a naval blockade. Meanwhile, the king met with his counselors and also with the king of Tabanan, his neighbor to the west. The poem continues:

The king of Badoeng spoke, "My lord princes,
and my lord King of Tabanan, I am greatly pleased
Even though disaster is coming, in your presence I feel
the pure emotion in confronting whatever approaches
Foretold in the Nitisastra* . . .
As humans we cannot avoid our fate
For all creatures life brings both happiness and sorrow."

[*Nitisastra=a classical religious text]

Later, the king spoke to a gathering of his ministers: "Kinsmen and counselors, because it is certain that we will be conquered, what is your counsel? According to my belief, to choose the good according to our philosophy, we must fix the hour of our deaths. I therefore choose to seek Nirvana." The ministers agreed, saying "let us not be small-hearted, our wish is to perish in battle, since your words are the truth we shall become corpses." When the invasion began, the king hurried to complete the funeral rites for several kinsmen, to fulfill his duties on earth. Meanwhile, the Dutch army advanced and was met by small groups of Balinese soldiers armed with lances, swords, and some antique firearms.

Evening fell and the soldiers returned to their quarters
But when the king arrived at his palace, he sought the high priest.

"Om, om. Your servant asks the pardon of my lord priest,
Tell me, what is the highest fate . . ."
"Lord king, aim for sunia mreta*
to purify your thoughts, by thinking of God
God will be present, goodness will dam up madness,
Strive to find clarity, focus your being." The king answered
"Yes, lord priest, that is what your servant truly desires."

[*sunia mreta = the void of death, perfect calm]

On the day of the final battle, the king gives the order to destroy the palace as artillery shells fall around him. As one hero after the next is killed in skirmishes with the Dutch, an old woman calls on her son to end her life with a sword stroke. Tears fall as she dies; the palace gates are opened and the entire royal court walks out to meet the Dutch, the twiceborn ladies adorned with their jewels. The king appears calm and assumes the posture of semadi meditation, before he is struck down by rifle fire. The court ladies, dressed (as we are told by Dutch journalists) in their white cremation gowns,

Marched forward like white ants,
but the bullets of their enemies were like fire
as they came forward and fell, their bodies piled up
a mountain of corpses in a sea of blood.

With the death of the king and 3,600 of his followers, the "world is washed with blood." Looking back, the poet sees that there were signs foretelling the end:

Now the kingdoms have been defeated, fated by the All-Powerful
There was a sign, the shrine of the king of Badoeng
    at the Temple of Suaragiri was inundated by rains
The shrine collapsed, and the place of the gods at Uluwatu
    likewise was destroyed by a thunderbolt.
The Hall of Audience at the palace of Pemetjutan,
    blown apart by the winds.
The beautiful beringan tree of Tabanan enveloped in spider's webs
    so that it turned white, a sign of great danger.

• • •

These two poems convey the heroic spirit of the aristocratic cult that the Balinese Brahmins fashioned from their metaphysical texts. In the *Purwa Senghara*, the task of rulers is to gain mastery over the bhutakala that threaten their kingdoms. This is inevitably a doomed struggle; even the

Buddha, as King Sutasoma, is unable to awaken the higher nature of the bhuta and so deflect them from mindless destruction. A similar ethos pervades the Brahmin's story of the death of the real king of Badoeng: the Dutch are depicted as an embodiment of the bhutakala of the final age of the world. Since military victory was out of the question, the king chose to meet this challenge by setting an example of superhuman courage, facing death with godlike calm. His example was later emulated by the kings of Tabanan and Klungkung.

The farmers of Bali drew different lessons from their metaphysical studies; their antagonists were not armies of demons or colonial soldiers, but the continuous entropy of petty quarrels, illnesses, and harvest failures. Yet the problems confronting the villagers were not entirely dissimilar to those of their former kings; in both cases calamities were understood to be the consequence of the disintegration of the bhuta. To the Dutch, the death of the king of Badoeng appeared to be an act of defiance, but from his writings it seems clear that his actions were modeled on the sacrifice of Sutasoma. His aim was to embody perfect control of his own interior bhuta, by refusing to give in to anger or fear.

The theory of the recombination of the bhuta centers on a concept of emergence, the achievement of higher forms of being. In the context of the aristocratic cult, this was accomplished through strengthening the powers of mind until they became superhuman. The challenges faced by the farmers called for less heroism, but their complexity gave rise to a more nuanced response, one that arguably embodied greater psychological depth. The recurrent problems of village life—jealous relatives, angry neighbors, overbearing leaders, lazy partners, and even outbreaks of leafhoppers—all threaten the desired order. None of these afflictions can be altogether vanquished, so the problem is to keep them under adequate control. (As the farmers say, kill a hunded rats and Durga may send ten thousand to replace them.) It is the task of each person and each household to manage itself, but when they fail and problems spill over the house walls, it becomes the community's business to cope with them. The concept of the bhuta bears on this formulation in two ways. First, it emphasizes the need for continuous attention to the problem of managing the bhuta. Dangerous passions like anger, grief, and envy are present in the subjective reality of every person, and in the chaotic Age of Kali they will never be altogether banished; the goal is to contain them. The second, less obvious idea derives from the assumption that the inner world or subjective reality of every person is constructed from the same elements, the same bhuta. From moment to moment, explains one Brahmin, the west wind is different, yet it is always the same, and so is the way that it feels on one's skin. The untrained mind experiences itself and its feelings as unique, but can learn to recognize underlying patterns.

The goal of religious instruction is to provide the tools to achieve this form of self-knowledge, and so gain control of the bhuta. The Brahman-ical tradition encourages the twiceborn to strive for control of the bhuta through a superhuman effort at self-mastery. But the rites of the water temples offer a different lesson. Here the limitations of the individual are transcended by emphasizing the universality of the bhuta that make up subjective reality. If an individual can gain mastery of his own bhuta by learning to recognize their universality, it follows that the collective can come to a similar realization, and in the process of comprehending itself gain a measure of control.

A metaphor drawn from the rites of the water temple cult may help to clarify this point. In a functioning subak, every farmer receives his per-sonal share of the subak's water when it enters his field. Upstream, at the main canal or spring where the water for the subak originates, there is always a small shrine. Dip a cup into the water by this shrine, and it will contain a few drops of everyone's water, mingled together since the flow has not yet been subdivided. Which drops are yours, and which are mine? Such a cup of water, sanctified at the shrine, signifies the subak as a social being, an entity that has the potential to master the bhuta that lie beyond the grasp of individuals, even if those individuals are not he-roes or princes but ordinary men. The question becomes how to enhance such awareness, to the point that the subak can cope with the bhuta that are beyond the powers of their individual members to control.

As we shall see, the farmers accept the metaphysics of the bhuta as an attractively grand framework in which to situate their observations of their own emotional states and those of their neighbors. But the Brah-manical textual tradition does not provide a rich source of insights into particular psychological states; its emphasis is rather on cultivating the ability to transcend the emotions. The challenge for the subaks is to pro-mote a shared and subtle understanding of real conflicts that threaten their welfare, in terms of underlying stereotypical patterns. In this con-text, one can begin to appreciate the significance of the water temples for the subaks. If problems and conflicts are to be seen in the light of these religious teachings, as typical manifestations of the bhutakala, and if the goal is to mobilize the powers of the collective to gain control, there is a need for a public venue in which to cultivate this awareness. Simply ask-ing for the blessing of the gods in conventional rituals will not serve the purpose. On the other hand a bit of theater, a well-told tale, can be an ideal vehicle to convey the essential message of the stereotypical nature of human dilemmas. For this reason, the farmers can be quite Jungian in their enthusiasm for explaining the workings of the mind in terms of myths. An interesting example is provided by a well-known myth that tells the story of the birth of the bhutakala. This story provides an explanation for the origins of witchcraft and sorcery, which as we have seen loom large in the affairs of the subaks as explanations for conflicts. This version of the myth comes from the *lontar* (palm-leaf) manuscript *Andabhuana*:

The supreme god Siwa wished to test the fidelity of his wife, the goddess Uma. He pretended to be ill and asked Uma to bring him milk from a pure white cow. Uma descended to the mortal realm and searched until she found the only perfect animal, belonging to an aged cowherd. Uma did not realize that the cowherd was actually her husband in disguise. Uma asked the cowherd for milk from the white cow, and offered to pay anything he asked, but the disguised Siwa answered that he would give her the milk only if she would have sex with him. With great reluctance, she agreed. Afterward Siwa returned to his divine realm of Siwaloka and asked his son Gana (the elephant-headed god) to ask his mother how she had obtained the milk. Gana trapped Uma into denying that she had had sex with the cowherd, and then read from the book of time (the *Wariga tenung*, which accurately chronicles the past, present, and future) to prove that his mother had lied. Furious, Uma cursed her son and threw the book into the fire. Gana rescued the book with some pages burnt and some still readable, which is why even the gods can no longer know the past or future with perfect accuracy. Siwa told Uma that her falsehood together with her anger against her son made her unfit for Siwaloka (Siwa's heaven) and banished her to the mortal world, where she would take the form of the terrible destroyer goddess Durga. There she took her place by the cemetery at the Pura Dalem (the village "Temple of Death"), where she was given the power to decide the life span of all living creatures. As Durga, she gave birth to all the bhutakala: those of the inner world of the self, including Banaspati, Anggapati, Prajapati, and Banaspatiraja; likewise the bhutakala of the outer world, which follow the movement of the seasons—all sicknesses, plagues, witches, and demons. But Siwa did not wish to be permanently separated from the goddess. He promised to rejoin her in his demonic form as Rudra, in the cemetery on the night of the ninth new moon.

Still the goddess longed to be reunited with her husband, not as Durga but as Uma. A second myth explains how she was able to do so. As Durga, the goddess brought illness to Dewi Kunti, mother of three of the Pandawas (the heroes of the epic Mahabharata). Kunti's twin stepsons Sadewa and Sahamara agreed to die in her place to satisfy Durga. Seeing this, Siwa manifested himself as the twins and Durga recognized him as her husband. She lost all her anger and having done so became Uma again, returning from the human world to Siwa's heaven.

As these myths show, the processes that transform Uma into Durga are reversible. At the instant she relinquishes her anger, the goddess ceases to be Durga. This story provides the commonly accepted explanation for witchcraft in Balinese villages. Persons who wish to explore the temptations of witchery must ask for Durga's assistance by approaching her in secret at her shrine in the Temple of Death. Because anyone caught practicing witchcraft risks being killed, the safest way to visit this temple is to send one's spirit there at night while one's body appears to be peacefully asleep at home. One acquires the powers of Durga by emulation, by cultivating one's own Durga nature. The dread goddess is thought to be especially sympathetic to ill-treated wives. Candidate witches learn to attack their enemies in secrecy and anonymity, by embodying dangerous bhutakala that can cause illness or death (figure 25). These beliefs have very real consequences. When unexplained illness or misfortune strikes a family, it will normally consult with a type of trance medium or sorcerer called a *balian ketakson* to determine the cause of the affliction. The most common diagnoses are either the wrath of neglected ancestors or a deliberate attack by a witch. The first problem can be avoided by paying close attention to the annual cycle of rites for the deceased, while the second requires regular offerings placed at the entrances of the house. Such offerings are thought to be an effective protection against witchcraft attacks from the outside. That being the case, if the family agrees that the protective offerings were not neglected, then suspicion of witchcraft falls on "insiders," on members of the household who are suspected of harboring envy or resentment toward the person who suffered the affliction. This belief is the source of acute psychological tension in many households. Uma's anger against her son and husband are thought to have been well merited, and women who find themselves in weak positions, or those who have been mistreated, are considered to be vulnerable to the temptations of their own Durga nature.

The ideal solution to these temptations is of course to master them. But because not everyone will succeed, there comes a point when a self-governing community must take an interest in controlling or suppressing the bhutakala that originate in unhappy households. We could, if we chose, examine other manifestations of the subak's interest in framing its problems in the imagery of the bhutakala. But the story of Uma's anger nicely illustrates the psychological complexities involved in the subak's struggles to comprehend and govern itself. Like the author of the *Purwa Senghara*, the farmers have an interest in discovering the conditions that give rise to the bhutakala, and exploring the effectiveness of strategies for coping with them.

By all accounts, the paradigmatic reason for conflict in farm families is the question of inheritance. The transfer of power from one generation to the next is acknowledged to be fraught with anxiety. In the rice-growing villages of China, farmland is divided with strict equality among all male

Figure 25. Images of witches and bhutakala. Reprinted by permission from Christiaan Hooykas, *Drawings of Balinese Sorcery*, Leiden: Brill, 1980.

heirs. But no such clarity exists in Bali. While only males inherit, there is much variation in the rules governing the respective shares of brothers. Everyone agrees that nominal rules exist, but precisely which rules are taken to be prescriptive varies from village to village and even from family to family. Sometimes the eldest son is favored, sometimes the youngest; in recent times there has often been an effort to make an equal division, but in every case the paramount interest of the household head in bestowing an inheritance is to ensure the continuity of the rituals at the ancestor shrine of his household, after he is dead or incapacitated. This shrine (*sanggah* or *mrajan*) is the active link of the family to its immediate ancestors, who are the intermediaries between the family and the realms of the gods. To break this link is to invite disaster. If the ritual cycle is not sustained at the sanggah, the family risks immediate retaliation by its own ancestors. Furthermore, the cycle of personal reincarnations will be broken, because after their own death the parents will lack descendants. The household head's interest in ensuring that the ritual cycle at the sanggah continues uninterrupted helps to explain the ambiguity attached to the question of inheritance. From the perspective of an aging patriarch, the bestowal of house and land on a male heir is a means to an end: to secure the perpetuation of himself through his ancestral line (*purusa*, a polite term for penis). If this aim is accomplished, he and his wife can rest easy, their duties done and their own future secure. But if he has more than one son, or no sons, then the door is open for conflict. Rice land is scarce and expensive, and until very recently, when new sources of employment appeared, the amount of land one inherited was the main determinant of a farmer's income.

These beliefs lay an enormous psychosocial burden on young women marrying into a household. In the marriage ritual, a bride severs ties with her father's ancestral shrine so that she can become a vehicle for the reincarnation of her husband's ancestors through their purusa shrine. From the day of her marriage, she takes up responsibility to perform rituals at this shrine, on which the ongoing welfare of her husband's family depends. She must be an effective and reliable performer of what is sometimes called "white magic," the ritual cycles at the household shrine and also in the temple rituals where she represents the family. In some villages there are annual rituals in which the wives of all subak members bring offerings called *tipat*, which consist of rice grown by the family and cooked by boiling inside woven palm containers. One by one, each woman submits a tipat to be sliced open by a committee of temple priests, who inspect the rice for signs of any impurities. If a speck of dirt is found, it is taken as a magical sign that the woman has failed to provide efficacious offerings during the past year. She is fined by the village, and may be quietly scolded for endangering her family. These inspections provide a means for the community to monitor its member families for signs of the appearance of dangerous bhutakala. The priests say that the purity of the offering does not depend on a woman's cooking skills or the cleanliness of her kitchen. Rather it is a way for the community to discover, by magical revelation, whether her prayers and ritual acts are sincere. To fail the tipat test is dangerous for a woman because it suggests that she may not have her family's interests at heart; that she may have strayed from the path of ritual performances laid out for wives; in short, that she may be a witch.

What might tempt a virtuous woman to yield to the temptations of witchcraft? This question also leads back to the purusa shrine, and the issue of inheritance. As every bride knows, the continuity of her in-laws' ancestral line depends on the availability of a son to inherit the family home and ancestor shrines. Young women are routinely warned by their mothers to expect rivalry, which may include witchcraft, from their sisters-in-law or other members of their husband's household. This rivalry is explicitly linked to inheritance. The mother of a male heir is in a much stronger position within the household than women who have no sons. The importance of the male heir is underlined by the custom of *sentana* marriages, in which household heads who lack a son offer to confer their entire undivided property to a man willing to marry one of their daughters. The bridegroom must renounce his own purusa shrine so that his children can become heirs for his wife's father. The purpose of a sentana marriage is thus to enable a daughter to try to produce a male heir. If this does not occur within a few years, the couple is left to choose between adoption, a second wife, or divorce and remarriage—whatever is required to obtain an heir.

Thus a woman who does not produce a potential male heir, or coheir, has effectively lost the key struggle for power in the household for women of her generation. Such women are the most likely candidates for witchcraft accusations.[12] Other likely candidates are abused or jealous women seeking power over their husbands, and the daughters or grand-daughters of suspected witches. The last of these candidates—women suspected of having a witch in their family tree—are particularly worrying to men in search of a wife. As women are taught to fear their sisters-in-law, young men are taught to beware of marrying a woman who may become a witch. These beliefs shed some illumination on one of the most startling results from our household surveys: the strong preference among members of subaks for marriage to the daughter of another subak member. The farmers' explanation for this preference follows logically from their views on the psychology of witchcraft. It is believed that witches possess tangible powers that must be passed on to someone else before

---

[12] If men study the black arts, it is politely assumed that they wish to use them to enhance their powers as balians, not to become witches. Balians are respected public figures, and a knowledge of black magic only increases their stature, while no one in their senses would admit to being a practising *desti* (witch). Villagers also agree that the most likely suspects in the case of illness or death caused by witchcraft (*gering manusa*) are jealous female relatives. This belief is linked to the assumption that the most likely targets of witchcraft are members of the witch's immediate family (although ascending the heights of witchdom is said to require a progression of more ambitious murders).

they die; otherwise their own funeral rites will fail. The most common victim is thought to be the witch's daughter or granddaughter, who may acquire witchcraft unknowingly in her sleep. For this reason, it is understood that the descendants of a witch are quite likely to become witches themselves, even without their own knowledge or volition. One young woman offered a story rather transparently based on her own experience: A powerful ancestress, seeing the predicament of a young wife who suspects that her sisters-in-law have used witchcraft to prevent her from having children, recalls having been in the same precarious position herself, and decides to gift her granddaughter with countermagic. Appearing in a series of dreams, she awakens the young woman to her heritage of magical knowledge. Soon after, a son is conceived.

But as everyone knows, someone who begins to make use of magic makes a Faustian bargain. For example, a witch can gain wealth in secret by means of a blerong, a particularly dangerous manifestation of bhutakala that roams at night in search of money to steal. (The fear of Blerong was the reason for the attempted resignation of the head of Subak Pakudui, as described in the previous chapter). To create a Blerong, one must sacrifice a living being one cares for, preferably one's own child. The Blerong thus becomes a manifestation of one's most vicious and greedy nature. This concept provides an explanation for both sudden unexpected wealth and the death of children. In general, it is thought that any woman who begins to dabble in countermagic will almost certainly wind up a witch, and her first victims are destined to be members of her own household. If her powers grow unchecked, eventually she will seek other victims. Rather shamefacedly, some people observed that the community may tolerate such behavior, as long as the witch has the good sense to choose her later victims from far away. The presence of a sufficiently powerful witch in the community might even have some benefit, since lesser witches from other villages might not wish to disturb her.

Given these beliefs, it is not surprising to find that young men are eager to avoid choosing a wife who might be the descendant of a witch. We asked about twenty married men in each of thirteen subaks, a total of 252 individuals, whom they had married. Eighty-four percent had chosen a wife from among the daughters of men belonging to their own subak. When pressed for an explanation, subak members often mentioned the desirability of marrying a woman from a family whose history was definitely known, or alternatively noted that marrying an outsider can be risky. It is thought that any family whose ancestors include an accused witch will certainly wish to conceal this knowledge from prospective suitors. Thus the most trustworthy prospective wives (and daughters-in-law) are the children of members of one's own subak. But even such women are vulnerable to the pressure to produce a male heir. Witchcraft beliefs are a kind of recognition that these burdens are sometimes too heavy to be borne, an acknowledgment that normal social life in the villages will routinely produce "witches" in every generation.

One of the consequences of these anxieties is that subak members are inclined to scrutinize the psychosocial health of their colleagues' households with at least as much attention as their own. Interestingly, a survey of marriage preferences in two highland villages (where subaks do not exist) showed that these men were much less likely to marry within their communities; the rate of endogamous marriages was only 34 percent. They also claimed to be less worried about the possibility that their wives and daughters-in-law might have succumbed to the temptations of witchcraft. The highlanders work as dry-field farmers, laborers, and merchants, so their livelihood is much less dependent on the close cooperation of their neighbors than is the case for subak members. A more comprehensive study would be needed to validate this comparison, but it does shed an interesting light on the psychology of subak members.[13] After several years of research on the Sebatu subaks, I find it hard to exaggerate the corrosive psychological effects of the fear of witchcraft. In general, Balinese are reluctant to talk about these fears, lest word get back to a real witch who, fearing discovery, will certainly retaliate. (On the other hand, it must be difficult to harbor such disturbing suspicions and have no one to confide in, unless one happens to know a discreet anthropologist.) In these communities, once a woman is suspected of witchcraft each new illness or misfortune suffered by her family is liable to be interpreted as further proof of her malevolence. In one notorious case, a woman accused of being a murderous witch felt compelled to stand at her own doorway and loudly proclaim her innocence to the community. Today, twenty years later, she is an isolated figure in her village, shunned by her neighbors and even by several of her own children. Indeed, it sometimes happens that children suspect their own mothers of witchcraft. For example, one colleague is burdened by the knowledge that two of his brothers harbor such suspicions, and take care to keep their

[13] The very high rate of endogamous marriage within subaks was also noticed by Leopold Howe in his study of the village (and subak) of Pujung in the 1970s. He writes: "Village endogamy is very high indeed. Out of a total of 399 marriages for which I have reliable information, 82% were village endogamous. Of the 72 marriages contracted outside the village 34 were into the nearby villages of Ked and Bonjaka, and both of these were thought to be offshoots of Pujung (Bonjaka indeed is, since it was settled within living memory by people from Pujung). There is therefore good reason to include these as endogamous marriages, in which case the total goes up to 90.5%." Leopold E. A. Howe, "Pujung: An Investigation into the Foundations of Balinese Culture," doctoral dissertation, University of Edinburgh, 1980.

mother apart from their wives and daughters. If their mother is aware of these suspicions, she prudently gives no sign. But sometimes suspicions lead to actions that become public knowledge—for example, in one family's treatment of an aged spinster aunt suspected of witchcraft. As the old woman lay on her deathbed no one had the courage to go into her room, lest she pass her witchcraft on to them (even if this did not occur, the possibility that it might would open the visitor to suspicion in later life). The dying woman's food was lowered to her from the roof, and a dog was left in the room to receive her witchcraft powers. After her death, the dog was killed. Given this atmosphere of pervasive suspicion and fear, one wonders how cooperation can be sustained in families, let alone by whole communities. No wonder, then, that the subaks regard their democracy as a precarious achievement.

• • •

The concept of the bhutakala provides an explanation for crimes, hatred, and the disintegration of society in the Age of Kali. But it also provides a model for the restoration of harmony, one that is connected in a curious way with the democracy of the subaks. In general, self-governing subaks need to cope with two kinds of problems, those that arise from discord among their members, and those that are inflicted on them by the natural world, such as water shortages or pests. Problems like an epidemic of rats can be devastating, but they are intrinsically simpler than the problems that originate in the bhuana alit (microcosm or subjective experience) of the subak itself. The question of how to cope with rats is something like a "toy problem" for the subaks, one that can serve to illustrate the conceptual framework within which the farmers approach the problem of controlling the bhutakala.

Rats in the fields are classified as *merana*, a type of bhutakala that has become what we would call an agricultural pest. It is possible for humans who fail the spiritual tests posed by their existence to be reborn as rats or other forms of merana. Rats have simple desires, for food and procreation, and by fulfilling their dharma they may hope to ascend to higher forms of being in future lives. It is normal for a small fraction of one's harvest to be eaten by merana; to begrudge them this food would show a lack of sympathy for less fortunate spirits, and might risk annoying Durga. (When agricultural extension agents began to promote the use of rat poisons in the 1960s, this created an ethical problem for farmers. Traditional remedies for too many rats include a wide variety of rituals, which do not emphasize killing the animals but rather offering them alternatives to eating more than their share. From a practical point of view, many farmers concluded that using pesticides and poisons was ineffective in the long run, since the merana vanished only temporarily, and often returned in much larger numbers within a few growing seasons. But other farmers continue to use pesticides.)

When the usual rituals of persuasion appear to be failing to control the depradations of the rodents, the farmers have the option of performing a more expensive ritual that goes to the heart of the problem. Each subak member is required to kill a number of rats, and afterward some of the corpses are given an expensive cremation ritual. This gives the spirits of the animals an extraordinary opportunity to be reborn as higher animals, perhaps even as humans. Their kin who are not cremated should also be impressed by the generosity of the farmers, and so also the gods who are asked to witness this rite. This ritual serves to model ethical behavior for subak members and society at large. It gives the simple spirits of the rodents a prize that is also greatly valued by the farmers. During the colonial period, several enormous rat cremations were organized by Balinese kings.[14]

Many of the offerings that are provided for this kind of ritual are of the type mentioned at the beginning of this chapter: colorful, symmetrical images of cosmological order. These objects are meant to serve as models for the desired state of order in the inner and outer worlds. But there are also other kinds of offerings that have a different purpose: to help facilitate the desired transformation or ordering of the bhutakala. For example, *bebangkit* offerings are gorgeous baskets that contain whimsical forms made of colored rice dough that depict the good things of the mortal world, like rainbows. Bebangkits are designed to attract any and all sentient beings. Their contents include pleasing images such as a mountain with four rivers flowing down its slopes, a road with a dog, a rich man enjoying his gold, and a poor man with his wife and many children. The exterior of the bebangkit is adorned with colors and images in mandalic form, showing the essence of the world as it ought to be. Even the crudest bhutakala are thought to appreciate the delights of a bebangkit; they may be initially attracted to the site of a ritual with offerings of blood and liquor, but once there they are invited to enjoy the bebangkit and in this way achieve a state of being that is not only less disruptive but also more sympathetic and appreciative toward their human hosts. The purpose of the bebangkit is to encourage such a transformation, prompted by the belief that no being is too depraved to resist the attractions of things like dogs, rainbows, and mountains.

---

[14] Several accounts are collected in an unpublished manuscript by V. E. Korn titled "Abenan bikul," in his papers (the Korn collection) in the Koninklijk Instituut voor Taal-, Land- en Volkenkunde, Leiden. Coll. Korn, Bijlage XXVII.

Offerings like bebangkit are routinely employed in the annual round of rituals in the water temples. For an institution that is based on the principle of self-governance the most difficult problems are internal conflicts, because they develop in the devious minds of mortals, not the simple minds of rats. Imagine, then, the subak members and their families, seated in prayer in the forecourt of a water temple, facing the gorgeous array of mandalic offerings they have created with a bebangkit at its center, and listening as the temple priests ring their bells to invite the bhutakala to enjoy the fruits of their labors. For the rite to succeed, this invitation must be well received by the bhutakala that make up the mental state of the subak members themselves, persuading them to temporarily neglect their evanescent desires in order to experience, in a moment of focused concentration, the satisfaction of creating a transcendent and harmonious order.

Still, in the Age of Kali it can take more than rainbows and rat cremations to bring every member of a community to the desired state of mind, and so prevent the subak from disintegrating into a collection of jealous and quarrelsome individuals. Fortunately the water temples need not rely entirely on rituals; major temple festivals are usually accompanied by dramatic performances. As the world knows, these often attain a very high standard; some Sebatu farmers can boast of having performed on the stages of Paris, Amsterdam, or San Francisco. By combining theater with ritual, the organizers of temple festivals can shape powerful imaginative experiences, attaching subjective meaning to the objective purposes for which the temples were created. As noted earlier, there is a division of labor in the temples of Bali: the water temples of the subaks are directly concerned with control of the natural world, and only indirectly with the human spirit. But as we have seen, the very freedom and autonomy of the subaks makes them uniquely vulnerable to the emotional currents flowing through their members. The question of how to channel these currents comes to the fore in the annual cycle of rituals and performances connected with Durga and her retinue of bhutakala, where all the imaginative energies of theater and ritual are mobilized in the interests of the community.

At the new moon of the seventh month, Durga takes up residence in her earthly temples in the villages, called Pura Dalem. Here she remains until the end of the year two months later, when in accordance with the myth she will be visited by Siwa in his demonic form, and afterward return to Siwa's heaven as the goddess Uma. In all other temple festivals it is considered desirable to vary the dramatic fare from one year to the next, but at Durga's temple the same tale is enacted nearly every year. This story is called *Calon Arang*, the "candidate witch." *Calon Arang* tells the story of a witch's anger when she finds that no one will marry her beautiful and virtuous daughter. The original story is set in an ancient kingdom of East Java. *Calon Arang* can be performed either as a shadow puppet play or a theatrical performance. In either case the performers are understood by the audience to be sorcerers, and in most performances they occasionally depart from the story to call out challenges to the local witches and sorcerers, testing the strength of their own magical powers. If the performers come from far away, before the day of the temple festival they make it their business to find which villagers are suspected of witchery, and use this knowledge to make innuendos during the performance. In this way the Durga myths are connected to the local scene, as the performers play up the specific manifestations of witchcraft thought to be taking place in the here and now (this may explain why the audience never tires of the *Calon Arang* story).

The performance is held at night at Durga's temple, and it is intended to be terrifying. Actors costumed as witches may fall into trance, possessed by the spirits of real witches, and in the final scenes a character called the *dulang* is carried off to lie in a real grave until morning, lying motionless as his spirit fights off attacks from invisible witches. It is said that if any of the witches prove to be too strong for him, the dulang will become a real corpse. As the identities of suspected local witches are often broadly hinted by the performers, one might expect that these individuals might be in danger of attack by other villagers in the aftermath of a *Calon Arang* performance. But when I asked about this possibility, my Balinese colleagues suggested several reasons why such attacks are rare: it is hard to prove the truth of witchcraft accusations; it is also dangerous to provoke suspected witches; and in any case witchcraft is so pervasive that it would be foolish for the community to try to take action against every suspect.

Instead, a more intriguing remedy for witchcraft is provided in the days following the *Calon Arang*. The goal is to facilitate the transformation of the various manifestations of Durga that exist in the community, in preparation for her departure. The full moon of the tenth month marks the start of the new year, and is preceded by a day called *nyepi* (silence, emptiness), when it is hoped that Durga and her dangerous bhutakala will depart. On nyepi, no fires may be lit, and no one should venture out of his or her house. Just before nyepi, many villages embark on a pilgrimage to the sea called *melasti*. Their pilgrimage commemorates the courageous journey of the hero Bima to the underworld, in a quest for the holy water called *tirtha kamandalu* that can restore life. The sea has particular significance in Balinese cosmology, representing death, dissolution, and the inhuman powers of chaos and the mahabhuta. The sea is the final destination of the ashes of the dead, which are ceremoniously cast into it so that they may dissolve into their elemental bhuta. But the rituals of the dead involve only family members, whereas the annual melasti pilgrimages require the participation of every family in the village. When the melasti processions reach the water's edge, icons of the gods of the village temples are arrayed in a line of shrines facing the ocean, and priests offer prayers to the mahabhuta. They also collect holy water from springs near the sea, called *tirtha pawitram*, which is carried back to the village and used to purify all the temples and household shrines, beginning with Durga's temple. There, on the new moon of the ninth month, a great sacrifice to the bhutakala is performed. The tirtha pawitram that the community bravely collected at the seacoast is sprinkled on offerings such as the bebangkit to encourage all the lesser bhuta to accompany Durga in the rediscovery of her Uma nature. Later, the holy water is ladled out by the temple priests to the village matriarchs, who carry it to their husband's purusa shrines for a cleansing ritual. On the following day, the ancestors and gods are invited to return to the village.

• • •

"The state," writes Hegel, "must be treated as a great architectonic structure, a hieroglyph of the reason which reveals itself in actuality." He is scornful of theorists who fail to recognize that political institutions are simply reflections of the consciousness of a society at a particular historical moment: "Mind is actual only as that which it knows itself to be, and the state, as the mind of a nation, is both the law permeating all relationships within the state and also at the same time the manners and consciousness of its citizens. It follows, therefore, that the constitution of any given nation depends in general on the character and development of its self-consciousness."[15]

Athenian democracy failed, according to Hegel, because it lacked a solution to the problem of transforming the "weighing of pros and cons" into decisive action. With no means to transform "la volonté des tous" into "la volonté general," the democratic assembly would "let itself oscillate perpetually, now this way now that," as each member articulated his own interests. When the moment came for decisions, the Greeks had to resort to oracles and natural signs, since they lacked institutions to embody ("objectify") the universal interests of society. Although he does not dwell on this point, it is clear that for Hegel, as political consciousness matures there is less need for conscious participation by the citizens, because the universality of the State is passively embodied in this struc-

---

[15] G.W.F. Hegel, *Hegel's Philosophy of Right*, translated by T. M. Knox, London: Oxford University Press, 1967: 179.

ture of institutions. The process of political maturation culminates in the constitutional monarch, who becomes the preeminent "hieroglyph of Reason." Since he represents and can act for the State, there is no further need for oracles.

Against this view, which in one way or another underlies much later Western political philosophy, the conceptual foundations of the democracy of the subaks stand out in stark contrast. For Hegel, the flow of history leads to the perfection of human institutions and the triumph of Mind, but in the Balinese view time is not an ally, and institutions exist to facilitate the active consciousness of their members in the struggle against Senghara. Balinese institutions like water temples are mere empty shells, sites where wisdom can be cultivated, not monuments to its steady accumulation. If one were to try to find words to summarize that wisdom, it would be something like the proposition that to gain mastery over one's desires, it is necessary to discover their universality. Such an awareness can be cultivated to serve as the foundation for forms of social existence that transcend the individual. Here we see the key innovation of the water temple cult and its point of divergence from the royal cult. In the Brahmanical tradition, the State is the creation of a universal monarch who has gained personal mastery over the bhutakala. The democracy of the water temples, in contrast, relinquishes the goal of developing superhuman powers and focuses instead on cultivating awareness of the universal elements that are the common human experience and mirror those of the natural world. Dharmasastric kings must continually test their powers against their foes; when they fail, the kingdom is lost. But the democracy of the water temples expects failures, because it is based on an attempt to mobilize the resources of a fallible human community. In both the Brahmanical tradition and that of the temple cult, the core teachings emphasize a process of self-discovery, in which aspects of the self that the untrained mind experiences as unique are objectified and shown to be universal. But subsequently the two traditions diverge. Brahmins and princes are taught to strengthen the mind through austerities, in order to achieve the capacity for heroic action. The temple cult does not provide guidance for such solitary struggles; instead it offers solutions for coping with the inevitable failures. The task of mastering the bhutakala is shifted from the heroic individual to the group as a whole, which is constituted as a unified and potent social being. To the extent that this is successful, problems that prove to be beyond the powers of an ordinary person—a plague of rats, a murderous spouse, a shortage of water, or one's own personal weaknesses—can be brought under control by the collective. The annual cycle of rituals is based on the premise that such failures are bound to accumulate, and that they will do so in a predictable pattern. By drawing attention to this predictability, the performance of the rituals heightens the participants' awareness of the powers of the collective to tame and domesticate the dangers that threaten it.[16]

From the perspective of Western political philosophy, it is remarkable that Balinese beliefs about witchcraft are closely entwined with the conceptual foundations of their democracy. Historians of early modern Europe often focus on witchcraft as the antithesis of rationality, as the foe that had to be defeated before democratic ideas could return to the West. Charles Taylor explicitly links the decline of witchcraft to the origin of the modern Western sense of individualism: "Disenchantment was driven by and connected with a new moral/spiritual stance to the world . . . what we see emerging is a new notion of freedom and inwardness." Lyndal Roper similarly argues that "our nineteenth century heritage is a conception of the rational which banishes witchcraft, spells, the demonic and the popular to the margins of society."[17] How, then, are we to regard the witchcraft beliefs of the Balinese?

Let me once again try to answer this question by reversing it. Even in early modern Europe, one need only think of Shakespeare's Ariel and Caliban to recognize that concepts of witches and the supernatural must sometimes have contributed to "inwardness" in Taylor's sense—to the enrichment of subjective experience and self-awareness. But there is a crucial difference: the European tradition lacks the mandalic "hieroglyphs of Reason" that the Balinese use to connect subjective reality with the representation of social institutions. In the absence of such explicit connections, individuals are left to discover for themselves what the creatures of the theater have to tell them about the workings of their own minds. Europeans did not lack objectified representations of the emotions, including those that threaten the social order, but they did not possess a philosophical and ritual apparatus to connect their discoveries about the self to human universals.

In Bali, this apparatus arguably worked too well. Believable witches are needed to justify the annual ritual cycle, the pilgrimages and purifications.

---

[16] Bryan Pfaffenberger makes a similar argument for a Tamil community of farmers in Sri Lanka: "What the Brahman achieves by separating himself from this world is easy enough, while Vellalars accomplish what had been deemed difficult, if not impossible: they throw themselves into this world with a profound lust for the mundane: for the soil, for farming, and for the battle to win fame. And yet at the same time they achieve a transcendence—not of the individual, but rather of the social collectivity, within whose ordered precincts flourishes sri, everlasting life." Bryan Pfaffenberger, *Caste in Tamil Culture: The Religious Foundations of Sudra Domination in Tamil Sri Lanka*, Syracuse, N.Y.: Foereign and Comparative Studies/South Asia Series No. 7, 1982: 225.

[17] Lyndal Roper, *Oedipus and the Devil: Witchcraft, Sexuality and Religion in Early Modern Europe*, London: Routledge, 1994: 21.

This creates a context in which ordinary domestic quarrels are liable to be magnified and take on mythical, even cosmological overtones. While the lessons of the Durga myths have to do with the cultivation of personal insights into the origin of negative emotions, the ritual cycle has its own imperatives, and easily leads to the portrayal of real people as the very personification of evil. When rituals and performances are so successful that they create what might be called an overstimulus of the imagination, they may function not to reduce psychological stresses but to ratchet them up. At the end of the year, when the Durga myths are so persuasively performed, not only do people often speak of the existence of witches; often they are convinced that they can actually see them.

But if the rituals and performances of the temple cult can heighten interpersonal tensions in this way, they also provide a remedy. If the community believes itself to be threatened by individuals who possess extravagant powers to cause harm, it must strengthen its own powers in order to prevail. In this way, the dramatization of perceived threats can increase people's willingness to invest in the rituals that promise to enhance the powers of the collective. A grand temple festival displays these powers in a way that is particularly satisfying, lending mythical stature to the community's sense of itself. But with grandeur come dangers of a different kind.

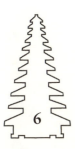

6

Demigods at the Summit

PERCHED DRAMATICALLY ON the rim of Mount Batur overlooking the crater lake, the supreme water temple Ulun Danu Batur is a collection of nested stone courtyards enclosing an array of towering shrines and pavilions, dedicated to the worship of a pantheon of forty-five deities, foremost among them the Goddess of the Lake, who is said to make the rivers flow and bring prosperity to the land (figure 26). From an architectural standpoint the temple seems ageless and serene, but for the past half century it has been a site of almost continuous turmoil. The explanation for this instability, I suggest, has to do with inherent tensions in the cult of water temples. At Ulun Danu Batur two distinct symbolic systems converge, but do not perfectly overlap. One of them identifies the volcano with the cosmic mountain, while the other places the temple at the apex of the hierarchy of water temples. The first of these ideas—the identification of the temple with the cosmic mountain and the great Goddess—lends it an importance that extends far beyond its significance as a water temple. Ulun Danu Batur is the only water temple whose rituals are often attended by representatives from many of Bali's royal families. For them, its role as a water temple is almost inconsequential; instead it is regarded as one of a pair of temples associated with Bali's two supreme gods. According to legend, in ancient times the supreme god who resides on Mount Meru broke apart the summit of the mountain and sent the pieces to Bali to become abodes for his son and daughter.[1] The son became the first male god of Bali and took up residence atop the

---

[1] An early version of this story appears in the Old Javanese *Tantu Panggelaran*. According to the story, Mount Mahameru was transported to Java. During the journey the mountain began to break apart. The pieces fell to earth, forming a chain of volcanic peaks. The base became Mount Semeru, Java's highest mountain, while the summit, Mount Pawitra, came to rest on the plains to the south of Surabaya.

Figure 26. A procession bearing images of the gods leaves the inner courtyard of the temple Ulun Danu Batur, March 2004. As the priests and deities exit the temple, they are joined by orchestras from 71 villages, which accompany the procession through the village of South Batur.

larger fragment, which became the volcano Mount Agung. The smaller fragment, which became Mount Batur, contained a vast and deep crater lake. On the floor of the lake the daughter of the high god built a palace and took the name Dewi Danu, Goddess of the Lake. Ulun Danu Batur became the temple for the Goddess, while an even larger temple called Besakih was constructed on the slopes of Mount Agung for the worship of her brother.

Although the two temples are often regarded as a pair, there are important differences between them. The temple of Besakih is associated with the Klungkung dynasty, whose rulers consider themselves to be distant descendants of the male god and claim spiritual supremacy over all the kingdoms and princes of Bali. Farmers play only a minor role in the affairs of this temple. In contrast, Ulun Danu Batur is supported not by a royal dynasty but by contributions from its enormous congregation of subaks. The priests of Ulun Danu Batur are commoners from the village of Batur who are believed to have been selected by the Goddess herself, or one of the other deities enshrined at her temple. When a member of the priesthood dies, trance mediums are summoned so that the gods may possess their voices and name the child whom they have chosen to become the successor. Priests who are discovered in this way enjoy a status unknown to other temple priests, and they make strenuous efforts to limit the role of the aristocracy in the temple. Thus Brahmin priests are excluded from the performance of most rituals at the temple. Shrines to the ancestral dynasties of several Balinese royal families are included in the temple's pantheon, but they are subordinated to the shrine of the Goddess of the Lake, and she is not considered to be their ancestress. The priests also forbid the expression of caste distinctions by the people of Batur.

To the extent that the leadership of the temple succeeds in suppressing or muting the claims of the aristocracy on Ulun Danu Batur, its second identity as a water temple comes to the fore. This identification has as much to do with the crater lake as with the volcano. The temple's supremacy is partly a consequence of the structural logic of water temples. In general, the congregation of a water temple consists of all the farmers who share water from a particular source, such as a weir or spring. The same logic applies to multisubak temples like the Masceti Pamos, whose congregation consists of fourteen subaks that share water from a cluster of adjacent weirs and springs. Because the crater lake is regarded as the ultimate origin of every spring and river, its congregation appropriately includes all subaks. As a water temple, the Ulun Danu temple is endowed with a unique collection of attributes: it is at once the most universal subak temple, the sacred summit of the cosmic mountain, the sole source of the most potent holy water, and the only temple where the priesthood is selected by the gods themselves. These impressive symbolic associations combine with its spectacular location on the crater rim to endow the temple with an aura of otherworldliness, especially on the days when its greatest treasure, an ancient gamelan orchestra, plays stately music while the temple's vast courtyards become carpeted with flower offerings left behind by thousands of worshippers. At such moments it is not difficult to believe, as a priest once told me, that if you look hard at the air over the crater lake, gods may appear.

Ulun Danu Batur plays a crucial role in my argument for several reasons. In earlier chapters I argued that the cult of water temples poses an implicit challenge to the ideologies of caste and kingship. This challenge becomes explicit at Ulun Danu Batur. According to legend, after the gods took up residence in Bali, the male began to press his sister to marry him. She resisted his advances, explaining that such a marriage would be incestuous, and refused to subordinate herself to her brother's authority. Within her domain, which includes the summit of Mount Batur, the lake, and the subaks that depend on her, she claims supremacy. Through a simple symbolic association, at Ulun Danu Batur the Goddess comes to stand for the subaks, so that her desire for autonomy becomes one with theirs. But unlike her brother, she makes no claim to universal authority; instead she upholds the principle of dualism, based on the complementarity of male and female cosmological principles. This becomes the charter for the temple's authority and the basis for its claims to autonomy. While caste reigns unchallenged at the temple of Besakih, at Batur the priests struggle to suppress it so as to bring forward the dualistic cosmology of the Goddess.

But this effort is only partly successful, and its failures expose certain limits to the powers of the subaks. Considered as a water temple, Ulun Danu is incomplete. All other water temples are associated with the control of some productive physical resource, such as an irrigation system or a block of rice terraces. As we have seen, the cooperative and egalitarian traditions of the subaks originate in the meetings that are held to manage these resources. But the crater lake has no outlets; its waters percolate slowly into the porous volcanic soil and become part of the groundwater system. Because there is no source of flowing water to be managed, there are no subak meetings at Ulun Danu. Instead the subaks come as worshippers, and the temple is managed by the priests and people of the village of Batur. For them, the fact that the temple does not actually control an irrigation system is not a great hardship, because the temple itself is an important source of wealth and prestige. But this highland village does not possess a subak; instead the villagers support themselves by dry farming and trade. Thus the largest and most important water temple is managed not by a collection of subaks but by the members of a village where the rituals and institutions connected with the subak system do not exist. This village is plagued by a history of violent factionalism; between 1948 and 1977 it divided into two, then three, then four separate communities.

This chapter has two stories to tell: the first concerns the temple, and the second the struggles of the village of Batur to manage it, or perhaps one should say to manage themselves. But before beginning, it may be helpful to explain why I wish to devote an entire chapter to a single water temple. The explanation has to do with the unique role played by Ulun Danu Batur in defining the water temple cult. While all other water temples are directly involved in some aspect of rice production, the Ulun Danu temple has a different agenda. In a certain sense its main business is to define itself, to articulate a cosmology in which the Goddess and her temples should occupy a central role in the Balinese world. While attendance at other water temples is restricted to their subak congregations, Ulun Danu seeks to attract the largest possible crowds to its major rituals. The temple bases its claims to supremacy on passages from purported ancient texts, but these claims would have little salience were it not for the priests' success at translating them into dramatic public rituals associated with the annual visitation by the Goddess. On these occasions, most of the male inhabitants of the village become full-time servants of the temple, as organizers, priests, musicians, cooks, dancers, or laborers. During the ten days when the Goddess is thought to be in residence, the temple becomes an enormous redistributive center where tons of rice and other foods contributed by the subaks are used to feed hundreds of people every day. But this accounts for only a fraction of the value of the subaks' contributions; the remainder is spent on the temple itself and its rituals.

This emphasis on the theatrical aspects of the ritual cycle, performed by priests for the benefit of crowds of worshippers, is quite unlike other water temple festivals. But it bears a striking resemblance to the great public rituals of the royal cult. In precolonial Bali farmers were taxed by their princes, and a substantial portion of this weath was expended on royal rites of passage such as weddings and funerals. Clifford Geertz has argued that such performances served an instrumental purpose; he suggests that they were not merely ostentatious displays of wealth, but the primary source of legitimacy for princes. According to Geertz, "If a state was constructed by constructing a king, a king was constructed by constructing a god. . . . Kings were all Incomparable, but some were more Incomparable than others, and it was the dimensions of their cult that made the difference."[2] The sheer magnificence of the ceremonies of the

[2] Clifford Geertz, *Negara: The Theatre State in Nineteenth-Century Bali*, Princeton, N.J.: Princeton University Press, 1980: 125.

"theatre states" thus served to validate a prince's claims to overlordship. In a similar way, the scale of the annual cycle of rites at Ulun Danu is meant to reflect the grandeur of its pantheon and so enhance its claims for recognition. The priests therefore devote much attention to the problem of organizing contributions from the farmers, using a system that resembles the one employed by the old royal courts. Subaks receive formal lontar-palm letters from the high priests of the temple each year, reminding them of the specific contributions that are expected from them. When the subaks arrive at the temple, these goods are carefully tabulated. In this way the subaks become "supporters" (*pengayah*) of the temple, just as in former times they would have been supporters of their rulers. By providing such support the farmers acquire a role at the temple or palace, and in return may expect to receive benefits from their gods or kings.

But the parallel with the royal cult breaks down when we consider the origins and purposes of the rituals held at the water temple. The rites of kingship draw on ancient precedents; as we have seen, they are closely linked to the ideology of caste and the Dharmasastric state. But what precedents are available to a water temple atop a cosmic mountain, the only institution of its kind? Especially if the temple does not control flowing water and is not managed by subaks? In a word, the priests of the Goddess are forced to improvise. This involves some rather delicate negotiations. The temple is managed by the people of the village of Batur by means of several governing institutions, which include not only the priests but also a group of trance mediums and a hierarchy of village Elders. These bodies have partly overlapping responsibilities and often yield to the temptation to compete with one another by emphasizing the importance of the rituals that highlight their own importance. In the absence of a stable authority structure, one group may urge the performance of *abiseka ratu* (sacred kingship) for the high priests, while others may hope to elevate their own status by emphasizing a different sequence of rites. There are special rituals for trance mediums, while others connect the birth of twins to the mythology of the Goddess, and at some point even a version of human sacrifice became part of the temple's repertoire. A skeptic might conclude that what unites these ideas is merely that they can all be used to embellish claims for an elevated status. And indeed the temple offers a seductive opportunity for the people of Batur to costume themselves in the larger-than-life identities that their association with the temple can provide. But the choice of rituals to be performed is constrained, I suggest, by the need to ensure that they resonate with the basic principles that helped Ulun Danu to emerge as the supreme water temple: the symbolism of the cosmic mountain, the Goddess, and the holy water of the lake.

I am suggesting two claims about the annual cycle of rites at this temple: first, that they broadcast a seemingly unified vision of the meaning of the water temple cult, and second, that this vision emerges from an ongoing historical process of give-and-take between various factions, constrained both by political realities and by certain structural imperatives. The emergence and articulation of this vision is the subject of the chapter.

Anthropologists have recently begun to chide one another for overemphasizing the exotic aspects of their subject matter. But try as I may, I do not see how Ulun Danu Batur could be made to seem prosaic. So I have decided to give up the struggle and begin the chapter with one of the most exotic aspects of the temple's governance: the responsibilities that are entrusted to a special group of men and women while they are in a semiconscious state of trance possession.

• • •

About eight o'clock one evening in July 2002 six trance mediums from the Ulun Danu temple gathered at the home of a married woman in the village of Batur who had been suffering from depression and distressing dreams. They were joined by two other women who also wished to discover whether becoming a medium (*premade*) might give them release from various physical and mental afflictions. A roofed platform of bamboo had been specially prepared to provide a place for them to sit, and along one side were placed an array of forty-five coconut shells on silver-colored plates representing the forty-five deities of the temple. Each coconut was partly filled with small objects such as colored rice grains and bits of metal to symbolize the bhuta. Similar objects are used to convey the ashes of the dead to the sea in the final rites after cremation. But here they were intended to help the mediums align their own inner worlds with those of particular gods. Often, illnesses of the spirit can be traced to the *sad ripu*, the six destructive emotions including, for example, anger, sadness, and envy. If a child is conceived when one of its parents is in the grip of such an emotion, the imbalance may persist in its own inner world and become a permanent handicap. In such cases becoming a medium may offer relief. As the ritual began, prayers and incense were used to invite the gods to appear, and then ceramic plates filled with burning charcoal were set in front of the mediums and the three candidates. Prayers continued as one by one the mediums fell into trance. One man began to cry out nonsense syllables, which onlookers interpreted as a dialect of Chinese, evidence that he had become possessed by a deity from the temple's Chinese shrine. He grew increasingly agitated, rocking back and forth and plunging his hands into the charcoal. Presently he reached into the charcoal, grasped several burning coals, and rubbed them into his hair. In seconds he lost consciousness and collapsed, as onlookers rushed to put out the fire. The other mediums were women and their trances were less violent, but soon all of them were interspersing loud cries with snatches of prayers as they handled the burning embers. Two of the three candidates seemed to fall into a much gentler trance, while the third remained immobile and continued to pray quietly with her eyes closed. This ritual was repeated for three more nights, and at the next major temple festival the two candidates who had shown their susceptibility to trance were welcomed as members of the *premade* for the temple. Henceforth they would make annual offerings at the shrine of the god who had chosen them. The mediums are called *penuntun*, guides, and they endow the priests with an authority that is not easily challenged.

Trance divination is quite common in Bali. Some mediums become professional diviners called *balian ketakson*, who are consulted by people when they wish to contact the dead in order to discover the causes of illnesses or misfortunes. But the trance mediums of Ulun Danu Batur do not attempt to contact the ancestors; their only role is to serve as mediums for the gods who selected them. Trance rituals occur after the annual visitation by the Goddess in the tenth month and at certain other times. The mediums gather as a group in the temple forecourt and are sent into trance so that they may dance and handle fire to prove that their possession is genuine; only then will the temple priests listen to them. On these occasions each medium speaks for his or her own god, but when a child must be chosen to replace one of the priests, somehow the mediums must reach a consensus while still in a trance state. The Ulun Danu temple is unique in that trance divination is used to select the governing priesthood and to maintain an unbroken relationship between the priests and the gods. The process resembles the Tibetan Buddhist procedure for discovering reincarnate lamas, but there are important differences. As in Tibet, the direct connection between humans and the divine realm that becomes manifest in this way is a source of temporal power. But in the case of Ulun Danu Batur, the aim is not to discover a single person, such as a reincarnate high lama. Instead a whole pantheon of gods must continually find replacements for their human acolytes. This is quite unlike the rituals of the water temples described in the previous chapter, in which all members of a congregation have an identical responsibility to honor all the temple's gods and to contemplate the universality of their own subjective experience or inner world. At Ulun Danu the emphasis is also on the universal, but it is discovered by a different route. Individual priests are concerned with the particular gods who chose them, and are occupied with a perpetual cycle of rites in which each god and each priest have specific responsibilities.

In this way the governance of the temple is partly given over to a kind of collective unconscious; it seems significant that the most important decisions of the mediums must be based on consensus. Clearly this has certain advantages: it is a check on the powers of the priests and Elders, giving voice to the concerns of the village; at the same time it insulates the priests and Elders from criticism by displacing ultimate responsibility for the governance of the temple to entranced mediums and the gods they represent. But the mediums are not mere colorless channels for the gods; it is significant that the most prominent mediums are usually pairs of opposite-sex twins. When such twins are born to a woman of the village, the entire village must undergo purification rituals, and it is expected that the twins will eventually become temple mediums. They are considered to be married from the moment of their birth, and these married siblings become focal points for anxieties about sexuality, pollution, and the supernatural that are connected with the gender-based cosmological dualism that pervades the symbolism of the temple. As we will see, they physically embody the emotional tensions involved in balancing male and female power, and connect this mystery to the charged moments when trance creates a bridge between the temple and its gods.

The connection of twinship to the Goddess and the temple is partly explained by one of the many legends that describe the arrival of the Goddess at the lake. Such stories form the repertoire of the gurus of the temple, a group of learned men who have an honored role in the hierarchy of village Elders, and who are consulted when questions arise concerning historical precedents or charters for activities at the temple. That these stories often provide alternative explanations for the same events troubles only the most literal-minded questioners. In this version the high god of Mount Meru visits his wife, who resides on Mount Sumeru in Java. They have three children, who express to their mother a desire to have mountains of their own in Bali. On arriving in Bali they seek the highest peaks, and their father tells them "near here would be a good place for your thrones." They respond, "let us ask our mother to give us a guide who will know where it would be best to build our residences." He agrees and asks his wife, who sends a human guide with the royal title Ida Dalem Masula-Masuli. Masula-Masuli suggests locations on three adjacent volcanoes, and then urges the gods to ask their mother for help in the contruction of their palaces. She sends the Naga (serpent) gods to provide foundations for the three palaces, and later sends humans to populate the island.

Having connected the Balinese gods to their mother, a Javanese mountain goddess, Ida Dalem Masula-Masuli now disappears from the story. But in the present day, when twins of opposite sex are born to a woman of the village, they are thought to represent the reappearance of the spirit of Masula-Masuli. Whether this event is taken to be a good or a bad sign depends on the order in which the infants appear. If the male appears first it is considered auspicious, a portent of prosperity. Nonetheless the children are considered to have become intimate while in the womb, and the entire village must undergo a month and seven days of ritual purification, followed by a procession to the sea at Keramas to seek holy water (*kamandalu*) for purification, as described in the previous chapter. But if the girl appears first, it is called *salah wadi*, a dangerous sign that Durga is restless in her temple. To avoid her anger the village must seek tirtha kamandalu and carry out purifications at her temple; here the story connects with the myth of Durga's desire to return to Siwa. In both cases the parents' house must be destroyed, and they and their children must live outside the village during the rites of purification, in a small community called Tasu that was created to provide a refuge for such temporary exiles. The birth of same-sex twins is also polluting, though much less so, and the parents must also live in the place of exiles while the purifications are performed. Interestingly, parents of three or more children of the same sex are also exiled to Tasu until a child of the opposite sex is born to them and restores the proper balance. These beliefs are not merely hypothetical: from time to time in the village, twins and triplets are born, houses are burned, processions are sent to the sea, and families are relocated to Tasu.

All this is in aid of maintaining a balanced gender dualism, an ideal that is depicted as fundamental to the organization of the temple and the village. Both the hierarchy of priests and that of the village Elders are divided into two groups. One is called *bedauhan* (west) and is associated with the female principle (*pradana*). The opposite is *bedanginan* (east), which is considered to be male (*purusa*). The monthly cycle of rituals is also divided into male and female categories according to the phase of the moon, with the east priests and functionaries responsible for the phase that begins with the new moon, and the west's responsibilities commencing at the full moon. The relationship between east and west is modeled on complementarity. For example, during the fifteen days that the east priests are performing the regular cycle of temple rituals and also attending to the rituals requested by visitors, their counterparts of the west are responsible for preparing the necessary offerings.

Yet while the activities of the temple are organized around the ideal of a balanced harmony between male and female, it is taken for granted that such perfection is hard to achieve. One sees this clearly in the marriage ceremonies at Batur. Folk wisdom in the village maintains that the prospect of marriage is disruptive and "confusing" to both partners. A remedy is provided in the form of a pair of chickens that the couple are told to hold atop their heads near the end of the ritual. The couple is

Figure 27. People of Batur seated in the middle courtyard for ceremonies concluding the rites of the tenth month, March 2004.

instructed to pray that all their negative thoughts about the marriage should be transferred to the chickens, which are promptly barbecued. Marriage, like twinship, represents a potential solution to the problem of balancing the male and female principles. When anthropologists encounter belief systems that seem to organize themselves neatly into such

Figure 28. Men of Batur preparing spices for meals that will be served to visitors to the temple during the ceremonies of the tenth month, March 2004. The color of their headband signifies whether they belong to the left (female) or right (male) moiety.

tidy categories, there is a well-known temptation to push the argument along, so that dichotomies like opposing male and female principles seem to pervade an entire system of thought. But in this case I suggest that it is the people of Batur, not the anthropologist, who exert themselves to emphasize the centrality of this idea. The degree to which the mysteries of marriage and twinship weigh on their minds is evidenced by another sequence of rituals involving the four most senior male Elders of the village. These men are expected to participate in a series of rituals that culminate in the marriage of both pairs of old men to one another, whereupon they are considered to be in a sense "twinned" (*pabuncing*). The completion of these rites vastly enhances their authority, bringing the village as whole into alignment with a dualistic universe. Because the village attachs such importance to these rites, it is worth noting some of the details.

Like other Bali Aga villages of the mountains, the village of Batur is governed by a hierarchy of elders who meet monthly in the village temple. The hierarchy is based on seniority, so that as time goes on and the most senior men die, younger men move up in station. Similar or identical hierarchies appear in thousand-year-old royal inscriptions addressed to the villages of the region, and persist today. But in Batur the hierarchy of Elders (*balai rama*) is concerned with the governance not only of the village but also of the great temple and its satellites. The Elders meet several times a month in the village temple (*pura desa*), a complex of shrines and seating pavilions adjacent to the Ulun Danu temple. The village temple is dominated by two long rectangular roofed seating pavilions, elevated high off the ground and oriented with one end pointing toward the entrance and the other toward a row of shrines in the Ulun Danu temple. On the full moon eight pairs of male Elders take their seats in these pavilions, facing the gods. Each seat is associated with a title and certain responsibilities; the lowest-ranking Elders are messengers while the highest are the ritual heads of the village.

Between the two long pavilions for the Elders and the shrines for the gods there is a smaller, square seating pavilion that is elevated even higher from the ground. Presently this pavilion remains empty, awaiting the arrival of the Beautiful King(s) of the Place of Opposite-Sex Twins (*I Ratu Ayu Karang Buncing*). The two most senior Elders are eligible to become Beautiful Kings, but to acquire this title and take their seats in the square pavilion they must undergo a dauntingly expensive series of rituals, which include feeding the entire village for forty-five days as well as performing many of the ceremonies that are normally required for Brahmins to become high priests. These activities culminate in a marriage ceremony in which the two would-be Beautiful Kings, who belong to the eastern group, marry their opposite numbers from the west. Evidently the marriages of the four old men have no domestic or sexual implications; instead they are seen as actualizing a model of the village as a well-ordered family. Once the rituals are complete, the two Elders from the west side are considered to be the wives of the Beautiful Kings, and all four men move to the square pavilion. The other fourteen Elders move up two slots, and four new men are inducted at the bottom of the hierarchy, bringing the total number of Elders to twenty. Lest there be any doubt about the broader significance of these rites, the highest-ranking Beautiful King also acquires the title of Jero Petinggi ("He who is Highest"). Henceforth the two kings are entitled to issue commands that their "wives" convey to the other Elders. Any Elder who refuses such a command three times is exiled. Once they are installed as Beautiful Kings, it is said that the authority of these Elders would rival that of the two high priests of the temple. But it would be very expensive to carry out all these rites, and the revenues that flow into the temple from the subaks are largely controlled by the high priests. To the chagrin of the Elders, for the past century the square pavilion has stood empty.

• • •

Dualism is also central to the authority of the high priests of the temple, but it arises from different sources that generate crosscurrents with respect to the symbolism of marriage. The rites of the Beautiful Kings propose marriage as a solution to the problem of achieving perfect order, by balancing the male and female principles. But the high priest of the temple is symbolically associated with the refusal of the Goddess to accept marriage and subordination to her brother. According to the myths, the Goddess defined her role as a Balinese deity when she founded a new pantheon on Mount Batur where she could retain her independence. This pantheon is replicated by each new generation of temple priests in an unbroken chain of reincarnations. Thus when the Greater High Priest (*Jero Gde Duuran*) of the temple dies and a virgin boy is selected as his successor, the child is taught to worship the previous Greater High Priests as his own ancestors.

At the apex of the temple's pantheon is the Goddess herself, represented by the Greater High Priest. Next comes the Lesser High Priest, who is identified with her brother (the male god of Mount Agung). Connections to the other forty-three gods of the temple are parcelled out by the mediums to the remaining twenty temple priests, all of whom are considered to have equal status. Thus the pantheon is dominated by the two high priests representing the pair of Balinese mountain gods. The claim that the Goddess reigns supreme on her mountaintop is directed at the whole of Balinese society, and bears only incidentally on the governance of the village of Batur. As the Goddess rejects the supremacy of her brother, so her earthly representative, the Greater High Priest, refuses to accept subordination to kings or Brahmins. Indeed it is by reiterating this refusal that the priests justify the temple's claim to a unique status. Every visitor to the temple soon learns that the Greater High Priest represents the Goddess who refused an incestuous marriage with her brother. The visible subordination of the Lesser High Priest to the Greater dramatizes this relationship, and their relationship supplies an explanation for the temple's existence in terms of the unwillingness of the Goddess to accept subordination to male authority. This theme runs counter to the idealization of marriage by the Elders and makes marriage itself a focal point of contention in the temple. For while the priests derive their legitimacy from the principled rejection of marriage by the Goddess, the Elders pine for the wedding of the Beautiful Kings, and the twinned trance mediums embody the ambivalence toward sexuality and marriage that is evident in the wedding ritual.

It seems possible that this contest could be resolved by several alternative outcomes. For example, presently the opposite-sex twins who represent King Masula-Masuli occupy a relatively inferior position in the status hierarchy of the temple, but it is not hard to imagine them as potential Beautiful Kings, occupying a position like that now taken by the two high priests. I suspect that this possibility is foreclosed because it would be difficult to deny the superior position to the female twin, which would certainly exasperate the Elders. Instead, as a medium she is relegated to the role of an intermediary who helps to validate the selection of a virgin boy to represent the Goddess.

This arcane arrangement (selecting mediums to choose priests who represent the pantheon) ensures that the human representative of the Goddess is a male from the village of Batur. But from the point of view of the Elders, it is hardly a perfect solution. Once the priests are chosen, as anointed representatives of the gods they have potentially slipped out of mere human control. The trance mediums provide a kind of check on the powers of the priests, but one that depends on the vagaries of their pronouncements while in trance. A much more powerful means of control is provided by entrusting the Gurus (who are all Elders) with the authority to interpret the myths that define the nature and scope of the temple's activities. These myths take on fundamental importance because of the belief that each new generation of priests is a replica of the original priesthood, so that their role was defined once and for all when the temple was created. As it happens there are a great many myths and legends, not all of which exist in written form. Consequently the Gurus

enjoy a certain latititude in their interpretations. The most detailed stories provide explanations for the origins of all the satellite temples as well
as the temples' orchestras, dances, and rites. Other versions are more
succinct. The simplest version that I have heard explains that in the beginning, before the volcanic cone came into existence by the lake, eighteen people lived in a community that would become the village of Batur.
Because they were equal in their knowledge and powers, they tended to
quarrel. So the supreme king of Bali, Dalem Baturenggong, sent four
married noblemen to rule them. Each couple tried to rule the village but
failed because the people refused to accept their authority. After several
generations of strife six descendants of the original inhabitants jour-
neyed to the empire of Majapahit in Java to ask for help. They returned
with a written charter and orders to accept a descendant of the Balinese
king of Mengwi as their high priest and ruler, with a descendant of the
king of Bangli as the second-ranking priest; everyone else would have
equal status. All the trance mediums were summoned for the first time,
and they recognized two virgin boys as descendants of the two kings. As
we will see, this story bears quite a resemblance to recent historical
events.

Various written texts, including the *Babad Patisora* and a recent com-
pilation of myths and stories by one of the Elders, tell more complex
tales. For example, in one version the brother of the Goddess becomes
angry at his sister's refusal to marry him, and burns her palace on Mount
Agung. Their father advises her to move to the crater lake and so end the
quarrel. The father sends a holy man, Empu Pucangan, to help the Goddess make the journey. When they arrive on Mount Batur she tells the
holy man to strike the crater lake with a whip four times, pointing it toward the four cardinal directions. Where the lake divides she builds her
palace, while the holy man constructs a hermitage for himself nearby.
The mother of the Goddess sends six people from Java to serve her, who
settle by the lake, and the Goddess gives them an orchestra. As time goes
on the village grows to seventy households; they build a temple for the
Goddess, and the village is divided into eastern and western halves. The
god Indra visits Bali and bestows the authority to rule Bali on the Goddess and her brother. Indra also decrees that there should be ceremonial
dances in the temple, of the kinds that are still performed. The Goddess
asks Indra to return to Bali each year on the day called *pagerwesi*, and
declares her intention to make the island fertile with the gift of flowing
water. After Indra departs, the Goddess selects six people from the village, three men and three women, to become trance mediums. The mediums then choose the first temple priests.

The role of the priests is described in greater detail in another version.
In this account the village of Batur is created by king Dalem Baturenggong

from the inhabitants of four villages, Tampurhyang, Sinarata, Gunung Lebah, and Sapura, at the site of Empu Pucangan's hermitage. Sixteen Elders are selected by trance mediums, along with the two high priests. The first high priest is a member of the commoner clan Pasek Kayu Selem, who discovers that he is also a descendant of the king of Mengwi, variously called Arya Murti, Gusti Agung Mengwi, and Dewa Gde Bencengah. Thenceforth all the high priests are considered to be descendants of this king.

The most important consequence of these beliefs, from the point of view of the subaks, is to load the two high priests of the temple with a great deal of rather diffuse authority. Much attention is focused on the rituals that take place when high priests die and their successors are selected. Some weeks or months after the ashes of the deceased priest have been placed in their chandi, the village gathers in the temple. With the eyes of every adult member of the village on them, the opposite-sex twins lead the temple mediums in a rite of trance possession that re-creates the guiding role played by Masula-Masuli when the Goddess first came to Bali. After the mediums reach a consensus (while still in trance), the priests lead a procession to the home of the chosen child, and bear him to the shrine of the Goddess in the innermost sanctum of the temple, which he ascends. Henceforth the two high priests personify the divine pair of siblings. Their relationship contains an interesting ambiguity: in the presence of the Greater High Priest, the Lesser signifies the god of Mount Agung. But this god has no role to play on the mountain of the Goddess, so his priest occupies a nearly empty slot in the ritual calender. When the Greater priest is absent, the Lesser assumes his identity as the representative of the Goddess.

For these reasons the rituals that confer supreme authority, such as the rites of sacred kingship (*abiseka ratu*), are restricted to the Greater priest. After he is chosen as a child, his family moves into a residence adjacent to the temple, and for the rest of his lifetime his living expenses are borne by the temple. On a more modest scale, financial support is also provided to an unmarried man and woman who agree to perform the priest's death rites. This pair must remain chaste for the remainder of their lives. In former times, it is said, the woman would have been required to immolate herself in the high priest's funeral pyre as a suttee. Today she is required only to collect the "corpse water" from his bodily remains and bear the remains to a small chandi near Durga's temple, where his ashes will be placed. The male's principal task is to roast the head of a bull. These funeral rites, modeled on those of kings, climax with the transportation of the body of the priest to the cremation grounds in a grand tower, with eleven roofs for the Greater priest and nine for the Lesser. All other citizens of the village, including the other temple priests and Elders, are permitted only one-story towers, signifying the absence of caste distinctions in the village. There is, however, one exception to this rule: the man and woman who perform the death rites of the high priests require no funeral of any kind; it is considered that their spirits are already fully prepared to accompany the priests to the afterlife. Currently the widow of the former Lesser High Priest and a male dwarf live in readiness to perform these funeral rites.

• • •

In the foregoing I have emphasized the behind-the-scenes contests for precedence among the Elders, priests, and mediums at Ulun Danu, as each group favors rituals that help to strengthen its claims to preeminence. One might imagine that this could lead to chaos, but in fact most of these rivalries remain hidden from visitors, and the various symbols and rites promoted by each group are not seen as incompatible or antagonistic. Instead they simply enhance the awe and mystery of the temple, from the dwarf who guards the main entrance to the mediums dancing with fire and the Gurus who sit in the "sacred kitchens," ready to place their encyclopedic knowledge of the myths at the disposal of visitors. Thus despite its internal conflicts, the temple presents itself to the world as a coherent and cohesive institution, one of the two supreme temples in the Balinese world.

And indeed, from the vantage point of a Guru seated at his post near the temple's storerooms, the world appears to be a very orderly place. Regional water temples such as the Masceti Pamos seem to be miniature replicas of Ulun Danu, each of them containing a shrine for the Goddess and a local pantheon appropriate to the temple's location. The regional temples function as nodes for local clusters of subaks, which generally also contain shrines for the Goddess. In this way the cult of water temples seems to center on the Goddess and the crater lake. Similarly, the grand ritual cycle performed at Ulun Danu appears to be the culmination of the myriad rituals that take place in field shrines and lesser water temples. Looking downslope from Ulun Danu, the entire cult of water temples appears as a distinct, coherent, structured, and systematic set of institutions and beliefs.

But to accept this view uncritically is to make the kind of mistake that Stephen Gould and Richard Lewontin identified in their celebrated critique of Panglossian explanations. Gould and Lewontin offer as an example the great central dome of the San Marco Basilica in Venice. The architecture of the dome includes four spandrels (tapering triangular spaces formed by the intersection of two rounded arches). These spandrels are decorated with Christian cosmological imagery (as it happens, they depict the four biblical rivers, the Tigris, Euphrates, Indus, and Nile). The whole design, according to Gould and Lewontin, "is so elaborate, harmonious, and purposeful that we are tempted to view it as the starting point of any analysis, as the cause in some sense of the surrounding architecture. But this would invert the proper path of analysis." For the spandrels with their quadripartite symmetry are merely by-products of the solution to the problem of mounting a dome on rounded arches.[3] The genius of the artisans lay not in the creation of spandrels but in finding ways to integrate them into a coherent cosmological design.

The Ulun Danu temple presents itself as the pinnacle of an orderly hierarchy of water temples, and its ritual cycle is regarded as the culmination of all the local and regional rites of fertility. But this should not convince us that it came into existence, like other water temples, as the planned creation of a group of subaks (or indeed a Goddess). Instead it is more likely that the antecedent of the temple was a regional ancestor-origins temple (*pura banua*) located in the village of Batur; several temples of this type are still to be found in neighboring highland villages. Because of its fortuitous location by the crater lake, a pura banua could easily take on another identity as the supreme *patirthan* or origin-place of holy water. Once this identification occurred, the mythology itself could help to steer an unplanned and opportunistic accretion of meaning. A temple that aspired to be the supreme patirthan would need to contain shrines for the entire pantheon of fertility gods, and its potential congregation would logically include every subak. But perhaps the most powerful impetus for positioning itself at the apex of a hierarchy of water temples would come from the preexisting pattern of rice cult rituals. As we have seen, whenever a farmer begins a new planting cycle, he performs a sequence of rites that are directed at his own particular fields and crop. These individual ritual cycles are considered to be joined together and amplified at the subak temples, where they are addressed to local deities. The same process of amplification occurs again in the regional water temples. Given this wheels-within-wheels pattern of expanding ritual cycles, once a supreme water temple came into existence it could hardly resist the logic that would define its rituals as the master cycle. What began with the prayers of innumerable farmers to the particular spirits that control life and death in their fields and progressed through a pantheon of fertility gods and goddesses in the regional water

---

[3] S. J. Gould and R. C. Lewontin, "The Spandrels of San Marco and the Panglossian Paradigm: A Critique of the Adaptationist Program," *Proceedings of the Royal Society London*, B 205: 581–98.

temples would culminate in universal rites of fertility itself (birth, life, and death: *utpeti, stithi, pralina*) at the supreme temple.

"A building is not finished," writes Hegel, "when its foundation is laid."[4] The hieroglyph of Reason becomes apparent only after a slow process of unconscious maturation. Once regional water temples such as the Masceti Pamos came into existence, the node-and-cluster structure of the temple cult would point inexorably toward a supreme water temple associated with the crater lake. And as soon as a temple began to fulfill this role, the water temple cult would achieve a new level of coherence as a system of thought (rather than a mere amalgam of local fertility rites), expressing universal principles that would eventually exert pressure on the subak temples to redefine themselves as branches of the cult of the Goddess of the lake. However, a mountain temple that redefined itself as a supreme water temple would lack any authority to enforce conformity, so that lesser water temples would retain considerable latitude in their rituals and architecture. But henceforth, to the extent that the supreme temple succeeded in its quest for recognition, a universal hierarchy of water temples would become a reality. "Once the realm of ideas is revolutionized," Hegel concludes, "actuality does not hold out."[5]

My claim is that the supreme water temple came into existence as the last phase in the formation of the water temple system, as a mountain village opportunistically redefined its pura banua as a universal patirthan, or source of holy water from the crater late at the summit of a cosmic mountain. Some of the evidence for this interpretation is historical, and will be taken up later in this chapter. But the strongest evidence is comparative: only a few small steps appear to distinguish Ulun Danu from the other pura banua of the mountains. There is even a rival candidate for the role of supreme water temple. In the village of Songan, at the northern end of Lake Batur, there is another important temple associated with the lake. The priests of Songan claim that theirs is the true temple of the Goddess, because unlike the temple at Batur it is physically located beside the lake. At stake in this rivalry is the flow of tribute from the hundreds of subaks and villages that wish to honor the Goddess. (As we shall see, the Ulun Danu Batur temple was formerly also located by the lake until a volcanic eruption in 1926 made it necessary to relocate the temple and village on the rim of the crater). In a broader sense, Ulun Danu Batur bears a strong resemblance to the entire class of pura banua.

[4] G.W.F. Hegel, *The Phenomenology of Mind*, translated by J. B. Baillie, New York: Harper Torch Books, 1967: 75.

[5] Briefe von und an Hegel I, 253–54, quoted in Shlomo Avineri, *Hegel's Theory of the Modern State*, Cambridge: Cambridge University Press, 1972: 68.

Like Ulun Danu, these temples are supported by dozens of villages, which supply materials for a monthly cycle of rites tied to the phases of the moon. Their obligation to provide tribute derives from the belief that each pura banua represents the origin of a banua or original human community; the villages that belong to its congregation are thought to be its daughter settlements. The word *banua* derives from the ancient Austronesian term for village or community (*wanua*); cognates exist in most Malayo-Polynesian languages. One of the most important pura banua is located just a few kilometers from the village of Batur, at the summit of the highest peak on the crater rim. This temple, Pura Pucak Penulisan, is supported by thirty small villages. It differs from Ulun Danu in that it makes no claim to be the creation of the Goddess. But like most pura banua, it is not supported by a royal court and does not employ Brahmanic priests to carry out its rituals.

A closer parallel to Ulun Danu Batur is the Pura Kehen, a pura banua located near the royal palace of the kingdom of Bangli. Like Ulun Danu, this temple combines several functions; both princes and Brahmins play an important role in its affairs. The primary deity of this temple is a male god who is understood to be the ancestor of the Bangli royal family. Support for the temple is shared between the royal court, powerful Brahmin families, and a cluster of nineteen nearby villages. The Pura Kehen functions as both a pura banua, or origin temple for these villages, and a royal origin temple for the Bangli dynasty. By assuming responsibility for the performance of major rituals in the temple, Brahmin priests demonstrate their importance to both the kingdom and the banua. There is also a hierarchy of sixteen hereditary temple priests who are not Brahmins. As at Ulun Danu, these priests are divided into male and female groups (called right and left). The most senior priest of the right (male) side bears the title of Jero Gde, like the two high priests of Batur, and like them is entitled to be carrried to his cremation fire in an eleven-roofed tower. But unlike the high priests of Batur, he may not look forward to the rites of saced kingship (*abiseka ratu*), for Bangli already has its king. Thus the leadership of the Pura Kehen shares most of the elements that are found at Ulun Danu, but they are configured in such a way as to pose no challenge to the authority of the rajah and the Brahmins.

The village of Batur and the Ulun Danu temple are located within the territory of the former kingdom of Bangli. If Ulun Danu were to be controlled by a king, the rajah of Bangli would presumably fulfill this role. The fact that he makes no such claim is explained by another myth. According to the Gurus of Ulun Danu, the male god of Pura Kehen was also once an unsuccessful suitor for the Goddess of the Lake. But she rejected him and fled to her lake. Henceforth she refused to visit his temple. Her refusal to submit to his authority is recalled each time the priests of Ulun Danu journey through the kingdom of Bangli on their way to the sea, as happens regularly in order to acquire holy water. On these occasions the Goddess and her retinue do not stop at his temple; instead they pay a fine to the Pura Kehen. The Gurus say that if the Goddess were to weaken and accept one of the dynastic mountain gods as her suitor, she would become subordinate to his authority and the male principle of caste would regain salience at Batur.

But the leaders of Ulun Danu seem quite unworried by this possibility, trusting in their Goddess; they are much more concerned about potential rivals such as the lake temple at Songan. If the subaks began to waver in their belief that Ulun Danu Batur is the preferred temple of the Goddess, the priests of Songan would be delighted to accept their tribute. This brings us to the final issue with regard to the functional role of Ulun Danu in the water temple system. Another anthropologist, Brigitta Hauser-Schäublin, has argued that Ulun Danu was "unquestionably a royal temple," one that demonstrated divine royal power by providing a means for coordinating the organization of irrigation. She attributes the high position of the Greater High Priest as deriving from his ancestry from a king of Mengwi in the age of Gelgel (fourteenth century), and sees him as a representative of the king of Mengwi or perhaps the king of Klungkung.[6] Her evidence for this view amounts to a literal interpretation of some of the myths mentioned earlier in this chapter. But the impetus for her argument comes from the assumption that the supreme water temple must play a central role in the management of irrigation, and that kings must surely have sought to maintain control of this vital source of power. I invoke her argument here partly to inform the reader that my views on this topic have not gone unchallenged but also to underline how much my explanation contrasts with this view.[7] Implicit in the argument I have presented so far is the assumption that the transformation of a pura banua into the supreme water temple happened as the last phase in the formation of the water temple system. I now wish to

---

[6] Brigitta Hauser-Schäublin, "The Precolonial Balinese State Reconsidered: A Critical Evaluation of Theory Construction on the Irrigation, the State, and Ritual," *Current Anthropology* 44, no. 2 (April 2003): 42.

[7] Hauser-Schäublin also criticizes my emphasis on the preeminence of the Goddess at Ulun Danu, observing that many other deities are included in the temple's ritual calender. But subaks bring their tribute to Ulun Danu because they wish to honor the Goddess "who makes the rivers flow." And the supreme rites of the annual cycle are carried out by the Greater High Priest at the shrine of the Goddess. Indeed the Greater High Priest's supremacy in the hierarchy of temple priests at Batur derives from his connection to the Goddess.

push this argument a step further, and suggest that its role in irrigation management was an incidental by-product of attempts to secure the status of the temple as the foremost patirthan.

In an earlier book I described two kinds of cases where the high priests of the temple become involved in irrigation management. The first kind occurs when subaks or groups of subaks become involved in disputes over water rights. These cases are often brought to the temple by one of the parties to the dispute, and quite often one or both of the high priests agree to become involved. The Gurus can recite no mythical or historical precedents for this involvement, but the authority of the priests as the chosen representatives of the Goddess makes them obvious choices to serve as honest brokers in disputes that cannot otherwise be resolved. The usual procedure is to send experienced temple messengers (*sinoman*) to sort out the facts on the ground, and then arrange for the members of the subaks to gather at a water temple to receive a ceremonial visit by the high priests. It should be emphasized that the priests of Ulun Danu can invoke no specific legal standing for themselves in such cases, but the compromises that they suggest carry the considerable weight of their authority. The current Lesser priest is fond of pointing out that all flowing water should be regarded as the gift of the Goddess, reminding his listeners that springs have been known to dry up.

The second kind of case occurs when a group of farmers desire to capture a new water source, either to augment their existing supply or to build an entirely new subak. Dozens of new subaks have been created within historical memory, many of them located at high elevation in the vicinity of Lake Batur. The priests of Ulun Danu appear to have the tacit authority to withhold permission to build new irrigation works if they feel that the resulting diversion will adversely affect existing subaks downstream. But if permission is granted, the priests offer assistance in planning the new temples and shrines that are necessary to bring a subak into existence. The creation of one such subak is shown in my film *The Goddess and the Computer*.

Both of these types of intervention by Ulun Danu priests occur in response to requests that are brought to them by the subaks or farmers; there is no attempt to actively manage the irrigation systems or temple networks. In other words, it appears that the functional role of the temple in irrigation is incidental and opportunistic. This role is not imposed from above, but emerges from below: disputes sometimes arise between subaks that are not members of the same temple congregation, and when this occurs the high priests of the supreme temple are well positioned to facilitate a persuasive compromise. The successful mediation of disputes and the creation of new subaks provide tangible proofs of the temple's supernatural authority. This, rather than the management of irrigation, is the goal of the temple priests.

• • •

In the second part of this chapter I turn to the story of how the village of Batur has struggled to contain the crosscurrents of envy and religious enthusiasm generated by its control of the great temple. In an earlier book I summarized historical observations of the temple's role by European visitors. I interpreted this evidence to suggest that by the early nineteenth century Ulun Danu Batur was functioning as the supreme water temple of central Bali, receiving annual pilgrimages and offerings from many subaks. It seems unnecessary to go over those sources again here. Instead I wish to move on to the twentieth century, for which the evidence is better, and to focus on two issues: the nature of the temple's role with respect to the water temple cult, and the internal struggle of the village to manage itself and its great temple.

In 1917 a major earthquake destroyed many temples and palaces in Bali. Some months later, a well-known Dutch architect, P.A.J. Moojen, was employed by the governor-general of the Netherlands Indies to undertake the first survey of major temples in the newly conquered principalities of south Bali. One of the temples that was severely damaged in the earthquake was Ulun Danu Batur. In his first report to the governor-general, Moojen wrote:

> There are six temples which are superior to the many village temples, which are most sacred to the Balinese and are honored outside the borders of the little kingdoms in which they are situated. Several authors on Bali give various names for these six, and Frederich mentions that in the Oesana Bali itself there are different temples mentioned. However, it is certain that the Temple of Besakih is the most holy, followed by the Temple of Batur, also called Temple of Mount Lebah. Further information given to me by knowledgeable sources also points to this, and I even received a written request to start quickly on the repairs to the Batur temple.[8]

By good fortune, the actual letter to which he refers to in this passage, urging the immediate repair of Batur, is preserved among Moojen's papers in the archives of the Royal Institute for Anthropology and Linguistics in Leiden. The letter was written by the *sedahan agung* (royal tax

---

[8] P.A.J. Moojen, letter of 21 January 1919, pp. 19–20. Archives of the Koninklijk Instituut voor Taal-, Land- en Volkenkunde (KITLV), Leiden: Stukken ajkomstig van P.A.J. Moojen (architect, kunstschilder), "Kultuurprobleme," stukken voornamelijk betreffende de restauratie van tempels op Bali, met platte gronded. Ca. 1930. 1 bundel. H 1169: 17.

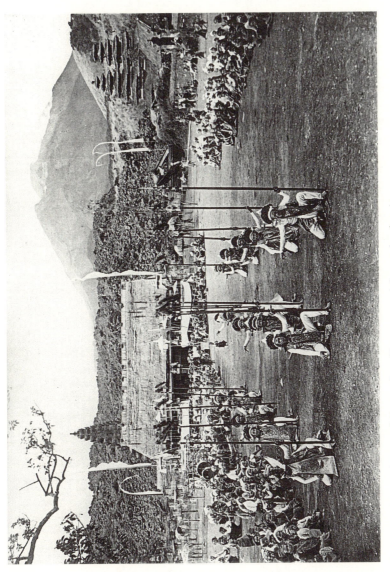

Figure 29. View of Batur showing the village, crater lake, and volcanic cone. From *Natuurkundig Tijdschrift voor Nederlands Indie*, Batavia, 1855.

collector) of the kingdom of Klungkung on 27 November 1918, addressed to a Balinese court official in Bangli and to the Dutch *controleur* of Klungkung. The letter is written in Malay, and reflects the struggle of the sedahan agung to convey the importance of Ulun Danu Batur to a foreign official. Interestingly, his explanation for the temple's importance echoes the mythological themes that were described above. The key passage is as follows:

> I hope that you will advise the (Dutch) Regent in Bangli, so that he will assist with the temple at Batur at the Ulun Danu, the home of the Deity called the Goddess of the Lake who has the power of control over water, the male has power over fire, this is very important according to Balinese religious custom, because the Deities of Mount Batur and Mount Agung are the children of the Deity of Mahameru who were given power over Bali . . . therefore it is extremely important that the two aspects of this, Mount Batur and Mount Agung, receive worship, as your servant advised earlier in Badung, and because it is easy to make things right at Batur if the people at Batur are assisted by their father.

Moojen wrote enthusiastically that "the fame of holiness, coming from this temple, has risen after the last eruption of Batoer in 1905 even more by the miraculous way by which it was then saved from total destruction. The glowing lava stream was stopped just at the main entrance in an inexplicable way!"[9]

This description is confirmed by the sketches of Nieuwenhuis, who visited the temple shortly after the eruption. Moojen estimated the cost of restoration of the Batur temple at thirty thousand Dutch florins (gulden), a small fortune in 1918. This included a sizable budget for labor. Batur was the only temple for which Moojen requested funding for labor, for a very interesting reason. As he explained in his report, "wages for labor are not budgeted (for other temples) since among the people it is the custom and tradition to supply this. But for one budget I have made an exception and that is for the temple of Batoer. . . . (Like Besakih), Batoer is of importance to the population of the whole of Bali, and from almost all parts of the island smaller or larger shrines have been built there, or the people have paid a share in their construction."[10]

Thus, according to Moojen's report, the importance of Batur transcended the boundaries of the former kingdoms. Unlike other temples,

---

[9] "De roep van heiligheid, die van dezen tempel uitgaat, is, na de laatste uitbarsting van den Batoer in 1905 nog zeer gestegen door de wonderbare wijze, waarop hij toen is gespaard voor algeheelen ondergang. De gloeiende lava-stroom werd immers juist bij de hoofdpoort op niet te verklaren wijze gestuit!" P.A.J. Moojen, letter of 21 January 1919.

[10] P.A.J. Moojen, letter of 21 January 1919, p. 38.

support for Batur came not only from nearby villages but from the whole island. These reports support the view that in the immediate pre-colonial era the temple of Batur functioned as the supreme water temple, much as it does today, and was neither a royal temple of the Bangli dynasty nor an ordinary pura banua. A few years after Moojen's report another major volcanic eruption again brought the temple to the attention of the senior Dutch official in Bangli:

> The village of Batur was situated before August 1926 at the foot of the volcano Batur. It was a neat, well kept village, which could be seen clearly from the crater. . . .
>
> On the third of August 1926, at 1 a.m., Mount Batur began to erupt. Along the north-western slope a long crevice appeared with a lot of noise and thunder, from which fires and many lava fountains spewed forth. I was informed of this and went to Kintamani, and descended to the village of Batur. It was impossible to get an overview of the situation: the inhabitants were not worried, and trusted in the power and will of the gods, and in the temple which already once before had stopped the lava-stream. From above you could see that the lava-stream was not moving towards the village. However, it seemed to me that the continuous eruptions would eventually fill the hollow in which the village was nestled. In the afternoon of the first day a new source of lava came into being at about 1200 meters distance from the village. With the sound of a diesel engine, it regularly emitted large waves of blood-red glowing lava. A lava stream started to move towards the village. . . .
>
> Above all this, the sky was blood-red, dyed by 21 lava fountains, glowering and spouting lava. Very heavy explosions made the surroundings resound; the echo went on and on against the rim of the crater.[11]

This report goes on to describe the abandonment of the village and the temple, which were slowly buried under a great tide of lava. The people of Batur had time to gather their possessions, including the orchestras and ceremonial objects stored in the temple, and climbed to the crater rim where they were invited to take refuge in the nearby village of Bayung Gde, where they remained as guests for three years. Soon after their arrival they began to solicit land and financial support from the colonial government in order to rebuild the temple and the village on the crater rim. This triggered another assessment of the importance of the temple by the colonial administration. A 1927 report by Controleur Haar describes the mobilization of funds and labor for the reconstruction of the temple from the whole population of Bali:

---

[11] "Memorie van Overgave der onderafdeeling Kloengkoeng," door Controleur J.C.C. Haar, 27 May 1926–3 February 1930, pp. 22–24, Leiden: Archives of the Koniinklijk Instituut voor Taal-, Land- en Volkenkunde.

At this moment the members of the new village of Batoer are busy preparing the terrain for a new temple. A request to have the whole of Bali participate in this new construction by means of handing over contributions was already made, but will later be prepared more closely by the Anak Agoeng (ruler) of Bangli and proposed again. It was thought to request a contribution of 5 cents per family head. If you count the number of people at around 1 million (in 1920 the census says that most families consist of 5 people), then approximately 200,000 people would bring in an amount of 10,000 guilders.

The rebuilding of the temple and its satellites was not completed until 1935. Meanwhile, soon after the move to temporary shelter in the village of Bayung Gde, the Greater Jero Gde died and was given a great funeral. The Dutch administration distributed land for houses and temples to the people of Batur, and arranged for a tax on transactions at an important local market located on the main north-south road to help support the temple. In 1935 a ceremony (*karya melaspas*) was performed to celebrate the completion of the temple and the rebuilding of the village.

A few years later the Dutch were expelled from Bali by the Japanese navy. This event is seen in retrospect by the Gurus as a turning point in the history of the village, the beginning of an era of factional strife that lasted until the 1980s. Initially the Japanese protrayed themselves as anticolonial liberators, and my elderly informants agree that at first the Japanese administration imposed few burdens on the people of Batur. In 1942 several new *sadeg* (trance mediums) were appointed, and subsequently with their aid a successor to the Greater Jero Gde was identified and installed. But later that year the Japanese sent one of their minions, a nobleman from Bangli, to Batur with the aim of obtaining a list of landless families in the village. The Japanese proposed to send these people to the island of Celebes as forced laborers. When this demand was conveyed to the village head, Pan Madri, he called a general meeting of the village to explained the situation and propose a plan. By then the Japanese had become unpopular because of their demands for forced labor and their contemptuous treatment of the Balinese. Madri suggested that the village take a unified stand against this demand, and urged everyone who owned land to sell a little at a very low price to the landless: "If anyone must go, then let us all go, so that the village becomes empty!" This plan was accepted, and in the end no one was exiled to Celebes. In later years Madri became widely known as a hero of resistance to the Japanese. But after the defeat of the Japanese in 1945, the return of the Dutch to Bali triggered a political crisis. The rise of the nationalist movement in the cities gradually affected the countryside, as the anticolonial *pemuda* (nationalist) activists and guerrillas sought the support of villagers. In 1945 Madri was approached by four leading nationalists. He agreed to join the nationalist cause and to help mobilize support in Batur. This decision had multiple repercussions that ultimately included the fragmentation of the village and the murder of Madri himself nine years later.

The first crisis occurred a few months later, when five jeeps carrying armed colonial police surprised a group of men seated at a food stand by the road in Batur, among them three suspected nationalists. The soldiers made ready to shoot as the men prepared to flee, but onlookers shouted "don't run" and instead the three were taken to Bangli for interrogation. Two months later they returned unharmed. But their capture triggered a polarization of the village into pro- and antinationalist factions, with Madri leading the nationalists. The antinationalists were led by the rajah of Bangli, who urged everyone to wear head scarves signifying that they were pro-Dutch. In response, the nationalist sympathizers organized a secret meeting in the forest, where it was suggested that all nationalists swear an oath and impress their thumbprints on a list. This plan was widely regarded as dangerous, and Madri suggested an alternative. He called the village together in the great temple and asked everyone to swear a secret oath that, while their bodies might appear to comply with the colonial government, in their hearts they were pronationalist. With this invisible but binding oath, instead of a paper document that could be stolen or copied, the subtlety of Balinese politics would triumph over the Dutch. But pro-Dutch sentiment remained strong among some villagers, who resented Madri's attempt to enlist everyone in the nationalist cause. In 1947 this dissatisfaction crystallized around a plan to create a village bank. The plan originated with the colonial government, and was supported by Pan Santi, one of the leading Elders of the village, who was regarded as the unofficial leader of the pro-Dutch faction. The idea was to require all citizens of the village to make a small initial contribution to the bank, which would then lend money to villagers and be administered by the village. But seven individuals refused to contribute to the formation of the bank and denounced it as a colonial political gambit. The issue of the bank thus became a focal point for pro- and anticolonial sympathies. Pan Santi became known to the nationalists as a pro-Dutch figure and may have been targeted for assassination. In 1948 Madri called another meeting in the outer temple and announced that everyone who supported the bank should get up and stand together at the north end. This group presently decided to secede from the village and form a new village, "North Batur." This decision was soon ratified by the provincial government. In retaliation, Madri forbade the people of North Batur to enter the supreme water temple (Ulun Danu Batur). Along with the ordinary citizens of North Batur, this prohibition fell on six temple priests, who were thus excluded from performing their duties at the temple. In their places, six new priests were selected by the mediums from among the young men of South Batur.

Pan Santi became the village head of North Batur, and sought allies among the antinationalist politicians of Bangli. Few among the elite high-caste strata of Bangli had supported the nationalist cause, and the defeat of the Dutch put them in an awkward position. But by 1950 the formation of new political parties gave them a chance to redefine their role in the new political climate. Pan Santi took advantage of support from the old palace elite of Bangli to pursue an issue in the courts involving the ownership of agricultural land. The volcanic eruption had created some confusion with respect to land that had formerly belonged to the temple but was now being farmed by people from South Batur, who saw no reason to let valuable land lie fallow indefinitely. Like the bank, this became a polarizing issue, as Pan Santi used his connections in Bangli to pursue the matter in the law courts, to the discomfiture of Madri.

Tensions between the North and South factions came to a head in 1953, when Madri objected to the treatment of his sister by her North Batur husband and brought her to stay with him. In October 1953 Madri was shot at by anonymous assassins but escaped injury. But on the morning of 15 March 1954, on his way to the temple, he was fatally shot by two men who were later tried and convicted as professional killers. One of the killers was identified by a handkerchief on which his name was printed, which he dropped at the scene of the murder. The killers were sentenced to ten and fifteen years, and at their trial a third man from North Batur was implicated as the instigator of the murder. This local man received a sentence of only two years in jail. The murder itself and the light sentences imposed on the killers infuriated Madri's supporters in South Batur, especially in light of Madri's status as a hero of nationalist resistance to the Japanese and the Dutch. In a matter of months, Madri's son Siyem was elected to succeed him as the village head of South Batur. Soon afterward, there were several retaliatory killings of men from North Batur who were accused of having spied for the Dutch.

In the early 1950s the rivalries between factions became cloaked with the identities of the new political parties. Rather ironically, North Batur supported the Partai Nasionalist Indonesia (PNI) while South Batur identified with the more progressive socialists (PSI). In this way the killing of Madri became associated with the PNI faction. As the rivalry between the two villages intensified, a group of fourteen families in North Batur decided to adopt a neutral position in this quarrel, and in 1955 petitioned the regional government to be permitted to form a new village, "Middle Batur." Permission was granted, but this plan was not a great success: the villagers' former allies in North Batur were annoyed, while the South Batur faction refused to give them permission to return to worship in the temple unless they rejoined South Batur.

Instead Middle Batur decided to remain independent, and gradually began to fulfill its promise as a mediator. In 1957 the Lesser High Priest died, and the village of South Batur carried out his elaborate funeral rites. The mediums selected one of his nephews, a young man from Middle Batur, as his replacement.[12] This young man soon began to play an important role not only in the temple but also in the political rivalries between the three villages. In the 1960s the Communist party began to gain a foothold in North Batur. At that time economic conditions were terrible, and promises of land reform and redistribution of wealth attracted the poor. Pan Santi (the leader of the faction that became North Batur) found himself becoming marginalized, and as his support weakened he struck up a new alliance with Siyem, the son of Madri and village head of South Batur. By that time, according to my informants, Pan Santi's association with the PNI party had placed him at odds with the Communist faction in North Batur. It is a tribute to his political skills that he was allowed to rejoin South Batur, and he soon regained prominence in the leadership of the village. By the early 1960s South Batur and the supreme water temple were controlled by a coalition of four powerful men: Siyem (the son and heir of the murdered Madri), Pan Santi, and two Elders, Guru Badung and Guru Suma. This group exerted itself to retain control of the temple, which meant keeping the young Lesser High Priest under their thumb. When the father of the Lesser High Priest died, his widow was taken to wife by Guru Badung, placing the young priest under his paternal authority.

By 1963 Pan Santi had reemerged as the second most powerful man in the village and the Ulan Danu temple, after the village head Siyem. That year he was able to push forward an ambitious plan to construct a new village temple (*pura dalem*) for South Batur. But when the killing of suspected Communists began in 1965, Pan Santi fell under suspicion because of his former association with the Communists in North Batur. Seven men from North Batur were slaughtered by death squads, and Pan Santi went into hiding. Siyem, the village head, placed Pan Santi under his protection and by so doing is credited with saving his life. This left Siyem as the undisputed head of the Ulan Danu temple and the village.

---

[12] As the old priest lay dying, he was asked how he wanted to dispose of his large collection of *lontar* manuscripts. He replied contemptuously that as no one else was competent to interpret them, they might as well be burned. Tragically, his wishes were carried out. His young nephew (the present Lesser High Priest) participated in the burning, an event that he now remembers as a catastrophic mistake.

Nonetheless, soon after the massacres ended, the irrepressible Pan Santi began to resume his rivalry with Siyem. In 1967, Pan Santi gathered a group of his followers and created a fourth village, "Fourth Batur" (Batur Catur). Once again Pan Santi petitoned the regional government for legal recognition of the new village, but this time permission was denied.

With Pan Santi temporarily quashed, the only potential rival that Siyem faced as village head was the Lesser High Priest, who had begun to ask awkward questions about the scope of his authority at the temple. At the time, like most citizens of Batur the young priest and his brother lived in poverty. Seeing little hope for improvement in his circumstances, the young priest began to consider volunteering for a government program ("transmigration") that would relocate him to the island of Sulawesi, where he would be given land to farm. Several families from Batur had already volunteered for this program. When his mind was made up, the priest walked to the lakeside temple Pura Jati to announce his intention to the gods. But while walking home from the temple he was struck by a car, and woke up to find himself in a hospital bed. Friends and supporters came to visit him while he was recovering. Several of them suggested that he interpret the accident as a sign that he should not leave, but on the contrary stay in Batur and assume his proper place at the temple. The priest was persuaded by this argument, and when he had recovered from his injuries returned to Batur and began to meet with leaders of the four villages to discuss the possibility of opening the temple to all the people of Batur. Siyem (the village head of South Batur) responded by pronouncing a kind of anathema on the priest, forbidding all citizens of South Batur to speak to him. The priest responded by embarking on an extended pilgrimage to other temples around the island, praying and asking for guidance from the gods. Meanwhile, support for him was growing not only in South Batur but also in the other villages. People remember the 1970s as a time when members of the four factions were often summoned by the slit drums to brawl in the streets with fists, rocks, and clubs. The heads of the three recognized villages were frequently summoned to Bangli by exasperated magistrates and administrators, and admonished to sort out their problems peacefully. When he had completed his pilgrimage, the young priest met in secret with leaders from all four factions at the lakeside temple and proposed a compromise: the three villages would remain intact as administrative units governed by their own elected representatives, but the village of Batur would be reunited in a spiritual sense, with all citizens permitted to worship freely at the Ulan Danu temple. The temple priests and Elders who had been banished from the temple would be permitted to return to their former status. A governing committee for the temple would be created, with representatives chosen by the village heads: two for South Batur because of its larger size, and one each for North and Middle Batur. Fourth Batur (the home of the priest) was left out of the planned governing committee because it did not officially exist. This plan promised to reduce the endless factional strife, and to permit all the people of Batur to return to the temple. It would also have the effect of restoring the priests to a position of prominence at the temple, while reducing the power of the four men who ruled South Batur.

When this plan was proposed to Siyem, the village head of South Batur, he bowed to the inevitable and agreed to it with the stipulation that he would retain full administrative authority in South Batur, without interference from the two high priests. On 20 January 1978, the entire community of Batur gathered in the Ulun Danu temple to celebrate the reunification of the village and the restoration of the exiled priests of North Batur to their duties at the temple. Almost immediately, affairs in both the village and the temple began to improve. Overt hostilities between factions ceased, and the temple began to attract ever-increasing support in the form of contributions from the subaks and princes. The timing of the reunification was especially opportune, because in the early 1980s government officials from the Department of Religion had begun a campaign to increase their role in the management of Bali's most prominent temples. This effort was notably successful at the sister temple of Besakih on Mount Agung, where effective control shifted from local villages and the Klungkung royal family to the Department of Religion and the Parisada Hindu Dharma, a quasi-governmental religious organization. The leaders of all the Batur factions had a shared interest in retaining control of their supreme water temple, which meant that they needed to demonstrate that they were competent to do so. Meanwhile, in the 1980s the Greater High Priest was reaching maturity. He married, became a father, and began to take an active role in temple affairs, where he combined a profound devotion to the Goddess with a lack of interest in internal politics. This was widely interpreted as evidence that the Goddess had chosen wisely.

• • •

My best excuse for the length of time it has taken to complete this book is the sheer complexity of the story of Batur and its temple. If, as several authors have argued, irrigation in Bali was centrally managed by the kings at some time in the past, and if the Ulun Danu Batur temple was constructed to assert royal authority over irrigation, then most of the arguments presented in this book would have had to be reconsidered. It was thus essential to clarify the status of the temple, a task that proved to be unexpectedly challenging. There were many inconsistencies in the information I obtained from the Gurus, Elders, and priests. At first I attributed these apparent contradictions to the tragic destruction of much of the temple's library in 1957. Indeed, several Gurus and Elders told me that the loss of many important manuscripts forced them to fall back on their fallible memories. But later on I realized that I was being offered not incomplete, but rather competing, versions of events by the members of rival factions. The depth of the antagonism between them became memorably clear to me when I learned about the anathema imposed on the Lesser High Priest in the 1960s. Evidently, for prominent men in Batur, talking about the temple often meant reopening old wounds.

Things began to become clearer in 1995, when Pan Santi published a lengthy monograph giving his own version of the history of Batur and its temple. By then the old man was living in a kind of self-imposed exile in another village. Even his friends agreed that he had accumulated too many enemies in Batur to continue to live there. The monograph gave him a chance to settle old scores by having, as it were, the last word. The fact that much of what he had to say was highly partisan did not diminish the value of the book for me; on the contrary it provided an opening to talk with his former rivals about their own memories of events in the village. Better still, there came a day when the two high priests decided that it would be in everyone's interest for me to produce an accurate and unbiased account. To that end, they offered to bring together the surviving protagonists from the old factions to answer my questions.

Three such gatherings took place inside the inner temple, where (as the Lesser High Priest reminded everyone) it is inadvisable to tell a lie. Pan Santi was not invited, but sooner or later the group included leaders from all four villages including Gurus, Elders, and priests. I was a little hesitant to ask pointed questions at the first of these meetings, but it soon became apparent that most of the old men were now willing to talk candidly about the past. Several of them began by expressing their relief that the era of brawls in the streets was over, and gave the Lesser High Priest credit for reuniting the village. Still, there were several heated exchanges, and I agreed not to publish controversial claims or acccusations. These meetings gave me an opportunity not only to check my impressions and gather new information but also to ask for critical comments on the conclusions I had reached. This privilege more than made up for my earlier frustrations.

The memories of even the oldest of the Elders did not extend to the time before the transfer of the village from the shore of the lake to the rim of the volcano, and of course they had no direct knowledge of the precolonial era. But in the twentieth century, based on the information that they provided, it is clear that none of the royal families of Bali played a governing role at the temple. Instead, they participated in temple ceremonies as witnesses (*saksi*) and guests. At other times, the priests of Batur were invited to attend important rituals at the palaces; for example, in 1965 the temple sent a large delegation of priests, dancers, and musicians to participate in the funeral rites for the prince of Klungkung. In addition, several of the old kingdoms still have a physical presence at the temple: there are shrines to the ancestor-deities of several dynasties in the temple. And for a time, the rajah of Bangli kept a house near the entrance where he could spend the night when he and his retinue came to visit.

However, these shrines and reciprocal visits do not signal the subordination of the temple to the rajahs, but rather the reverse. The Batur elite are proud that they annually perform the most complex and elaborate series of temple rites in all of Bali. Kings are not merely superfluous to this ritual cycle; at its culmination they are explicitly subordinated to the Goddess. This is most clearly apparent in a ritual called *pulakerti*. *Pula* means "to plant," while *kerti* means goodness, or good things. The planting of goodness marks the climax or "peak of the ceremonies" (*puncak upacara*) at the temple. It takes place at the foot of the two principal shrines: the eleven-roofed tower to the Goddess and the nine-roofed tower to her brother, the Lord of the Earth (*batara meduwe gumi*), who is identified with the god of Mount Agung and the supreme royal dynasty of Klungkung. The pulakerti rite centers on the planting of a basket of symbols not unlike the bebangkit described in the preceding chapter. But whereas the bebangkit is made up of charming objects designed to attract and beguile the bhutakala, the kerti is intended to represent the irreducible components of the inner self and the living world. It includes the five precious metals; specimens of 108 plants and animals, both wild and domesticated; and the fifteen alphabetic symbols that can be used to represent all words, music, poetry, and magical signs. With the notable exception of the two high priests, all of the priests of the temple participate in the assembly of the kerti, in the names of the gods whom they represent.

Two pulakerti offerings are prepared, the larger one destined to be offered to the Goddess by the Greater High Priest, and the smaller to her brother by the Lesser High Priest. They are placed on the main altars at the beginning of the rites of the tenth month, when dozens of village orchestras come to greet the Goddess as she descends into her tower. During the ten days that follow, the kerti are soon surrounded by offerings that are piled up around them by the subaks. On the final day of the ceremonies, the two high priests dig up the remains of the pulakerti offerings from the previous year at the foot of the two shrines, and then bury (or "plant") the new ones. While this is going on, mantras are spoken expressing the request that the two deities animate all that the kerti contain, and so bring growth and prosperity in the new year. The Greater High Priest also performs a secondary rite called *penyejeg*. This interesting word means something made firm, so that it will not waver or fall apart. The ritual is intended to strengthen the growth of the kerti.

The claim that the Goddess and her priests reign supreme within her domain is explicitly conveyed by an admittedly subtle distinction, and one of my chief goals in talking with the assembled priests and Elders was to make sure that I understood it correctly. When the Greater High Priest offers the pulakerti to the Goddess, he is called Wibusakti. Meanwhile, the Lesser priest acquires the title of Prabusakti as he dedicates his pulakerti to the Lord of the Earth. However, as the priests and gurus take care to point out, at the royal temple of Besakih on Mount Agung, the rank of these titles is reversed. At Besakih, the Lord of the Earth is supreme, and consequently Prabusakti is superior to Wibusakti. The planting of the kerti takes place behind the main altars of the temple, out of sight of most of the congregation. But it is this rite that the royal families of Bali are specifically urged to witness. According to the priests and Elders, it represents the culmination of the annual cycle of rites, for which all others are preparatory. They say that it is intended to curb the forces of dissolution and chaos, to restore the balance of male and female power, and to animate the elements that bring life and growth to the living world. I wish to push their interpretation a step further, and argue that these rites serve to amplify the ritual cycles of the fields, subaks, and regional water temples so as to express the universality of the feminine principal of growth, extending it beyond the crops that are the focus of subak rituals to encompass "all beings that have breath"(*sarwwa prani hitangkaram*).

But we are not quite done with the people of Batur. Their very success in bringing off these grand celebrations of growth and harmony serves only to heighten the mystery as to why they seem to find it so difficult to take their own message to heart. Why are the factional rivalries in this village so intense? A comparison with the subaks suggests an answer. When a child of Batur is chosen to become the earthly representative of a god, the boundary between the divine and mundane worlds becomes a little blurred. Nearly everyone in the village has some type of special costume denoting his or her role at the temple, even if it is only a red or green turban denoting whether one serves the gods at the beginning of the full or new moons. These symbols are of course a source of great pride. Most of the priests and Elders choose to remain in their temple costumes a good deal of the time, and the Greater High Priest has not worn ordinary clothes since the day he was selected. In this identification with the divine world they resemble twiceborn princes and Brahmins more than ordinary farmers, who learn a very different lesson from the rites of the subaks: their shared humanity, and the need to rely on one another when addressing the gods.

Achieving Perfect Order

THE INITIAL IMPETUS for the research that led to this book was the discovery that computer simulations of Balinese water temple networks will self-organize, provided each node of the network is given the capacity to adapt to its local environment. As simulated networks coalesce, their ability to solve problems expands from the level of individual nodes to that of the network as a whole. In this way, the whole becomes something more than the sum of all the parts, a phenomenon noted by Aristotle.[1] Viewing the water temples from this perspective offered an opportunity to make use of the mathematical tools that have been developed to study adaptive networks. But the usefulness of the mathematics depends on how closely real water temple networks resemble those in the simulation models.

The fieldwork that my colleagues and I undertook to answer this question eventually led us to think about emergent processes from a second perspective, one that stems from Hegel rather than Aristotle, as the progressive embodiment of Reason in institutions. Although the two approaches are quite different, in the end both are concerned with understanding the moments when change becomes discontinuous, when it leads not merely to more of the same but to something truly different. So far we have pursued these two strands as separate topics. In this concluding chapter I will revisit what has already been said about each of them, and then move on to the question of how they may be related.

The first question is whether we gain anything by viewing water temple networks as complex adaptive systems. To answer this it is necessary to consider their origins. It was probably inevitable that paddy rice would be grown on Bali. The first Austronesian colonists may have introduced

[1] Aristototle, *Metaphysics*, Book H, 1045: 8–10.

rice to coastal settlements on Bali, and in any case by the first millennium A.D. rice was being grown by farmers on neighboring islands such as Java, with whom the Balinese were in contact via trading networks. But it was by no means certain that rice cultivation would expand into the steep interior of the island. For this to occur, ancient Balinese farmers had to find ways to move water through kilometers of solid rock, and to persuade themselves that the potential benefits from building irrigation systems in the mountains outweighed the costs. Those who chose to undertake such risky projects doubtless hoped to reap substantial rewards. Early royal inscriptions indicate that rice paddies were treated as private property in the early kingdoms, unlike the communal lands controlled by the villages.

The inscriptions also permit us to glimpse the origins of the subaks and water temples. The rugged topography in the interior created a need for institutions that could manage irrigation works that were not contained within the territory of single villages. Subaks appear in the text of royal inscriptions by the eleventh century. As is still true today, the first subaks consisted of small groups of farmers who shared a common irrigation source. But as cultivation expanded, eventually the farmers faced the problem of coordinating irrigation at a larger scale. The obvious solution—expanding the size and scope of the subaks—did not occur. Instead, clusters of subaks interacted by means of water temples.

The invention of temple networks was made possible by the evolution of the concept of patirthan from a sacred pool to a source of holy water signifying the blessing of a god. Every source of flowing water is considered to be a gift by the farmers who use it. By requesting tirtha from a shrine at the site where the water originates, they may obtain a visible sign of the blessing of the temple's deities. It follows, then, that the origin-point for every flow of water in an irrigation system needs a shrine or temple. In this way, water temple networks create a map of the physical irrigation systems. By positioning themselves at different nodes, the farmers can exert control at any point, from a single field to an entire watershed.

In ancient Bali, local experiments in coordinating irrigation among several subaks would have produced small networks. As irrigation expanded, these networks would gradually have merged, and it is at this point that the concept of complex adaptive system becomes relevant. Viewing water temples in this way leads to several conclusions:

Networks can solve problems

Modeling the selection of cropping patterns in water temple networks quickly generates a solution that predicts with remarkable accuracy the actual synchronized cropping patterns. This self-organizing process optimizes environmental parameters, raises mean crop yields, and reduces variance in yields.[2]

There is a progression from local to global solutions

As the simulations proceed, patches of syncronized cropping grow, improving crop yields by reducing pest damage. Later, the borders of patches change as water allocations are adjusted, further improving yields. Ultimately, mean yields in the entire network improve while variance decreases.

Network structure matters

Changing rate constants, such as irrigation flows or the population dynamics of pests, has no effect on the qualitative behavior of the model. In contrast, the connection structure of nodes and k, the search parameter, have significant effects.[3]

Higher-level control is not required

In our simulations, the highest mean rice harvests are produced by self-organizing networks, rather than those which simulate higher-level control. The superior capacity of networks to rapidly adapt to changing environmental conditions is the main reason for this effect. In the real world, it appears that subaks gather and discuss information about their local environments, but there is no higher-level, watershed-scale attempt to plan irrigation or cropping patterns.

The dynamics are not tied to the particularities of Bali

This was a surprise. Our mathematical analysis showed that the key innovation is the ability of networks to self-organize. This capacity is not dependent on the specific hydrology of the rivers we studied, or the biology of rice and rice pests. If the subaks were growing roses and managing aphids, some form of network structure could still emerge. Similar self-organizing networks may exist elsewhere but go unrecognized because in the past we have lacked a conceptual model for bottom-up control networks.

How much do these abstract models of network behavior tell us about the management of rice terraces in Bali? Our first model of the Oos and Petanu rivers shows that the scale of synchronized cropping has a large effect on rice yields because of its impact on water sharing and pest population dynamics, and these results were borne out by comparisons of model predictions with harvest data. Using sample surveys, we also confirmed that the relationship between synchronized cropping and pest

---

[2] We published a mathematical analysis of this process in 1999: J. S. Lamsing, J. N. Ktremer, and B. B. Smuts, "System-Dependent Selection, Ecological Feedback and the Emergence of Functional Structure in Ecosystems," *Journal of Theoretical Biology* 192 (1999): 377–91.

[3] See Lamsing, Ktremer, and Smuts 1999, where this topic is thoroughly discussed.

control was well understood by the farmers. Moreover, our records of subak meetings show that they adjusted the scale of synchronized planting in response to changing environmental conditions, and worked hard to make sure that irrigation schedules were obeyed by all their members. But the best evidence that water temple networks function as complex adaptive systems is the experience of the "Green Revolution," when the farmers were told to plant as often as possible and abandon the temple-based scheduling system. This was like running our network models in reverse, and led to similarly chaotic results.

Overall, it appears that water temples function like nodes in a network, enabling subaks to adapt to changing conditions so as to maximize rice harvests. But for this possibility to be realized, it is necessary for the farmers to cooperate effectively at several scales: not only within subaks, but also in multisubak clusters. Standing in the way of such cooperation is the "tragedy of the commons" issue. For while it is in everyone's best interest in the long run to share the available water equitably, any single farmer could do better in the short run by taking more than his fair share, and contributing less to the upkeep of the irrigation works.

We formulated this problem in the abstract language of game theory, and came up with a possible solution. The ability to control irrigation flows is not identical for all subak members. Upstream farmers have their hand on the spigot, while downstream farmers do not. But the downstream farmer can choose his cropping schedule in a way that affects the likelihood that rice pests will migrate to the fields of his upstream neighbors. This gives him a bargaining lever in negotiations over irrigation, so that cooperation becomes the best strategy for the upstream farmers too. Sample surveys in ten subaks indicate that the attitudes of the farmers were in accord with the predictions of this model: upstream farmers worried about pests, while downstream farmers were more concerned about possible water shortages.

This insight provides a logical explanation for the emergence of cooperation in temple networks. Less formally, it is clear that farmers are fully aware of the practical benefits of cooperation. Yet despite all this, our observations of the fourteen subaks in the Pamos water temple network showed that subaks are surprisingly fragile institutions. In particular, they are vulnerable to disturbances created by selfish or ambitious men. This is due partly to the nature of the physical irrigation systems, but more importantly to the fragility of the social framework that sustains cooperation. With regard to the physical infrastructure, irrigation systems in the mountains of Bali generally consist of long threadlike canal systems, so that water thefts or badly maintained canals can have catastrophic consequences downstream. But such disruptions are usually quickly discovered and fixed, provided the system as a whole is well managed. The greater danger is that farmers may lose confidence in the subak itself. The main business at most subak meetings is to make collective decisions about the kinds of costs that members are willing to impose on themselves, either to maintain the irrigation works or to carry out rituals at the water temples. There is generally a range of choices available, especially in the area of religious ceremonies, where it is always possible to do things on the cheap. Active, democratic subaks seldom decide to cut back on either form of investment. But when powerful men begin to use the subaks for their own ends, trust can quickly erode. Ordinary members become less willing to contribute their labor and resources, meetings are held sporadically, and the subak begins to falter or even fail.

So it seems that high levels of investment in what economists call public goods—in this case, maintaining the canals and performing rituals in the water temples—are typical of subaks, and may even be a necessity. The significance of this commitment becomes clearer if we compare the functioning of the subaks and water temples to another kind of economic institution. The most intriguing aspect of the water temple networks is surely their ability to optimize rice harvests at a global scale, without the need for centralized planning or control. Interestingly, economists since Adam Smith have made similar claims about the institution of the market. As Smith first observed, the invisible hand of the market can find a globally optimal solution to the problem of maximizing the utility functions for all participants, buyers and sellers alike. Greed is good, according to economists, because if each individual pursues his or her own selfish interests, a maximal state of satisfaction is achieved by all. When the market clears, everyone's utility is maximized. As in the water temple networks, countless local interactions eventually produce a global optimum, with no need for centralized planning.

In the view of classical economists, the magic of the invisible hand requires no investment in public goods, except for the minimal institutions of the market itself. Indeed, some economists conclude that any additional investment may be a waste of resources that would be better utilized in the private sector. The network structure of markets is very simple: all that is required is that buyers and sellers be connected. Adding or removing specific nodes or clusters of nodes will make no difference to the functional structure. It is otherwise for the farmers in a water temple network. The strictly selfish and short-sighted behavior that facilitates market interactions would be fatal to the subaks. In order to function, they must find ways to reduce their vulnerability to the consequences of such behavior. Individuals must be persuaded to bear in mind their dependence on the goodwill and willingness to cooperate of other subak members. They must actively participate in the process of self-governance, and choose to bear the high costs of contributions to public goods. They require, in short, a state of mind that is in many respects strikingly different from that of *homo economicus*.

•   •   •

The emergence of a farmer's cult of water temples was not supposed to happen. As we have seen, the farmers did not even have permission to read religious texts. Instead they were supposed to pay their taxes and play a supporting role in the dramas of the twiceborn elite. When the water temple cult came into existence, it did not pose an explicit challenge to this Brahmanical worldview, nor did it concern itself very much with the issues of personal spiritual development that were central to the Brahmanical tradition. Instead, it developed a rich symbolism to express connections between the living world and the inner self. The natural world became suffused with subjective meaning, while the inner world of emotions became objectified. One's own emotional state became a matter of intense interest. Farmers found themselves endlessly touching their cakra points with flower petals or eggs, and trying to master the demons contained within themselves, their children, and their communities. They also persuaded themselves that the world around them was constantly threatened with disorder, and in need of their attention.

Yet all this may not be quite so exotic as it first appears. An intense interest in the workings of human emotions is not uncommon when societies begin to experiment with self-governance. For example, Seneca's writings on the relationship between the control of the emotions and the problems of governance were carefully studied in the self-governing Italian towns of the twelfth and thirteenth centuries. In republics such as Siena, Orvieto, and Florence, the new guilds and commercial elites also invested as never before in civic institutions, choosing to impose on themselves the cost of building great cathedrals and town halls. Interestingly, this occurred at a time of such violent factional strife that rival groups found it necessary to build fortified defensive towers within the city walls. For civil society to function in a world no longer controlled by feudal aristocrats and monarchs, it was clearly necessary to find ways to restrain ungovernable ambitions. By the thirteenth century, Stoic views on the management of the emotions were becoming codified as civil law in Bologna, creating what the legal historian Robert W. Gordon has called "pictures of order and disorder, virtue and vice, reasonableness and craziness."[4] These laws defined the outer limits of acceptable behavior. Whenever destructive emotions gained the upper hand, they would have to be contained by the state, for "if each man follows his own individual will, the government of men's lives is destroyed and totally dissolved."[5]

As we have seen, the subaks took a broader approach to the problem of restraining destructive or antisocial behavior. Many chose to impose on themselves a written legal code, called *awig-awig*, which defined penalties for breaches of etiquette in subak meetings as well as for water theft or failure to participate in subak activities. But in addition to these laws, they also sought ways to enhance the ability of individuals to master their own emotions. This was a much more ambitious goal, and required a different kind of social institution. The elaborate rituals of the water temples convey a powerful message: that when individuals and subaks succeed in mastering themselves, the world (or at least the microcosm controlled by the subak) becomes more orderly. The flooded terraces resemble sparkling jewels, there are no plagues of pests, and the social life of families and communities is harmonious. On the other hand, when Reason gives way to destructive emotions, the effects are soon seen in quarreling families, disorderly fields, sickness, poverty, and pests. This is partly what I mean by the subjectification of the world. The farmers came to believe that the state of the world they inhabited was critically dependent on the condition of their own inner worlds, on the balance of emotional currents within themselves and their communities. Implicit in such beliefs is an enhanced sense of efficacy—an assumption that if a subak can manage to achieve a state of collective harmony, the effects will permeate the living world.

These beliefs run counter to the Brahmanical tradition, which envisions kings rather than mere farmers as the source of order and prosperity in their realms. We are back to the problem first posed in the introduction to this book: the contest between two concepts of governance, one based on a hierarchy of caste and the other on the powers of the collective. As we have seen, there is good evidence that Balinese farmers as well as Western social scientists view these as opposing principles. In order to function, subaks find it necessary to enforce rules prohibiting the expression of caste, yet from a Brahmanical perspective hierarchy is the organizing principle for human society. But it would be surprising if a society so fascinated with the origins of order were to leave the relationship between

---

[4] Robert W. Gordon, "Critical Legal Histories, *Stanford Law Review* 36, no. 57 (January 1984): 57–125; the quotation is on p. 109.

[5] Brunetto Latini (c. 1220–94), teacher of Dante, quoted in Quentin Skinner, *The Foundations of Modern Political Thought*, Cambridge: Cambridge University Press, 1978: 44.

homo hierarchicus and *aequalis* as an unresolved paradox, a perpetual contest between two irreconcilable principles.

And indeed, as we have seen, this conflict is generally portrayed rather differently. Caste is viewed as masculine, as deriving from the progenitive powers of male ancestor-gods, while *homo aequalis* serves the pantheon of goddesses associated with fertility. The relationship between male and female principles is defined as balanced and complementary, rather than oppositional, by the doctrine of dualism (*rwa bhineda*).[6] But there is more to this relationship than one might suppose, for the English words "male" and "female" do not capture the full meaning of this contrast. In Balinese, *purusa* means not only male, but also penis and the ancestral line of male descent. In this way it directly connects maleness with the origin of *homo hierarchicus*, because the potency of its purusa determines the rank of each male descent group. *Pradana* means "female" or "woman," but it also refers to the elements that make up the natural world. It derives from the Sanskrit (and Old Javanese) term *pradhanatattwa*, meaning the original source of the material universe, unevolved nature. The opposition between purusa and pradana thus evokes two quite different sources of order. Purusa conveys the image of a wellspring of male power that persists from one generation to the next, while pradana draws attention to the feminine qualities of the natural world, in particular the capacity for growth.[7]

Yet to clarify the meaning of this contrast only heightens the mystery. Purusa defines the powers of kings and patriarchs in purely masculine terms, proclaiming them to be guardians and protectors whose strength enables them to crush their enemies. They will inevitably compete for dominance (indeed, Clifford Geertz identified this competition as the driving force in the politics of the precolonial kingdoms). And as the masculine powers of purusa achieve dominance, those of the feminine pradana must recede. In what sense, then, can they be understood as complementary—particularly if it is necessary for rulers to "make inequality enchant," as Geertz argues, by celebrating the supremacy of their

---

[6] On the meaning of *rwa bhineda*, see *Jnanasiddhanta*, edited and translated by Haryati Soebadio, The Hague: Martinus Nijhoff, 1971: 57–58.

[7] These symbolic associations evoke those of republican Rome. The word "tribe" comes from the Latin word *tribus*, which may have derived from the three original tribes of the plebs. In ancient Rome the three tribes claimed power over the female powers of growth, especially in an agricultural context, while the patricians associated themselves with the masculine powers and gods relating to descent (cf. *Oxford Classical Dictionary*, 3rd ed., 1996: 1550). The plebs developed their own cult centering on Ceres, the goddess of grain, and Liber, god of fertility, centering on the Aventine Hill. John Boardman, Jasper Green, and Oswyn Murray, *The Roman World*, Oxford History of the Classical World, New York: Oxford University Press, 1986: 18.

purusa?[8] To answer this question, I propose to return to the poem composed in 1905 by the last king of Badung, which was briefly introduced in chapter 5. The central theme explored in the story is the nature of purusa: is there a point beyond which its powers lead not to order, but rather the reverse? What is the nature of the relationship between the qualities of maleness and the responsibilities of kings?

• • •

Toward the middle of the *Purwa Senghara* (Origins of Chaos), the king describes the wanderings of the Buddha on earth in the next-to-last age of the world. Wishing to hasten the pace of destruction, the destroyer gods Rudra and Kala have strengthened the powers of a flesh-eating demon called Purusada, whose name evokes the term for male lineage or penis (*purusa*) and thus suggests maleness itself. The Wairocana Buddha responds to this crisis by taking human form as Sutasoma, and begins a solitary journey in the world of men. His aim is not to engage in combat with Purusada and the *raksasas* (demons), but rather to awaken their capacity for compassion. The focus of the story is not on the simple contest between Buddha and the destroyers, but rather on the more complex choices faced by humans, more particularly by heroes and kings whose powers also derive from purusa. One of the minor incidents in Sutasoma's long journey offers an insight into the king's views on the significance of these choices.

Sutasoma encounters Sang Boja, the king of Widarba, who is engaged in carrying out the rituals of Dewa Yadnya (the worship of the gods). A great number of priests and noblemen have come to participate, and all are given gifts and prizes by the king. In their midst appears a very noisy priest who brokenly mispronounces the Vedic prayers. The king asks himself, who can this be? Approaching the king as if he were bearing a message from the gods, the noisy priest predicts that the rites will be unsuccessful because the soldiers and noblemen attending are armed as if for war, which is unsuitable for a ceremony that must be carried out with pure intentions. The king answers that his men are armed so that they will be ready in case raksasas who are *adharma* (lawless and without compassion) should appear. But the king is half-persuaded by the priest's words, and in his uncertainty becomes distracted. The priest, who is actually the demon Purusada, seizes the king and bears him away on a flying chariot to become one of a hundred kings that Purusada intends to offer as sacrifices to the destroyer gods.

[8] Clifford Geertz, *Negara: The Theatre State in Nineteenth-Century Bali*, Princeton, N.J.: Princeton University Press, 1980: 123.

The people of Widarba are left in terror and grief, helpless prey for the raksasas.

In this poem, the dharma of nearly every actor is fixed before the story begins. Demons, gods, ascetics, sages, and ordinary mortals fulfill their unchanging roles; only heroes and kings must struggle to understand what is required of them. In each successive age of the world the balance of forces shifts inexorably toward adharma, creating the stage on which successive generations of rulers must try to find their way. The *Purwa Senghara* comprises 1,732 verses in 323 folios and is divided into three parts. Each of them tells essentially the same story set in a different age of the world. This structure allows the poet to explore the nuances of choice; as the world becomes progressively darker, the opportunities for heroic action increase. The background is the same for all three tales: as one nymph is made to explain to another early in the poem, "I overheard Bhagawan Wrehaspati just now in the palace. He said that the problems of this age are the result of the failure of men to practice asceticism (*tapa*), the kind that aims for the good."[9] But for kings, asceticism and the worship of the gods are not enough, as shown in the story of the capture of Sang Boja. Instead, it is uniquely their task to try to comprehend the entirety of the balance of forces that confront them, which is to say the workings of dharma in their own age. Later on in the poem, Sutasoma is able to effect the rescue of the hundred kings, and takes the opportunity to preach a sermon on what is required of them: "Don't be sly, or arrogant about your position or wealth, do not kill needlessly, speak the truth carefully, pledge your soul only with great care, do not (blindly) follow your desires, as to all who serve you, bring much perfection to the people, whose fault is ignorance not sin."[10]

Yet as the story continues, it is clear that even those heroes who comply with all these precepts can hope for only temporary victories. Later in the poem, in the next age of the world, the role of Sutasoma is taken by the human king Suprasena. Suprasena is confronted by a demon-king, Rudradasa, who is allied with eighteen human kings. After a climactic battle, King Suprasena takes on the form of the Buddha Wairocana and restores all the dead to life, both human and raksasa. They leave the field

[9] Kocap wecanan sinuun, Begawan Wrehaspati, masaning kali sengara, kocap masane puniki, wantah arang ada tapa, tapane mamerih becik. Kranane mangkin pakewuh, baose wau ring puri, kaula miarsa matra. Geguritan Purwa Senghara, Pupuh 24, verses 27–28, original manuscript housed in the library of the Fakultas Sastra, Udayana University, Bali (my translation).

[10] Eda cinging da ngaguang luih, dadi ratu da ngaguang kasugihan, miwah mamati-mamatine, plapanang mangde patut, rangkung abot yen mutang pati, ring jadma tan pa-dosa, da mapilih kayun, ring sarwa-sarwa sewaka, mangde katah sampurane ring wong alit, tambet tan saking cekap. Geguritan Purwa Senghara, Pupuh 21, verse 27.

of battle and journey together to Suprasena's palace: "Arriving at the palace of Kapila, they enjoyed themselves for forty days, feasting and drinking, humans and demons, all inwardly calm. Then King Rudradasa was allowed to return to his country, Jwotispraba Mandala."

This passage was the subject of a commentary in 1985 by three Balinese writers who concluded that "the peace that is intended in this passage certainly refers to both inner peace and peace among men living together, avoiding conflicts and emnity such as that which formerly existed between men and demons."[11] But this peace lasts for only forty days; soon all the actors are again pursuing their dharma, the raksasas once again bent on tasting the pleasures of violence, lust, and power. Thus in the first incident recounted above, when Sang Boja begins to waver in his concentration, the way is open for the allegorical Purusada to capture him, leaving his people defenseless to male lust and violence personified by Purusada's army of demons.

Dharmasadhana, a Sanskrit term that appears in Balinese literature, is a means of fulfilling one's dharma. For kings, this may involve not merely passive study or submission to the law, but active critical reflection. The *Purwa Senghara* depicts dozens of set-piece conflicts following one after another, like a catalogue of chess matches. The moves available to each player—sage, demon, nymph, or goddess—are stereotypically fixed by their roles, with the exception of the kings and heroes, who must try to comprehend the whole chessboard in order to find a path that will lead to victory. Thus each episode can be interpreted as an allegory. The task that the king of Badoeng set himself in 1905 was to penetrate the meaning of these conflicts, not only as discrete stories, but as a cumulative narrative unfolding over three epochs of the world. Soon he would write his own chapter, one that (as he foresaw) would almost certainly encompass the destruction of his own kingdom. But with the insights gained from his analysis, this temporal defeat might be redeemed by a victory of Spirit over the soul-destroying poisons of the Age of Kali.

Hegel famously wrote in the preface to his *Philosophy of Right* that "philosophy is its own time apprehended in thought." He was the last major European philosopher to attempt to situate humanity within a meaningful cosmos, and he shared with the author of the *Purwa Senghara* the belief that the hieroglyph of Reason becomes apparent only in retrospect, when the mind can retrace the path of its own development;

[11] Made Sukada, Made Suarsa, and Wayan Suarya, *Amanat Geguritan Purwa Sengara*, Yogyakarta: Departemen Pendidikan dan Kebudayaan, Direktorat Jendral Kebudayaan, Proyek Penelitian dan Pengkajian Kebudayaan Nusantara, 1985: 103.

"the owl of Minerva spreads its wings only with the fall of dusk."[12] The *Purwa Senghara*, like Hegel's *Phenomenology*, is an ambitious survey of the movement of Mind in successive ages of the world. And like the *Phenomenology*, it accords a special role to kings. For Hegel, "the personality of the state is actual only as one person, the monarch."[13] A monarchical state is more than a system of governance, because it represents "the actuality of the ethical idea."[14] A similar theme runs through the *Purwa Senghara*. For example, in a typical passage King Ugrasena addresses the people of the kingdom of Yadu: "Danger originates in our minds, in the six enemies (destructive emotions) that make one prey to jealousy or evil; these can cause a general dissolution or downfall (of society). If our minds and character are clear and pure, grounded in ethics, then there is no danger of disintegration."[15]

But even if each person strives to follow the dharma in their own lives, the people cannot succeed without a king, because kings create a social order governed by manifest ethical principles. Indeed, as Sutasoma explains to the hundred kings, an inactive monarch is like a ghost who seeks a quiet place to hide, and has no purpose in his kingdom.[16] Balinese kings saw themselves as responsible for actively sustaining the sovereignty of dharma in their realms, holding great annual sacrifices at the end of the rainy season to reestablish control over the bhutakala. If kings stopped performing these functions, the forces of adharma would quickly gain ascendancy.

For Hegel the great fact about the state is that it is the embodiment of Reason itself, the materialization of rational ethical principles. But for the author of the *Purwa Senghara*, this idea is simply taken for granted. The great fact about politics is not that the state is a realization of dharma, but that the victories of dharma are always precarious because of the fallibility of human character. Reason is constrained by the emotions, which are the cause of turmoil and disorder not only in the mind but also in the wider world. Kingdoms and communities are threatened by *senghara* (disorder or chaos), and the origins of senghara, the *purwa senghara*, lie in the vulnerability of human minds to unruly passions. This theme is hardly present in Hegel. But it was the point of departure for the architects of civil law in thirteenth-century Italian republics, and it is central to Balinese ideas about governance.

[12] G.W.F. Hegel, *Hegel's Philosophy of Right*, translated by T.M. Knox, Oxford: Oxford University Press, 1967: 13.

[13] Hegel 1967: 182.

[14] Hegel 1967: section 257.

[15] Geguritan Purwa Senghara, Pupuh II, verse 16, p. 58.

[16] Geguritan Purwa Senghara, Pupuh XVII, verse 23, p. 90.

• • •

Surprisingly, the idea that kings are the prime source of order in the world did not disappear when the Dutch removed them from power. Instead, as I will show, this belief continues to play a vital role in the governance of the former kingdoms. There is a moment, at the end of the Balinese year, when society is considered to be at its most vulnerable. The powers of witches and other turbulent forces are at their zenith, and need to be contained lest they pass beyond human control. The cult of kingship offers a solution founded in masculine power or purusa. But as the author of the *Purwa Senghara* glimpsed, the ultimate source of disorder may be the purusa itself.

Each year the senior civil servants who now govern the former kingdom of Bangli join with the royal family to carry out the rites that mark the end of the year, at the new moon of the ninth month. Delegations are sent in advance to seek holy water from Ulun Danu Batur and also from a sea temple. At the crossroads outside the gates of the former palace, offerings are arrayed before a large statue of Siva. The focal point of the ritual is an ancient royal sword or kris, which symbolizes the purusa of the Bangli royal dynasty. The sword is called *batara kawitan*. *Batara* is the term for deified ancestors, and *kawitan* means sacred origin, so the sword represents the connection of the royal family to the virility and power of the founders of its dynasty. In preparation for the rite, the kris is wrapped in sacred white cloth and raised up above the altar on an ornate yellow palanquin. As noon approaches, members of the royal family, senior civil servants, aristocrats, and village heads take their seats outside the palace gates, facing the altar and the kris. In their midst is a raised platform where three Brahmin priests are seated with their bells, bowls, and flowers. The Brahmins perform a series of prayers, first to purify themselves, and then to invite the ancestor of the dynasty to enter the kris and accept the offerings prepared for him. When these prayers are concluded, the eldest male descendant of the last king of Bangli approaches the offerings. He touches the point of the kris to a container of holy water placed beside it, and in this way creates tirtha imbued with the male essence of the Bangli dynasty. He pours this holy water into a larger vessel, and adds the tirtha from the mountain lake and the sea. Next he sprinkles a little of this mixture on the assembled dignitaries, beginning with the civil head of the government of Bangli, who thus takes on the symbolic role of king. Ordinary temple priests now take over, sprinkling holy water on all the guests, and pouring out small quantities into containers that will be carried to the major temples of Bangli. At each of these temples, more holy water is added, representing the blessing of the temple's deities. The mixture is then carried to each community (*banjar*), where there is another purification ritual. Every family sends one of its members to the banjar, to request a cup of the holy water and a handful of rice. On arriving home, the tirtha and rice are used to purify the entrance to the house, to protect it against witches and other malignant bhutakala. Finally, the holy water is taken into the house and carried to the shrine for the ancestors, who are asked to add their blessings to it. Then the entire family undergoes a cleansing ritual, *mabiu kala*. At the conclusion of this ceremony, everyone drinks a little tirtha, and the head of the family sprinkles the remainder on the household. The next day is nyepi, the beginning of the new year, when people pray that the dangerous bhutakala will pass them by.

This ritual symbolically mobilizes the powers associated with the purusa of the royal dynasty of Bangli. Those powers are associated with the origin of the dynasty and with the potency of former rulers who were deified after their deaths. While Bangli is no longer governed by kings, the vital forces that brought the dynasty to power still represent the apex of masculine power in the realm. The ritual depicts these powers as augmenting those of the current rulers of the realm, a masculine hierarchy that includes the heads of every household. Their united strength is needed to overcome the dangers that threaten the kingdom, which are explicitly identified in the prayers of the Brahmins: enemies, sicknesses, raksasas, earthquakes, rats, and more generally a state of turmoil or senghara. The theme of resisting senghara is identical to that of the *Purwa Senghara*, and the author of the poem undoubtedly participated in similar rites at the gates of his own palace a century ago.

In Balinese eyes, the effectiveness of these rites depends on the potency of batara kawitan (ancestor-god of the lineage), the wellspring of dynastic power. When princes die, they return to the purusa, and the grandeur of their funeral rites is thought to index the power of batara kawitan. As Clifford Geertz showed in his study of nineteenth-century Balinese kingdoms, there was a competitive aspect to these spectacles. Kings presided over shifting coalitions of feudal lords, any one of whom might hope to found a dynasty and make his own purusa preeminent in the land. The death rites for nineteenth-century kings often mobilized entire kingdoms: in 1847, forty to fifty thousand Balinese witnessed a royal cremation in which three young women became human sacrifices, demonstrating, according to Geertz, "that worldly status has a cosmic base, and that hierarchy is the governing principle of the universe."[17] These competitive celebrations of hierarchy continue to be performed today; the only missing element is human sacrifice. For example, in 2004 the body of the last of the nine children of the former rajah of Ubud was carried

[17] Geertz 1980: 102.

to her cremation in an ornate eighty-foot tower. Most families living in the territory of the former princedom sent representatives to help with preparations, and in return received food and gifts from the royal family. The tens of thousands of dollars expended on this funeral were intended to create a spectacle that would match or exceed the splendor of other recent royal funerals. This ongoing competition in funeral rites among the surviving Balinese royal dynasties is echoed, on a smaller scale, in the death rituals that take place in the villages. Where competition among purusa is intense, it is not uncommon for patriarchs to pawn or sell their farmland in order to afford the desired degree of magnificence.

Geertz sees these rituals as "an illustration of the power of grandeur to organize the world."[18] But because of their great cost, the rites themselves can also have the opposite effect, driving families to ruin. More generally, as the author of the *Purwa Senghara* clearly believed, purusa is not intrinsically constructive; it becomes so only when firmly controlled. At one point he lists sixteen forms of mindfulness needed by his fellow kings, ranging from *Giribrata* (the aspect of mind that makes one stubborn as a mountain in the face of one's enemies) to *Indrabrata* (skepticism toward what one is told, especially when commanding the people or the army). To falter in any of them risks releasing the destructive aspects of purusa.[19] For even when a firm hierarchy of masculine power has brought order to a nation, its effects are bound to be temporary. Kings who manage to dominate their rivals and achieve supremacy remain vulnerable to their own passions, which can be even more dangerous than their external enemies.

• • •

The dualistic doctrine of rwa bhineda asserts that the powers of purusa to order the world are not unlimited, because masculine power invariably requires a feminine counterpart. It would be natural to assume that this female principle functions to restrain the masculine drive for dominance. But such an assumption would reflect Western ideas about the relationship between male and female more than the Balinese concepts of purusa and pradhana. Purusa involves powers that descend from sacred ancestor-gods to each generation of patriarchs, enabling them to engage in the struggle for dominance. But the female rites of pradana are unconcerned with dominance or the ancestors. Instead they consist of symbolic arrays representing the essential components of the living

---

[18] Geertz 1980: 102.

[19] Purusa may be understood as a cosmological principle. *Tri purusa* (the three purusa) refers to the Hindu trinity of supreme gods, Brahma, Wisnu, and Iswara.

world, which are symbolically transformed into higher or more perfect forms. The symbolic focus shifts from the capacities of individuals to those of collectives, and from the past to the future. In this way pradana offers an alternative conception of the origins of order in human affairs. However, while pradana does not directly challenge male dominance, it can have a damping effect on competition among purusa. This can be clearly seen in the end-of-year ceremonies in the village of Kedisan. These rituals have the same overall goal as those performed by the royal family of Bangli, described above. But they offer an entirely different solution to the problem of protecting the community from the dangers that threaten it.

The reader may remember Kedisan as the village where the rivalry between purusa (male descent groups) became so intense that for a year it was impossible to hold subak meetings. Peace was restored for a time, but in 2002 the members of one purusa startled their neighbors by insisting that their family priest should be permitted to conduct rituals on behalf of the entire community at all village temples. This was interpreted as an attempt to assert the supremacy of their purusa. Members of rival descent groups were incensed, and the village head began to take the precaution of asking the police to send a carful of uniformed officers to the village on the days when he had to call meetings.

It was in this atmosphere of disintegrating trust that the women of the village began to prepare the offerings needed to mark the end of the year. On the morning of the last day of the year, as members of the royal family of Bangli were gathering at the gates to their palace, the women of Kedisan brought their offerings to the crossroads in front of the principal village temple, and began to organize them into a mandalic pattern. None of the masculine symbolism of purusa enters into these feminine rites; there are no jeweled krises or invocations to ancestor-gods. Instead the women of every household take turns creating arrays of offerings intended to represent the essences (*sarin*) of the living world. Collectively these offerings are intended to signify both the inner and outer worlds and also three ranked metaphysical levels of being. In the original Sanskrit the latter refer to the first of the three upper worlds: the earth (*bhur*), sky (*bhuwah*), and the space beyond the sun (*swah*). But in Balinese these terms came to mean the respective domains of plants and animals, humans, and gods. The overall goal of the ritual is to encourage a process of ordering and movement up the metaphysical scale for all living beings that exist within the domain of the village. The lowest level of plants and animals (*bhur*) is represented by several chickens, a goose, a goat, a pig, and a dog. They are selected for sacrifice according to their color, which is interpreted as a sign indicating their place in the abstract system of mandalic order. Red, for example, is the color of the direction toward the sea, the god Brahma, his equivalent within the self, the letter *B*, a musical tone, the blood that accompanies childbirth, and so forth. In general, red dogs seldom live to an advanced age in Balinese villages, because their rare color indicates that they are suitable candidates for an early opportunity to be reborn higher up the scale of being. Beneath red, yellow, black, and white flags, offerings representing all living plants and animals are laid out in symmetrical patterns around a bebangkit.

At the middle level of humans (*bhuwah*), prayers are directed toward the dangers that may threaten the village in the coming year. Attention is directed toward the dangerous bhutakala lurking in the village, which can easily slip out of control at year's end. These bhutakala are usually represented as humans distorted by uncontrolled lusts: bulging eyes or genitals, upside-down bodies, or gaping mouths with sharp pointed teeth. Because the bhutakala are considered to be the children of Durga, regaining control over them involves encouraging the annual transformation of Durga into the goddess Uma. This event is symbolized, at the level of bhuwah, by the timely departure of Durga from the local cemetery and her simultaneous reappearance as Uma in a village temple. At the highest metaphysical level, that of the gods (*swah*), the transformation of Durga into Uma is symbolically marked by the moment when Gana, the elephant-headed son of Uma and Siwa, can once again worship his mother as a goddess. Previously, as long as she remains in her Durga form, she is imperfect and may not be honored by her son. Durga's rediscovery of her divine nature restores order to the bhutakala, and provides a model for emotional realignment among the human inhabitants of the village.

This complex ritual offers both a diagnosis of the sources of disorder in the human world and a model for the restoration of order. It is not considered to be an alternative or substitute for the rituals performed by the kings. If the village of Kedisan happened to be located within the borders of the kingdom of Bangli, the village patriarchs would doubtless be pleased to accept the holy water offered by the royal family. But acceptance of the royal holy water would not relieve them of the need to perform their own rites of purification at year's end.

It could be argued that the symbolic focus of the villagers' rite is the restoration of order in the archetypal family, achieved by bringing dangerous emotions under control. It is Gana, the dutiful son, who first exposes his mother's shame and later judges her fitness to return to the family. Pictures of Gana are usually displayed at rites of purification, because it is said that all bhutakala fear him. The theme of the Durga myth, that one's very being depends on mastery of the emotions, is generalized and extended to all forms of life. Humans are depicted as very close to both demons and gods, so close that it is easy to become either more or less than human. It is the struggle to master one's emotions that propels a soul in one direction or the other. In the classical Brahmanical tradition this struggle is performed by heroic male aristocrats, aided by their priestly advisers. But in the feminine rites of pradana, human communities are mobilized to aid "all beings that have breath." In Kedisan, where rivalry between purusa threatened to become violent, these end-of-year rituals served as a powerful reminder of how much the village stood to lose if this rivalry could not be contained.

• • •

The French historian Nicole Loraux argues that the creation of a democratic system of governance in ancient Greece led to the removal of women from public life, because they were seen as embodying qualities that threatened order. The political community was to be a community of men.[20] Loraux and others argue that this policy derived from the Athenian notion of the irrationality of female nature, "women's endowment with those characteristics inimical to ordered life."[21] The extreme examples are the nightmare creatures of Greek myth, all savage, uncontrollable, and feminine: the Harpies, the Furies, Medusa.[22] The dangers posed by women's emotional weakness, and the consequent need to exclude them from public life, are also prominent in the writings of Stoic philosophers in the era of the Roman republic, and were picked up again by the political theorists of the Italian Renaissance. Seneca's warnings against "womanish weakness of mind" (*infirmitate muliebris animi*)[23] were echoed by the proponents of democracy in republics such as Siena, Florence, and Orvieto. This theme is vividly depicted in the fresco representing Good and Bad Government in the Sienese Palazzo Pubblico, created at a time when the Sienese were struggling to sustain a system of self-governance, early in the fourteenth century. Tyranny is portrayed as the Whore of Babylon, holding in her hand a golden wine cup "brimming with her fornications" and under her foot a goat representing lust. She presides over the court of bad government, which includes a trinity of negative emotions (avarice, pride, and vainglory) as well as cruelty,

---

[20] Nicole Loraux, *Mothers in Mourning*, translated by Corinne Pache, Ithaca, N.Y., and London: Cornell University Press, 1998; original edition, 1990. See also Roger Just, *Women in Athenian Law and Life*, London and New York: Routledge, 1989: 198. He cites Demosthenes 43 [Makartatos]: 62; Loeb translation, modified.

[21] See Just 1989: esp. chap. 9; the quotation is on p. 218.

[22] Just cites John Gould, "Law, Custom and Myth: Aspects of the Social Position of Women in Classical Athens," *Journal of Hellenic Studies* 100 (1980): 38–59.

[23] Seneca, "De Consolatione ad Polybium," in *Moral Essays*, vol. 2, translated by John Basore, Cambridge and London: Harvard University Press, 1932: 365–67.

treachery, fraud, rage, division, and war. This fresco has been extensively studied as a reflection of contemporary political ideology, by scholars including Nicolai Rubinstein, Chiara Frugoni, Quentin Skinner, and Randolph Starn.[24] They argue that the fresco depicts the core problem for democratic rule as the gratification of self at the expense of the community. The rational self-control needed for an orderly political community is equated with the male nature, as opposed to disorderly emotional display, which is associated with the feminine.

The Balinese, as we have seen, adopt a somewhat different view of these relationships. On the one hand, the dread figure of Durga, queen of the witches and mother of the bhutakala, represents the evils of unrestrained self-indulgence. And women are said to be particularly vulnerable to Durga's temptations. But the solution is not to exclude the feminine from public life. Instead, Durga's transformation into a benign goddess becomes a model for the capacity of all living beings to undergo positive growth. This introduces a novel theme into Balinese ideas about the governance of society, one that appears to be absent from the European tradition. Like the Stoic philosophers, the Balinese believe that a feminine nature exists in men as well as women. But whereas the Stoics associate the control of the emotions with maleness, the Balinese connect the control of female emotion with the capacity for growth. In the rites of pradana, this idea is articulated as a cosmological principle: the tendency of the living world to become more chaotic and disorderly can be overcome. An omnipresent mandalic symbolism tirelessly repeats a simple message, that all things are constructed from a set of common elements, which have a natural tendency toward disorder. Bring them into correct alignment, and a new and greater whole can emerge. This capacity for growth or positive transformation (*nyomian*) is seen as feminine, and women have a special role in bringing it about. The "feminine" approach to governance also provides a model for the interactions of males when cooperation is necessary. The model for *homo aequalis*, for cooperation among equals, becomes female in a world where maleness is expressed in terms of a struggle for dominance among rival purusa.[25] In support of this interpretation, I offer the following evidence:

[24] Chiara Frugoni, *Pietro and Ambrogio Lorenzetti*, Florence: Scala, 1988: 63–66. See Randolph Starn and Loren Partridge, *Arts of Power: Three Halls of State in Italy, 1300–1600*, Berkeley: University of California Press, 1992, which cites the extensive bibliography on the frescoes.

[25] Following Joan Scott, it is worth pointing out that this concept of the female as pradana is essentially metaphysical. On the other hand, it undoubtedly plays an active role in defining cultural expectations of women's social roles. Cf. Joan Scott, "Gender: A Useful Category of Historical Analysis," *American Historical Review* 91, no. 5 (December 1986).

The source of both order and disorder is the archetypal family

Men can acquire the patriarchal powers of dominance through the purusa, but the ensuing competition creates emotional turmoil. There is an ongoing struggle for supremacy among brothers in a family, families in a purusa, rival purusa in a village, and lordly families in a kingdom. Success requires public acknowledgment of one's superior patriarchal authority. This struggle is purely masculine; there is no comparable hierarchy of female descent groups to rival that of males. Instead, women create bonds between families by adopting the purusa of their husbands. But they are vulnerable to the crosscurrents produced by the tides of masculine competition. The ongoing struggles for dominance produce resentful victims, including wives, brothers, and nephews who must bow to the authority of the dominant patriarch. Following Durkheim, I suggest that the cosmological principle of senghara, the idea that the human world is constantly threatened by disorder, may have its origins in this experience of social life.

Emotions can have terrifying consequences

Families and villages are prone to violent quarrels, which are especially threatening in rice-growing villages, where everyone's livelihood depends on sustaining high levels of cooperation. It is assumed that jealous or unhappy women will inevitably begin to secretly cultivate their Durga nature, and begin to work against the family's interests. The imagery of bhutakala and witchcraft vividly depicts the horrors that may ensue.

Pradana is about the creation of order

The feminine principle of pradana aligns the role of women with that of goddesses. In the divine realm, the growth of living things is jointly accomplished by cooperation among many female deities, including Pretiwi, the earth goddess; Sri, the rice goddess; and Dewi Danu, the goddess of waters. In the human realm, women belonging to rival purusa join together to carry out the rites promoting fertility and (self-)purification. For these rites to succeed, women must emulate Uma and the goddesses of fertility, while they avoid the temptations of Durga. The feminine nature of these rites is also apparent from the absence of masculine symbolism: there are no appeals to the ancestor-gods of male purusa. Women from every family in the community or subak participate in pradana rites as equals, and individual identity becomes submerged in the collective.

Order is achieved by realignment of elements

Disorder is averted by bringing the elements that comprise the inner or outer world into proper alignment, represented by mandalic patterns. The explicit goal is to achieve a higher unity in which the whole is greater than the parts.

Symbols resonate because the human environment is configured to reflect them

The mandalic patterns depicted in ritual offerings are replicated in everything from architecture to music, calenders, and descriptions of the workings of the human mind. In this way, a kind of formal logic progressively permeates the environment, which is seen and felt to embody a consistent set of ideas.

In water temples, men follow the pradana model

The rituals of water temples reflect and embody the feminine logic of pradana. Men set aside their differences of rank in order to configure themselves as members of unified social groups for the purpose of promoting the fertility of their crops and harmonious order in the local community. These groups range in size from single subaks to multisubak water temples to the congregation of the Ulun Danu Batur temple. Water temple rites follow the logic of pradana, in which the problem of promoting fertility and growth is defined in terms of the alignment of elements. This symbolism reflects the farmers' awareness that when they act in unison, small miracles of order regularly occur, as the jewel-like perfection of the terraces produces general prosperity.

Water temple rites are the subjective realization of the network structure

The irrigation systems of the subaks are engineered to facilitate cooperative management. Only a small proportion of subaks are in full control of their source of water: those that are situated at the head of a canal or spring. All others must rely on water-sharing agreements with other subaks. Great care is taken to maintain the system of proportional dividers, which make it possible to verify the fairness of water distribution. There is no attempt to protect the fragile canal systems and aqueducts from upstream subaks, for example by tunneling under them. Consequently, the price of a breakdown in cooperation is very high. Water temples provide convenient sites for farmers to hold meetings and express their gratitude to the gods. But more importantly, their rituals manifest a solution to the problem of cooperation on which the physical irrigation systems depend.

The last person to join our research team was Sang Kaler Surata, a Balinese biologist. While Kaler's initial interest was in the ecological aspects of our project, he soon became intrigued by the question of cooperation. He was particularly interested in the idea that marriage helps to sustain social bonds within subaks over long time periods, providing a counterweight to competition between male descent groups. Kaler suggested that we could subject this hypothesis to a further test by investigating marriage patterns in an unusual village, home to many of his own cousins. This village, called Tampuagan, is located at a high elevation in

TABLE 14
Marriages in the village of Tampuagan, Bangli

	Same Purusa?		Same Subak?		
	Mother	Wife	Mother	Wife	Sample Size
Wet subak	59%	54%	95%	92%	56
Dry subak	49%	37%	71%	69%	41

We asked farmers about their own marriages and those of their mothers. The first column shows responses to questions about kinship relations prior to marriage: was the woman born into the same descent group (purusa) as her future husband? The second question asks whether the woman's father was a member of the same subak as her husband.

the district of Bangli. Tampuagan resembles Sebatu in that it contains several large springs that are used for irrigation. But unlike Sebatu, in Tampuagan there is also a large dry-fields subak, which utilizes farmland located upstream from the springs. According to our hypothesis, the greater need for cooperation in the "wet" subak should encourage a higher rate of endogamous marriage.

Following Kaler's suggestion, we undertook a survey of marriages in Tampuagan. The results are shown in table 14. While the rate of endogamous marriages within subaks is high for all farmers, it is substantially higher in the wet subak.[26]

Our survey also showed that half a dozen major purusa (male descent groups) flourish in Tampuagan. According to Kaler, for as long as anyone can remember they have been engaged in a perpetual competition for status, similar to what we observed in the subaks belonging to the Pamos water temple. There is a strong preference to select a bride from one's own descent group, but this desire is balanced by an even stronger need to marry the daughter of a member of one's own subak. The tension between the claims of purusa and subak may have persisted for centuries: the springs of Tampuagan are ideally situated for irrigation on gentle slopes above a wide valley, and it is likely that the wet subak has existed in some form since ancient times. The experiments in democratic governance that began in some Italian cities in the thirteenth century met a different fate. In all cases they lasted less than a century, as strong men or oligarchies seized power from the governing councils.

[26] We did not try to investigate attitudes toward witchcraft in Tampuagan, because this topic is so sensitive. But it is probable that in Tampuagan as elsewhere, the preference for marrying women from one's subak reflects the fear of marrying outsiders who may not have the patriline's interests at heart.

Additional Publications from the
Subak Research Projects

MASTER'S THESIS

Daniel R. Latham, "Temporal and Spatial Patterns of Asynchronous Rice Cropping and Their Influence on Pest and Disease Occurrence in a Balinese Landscape: Developing Predictive Models for Management," M.S. thesis, School of Natural Resources and Environment, University of Michigan, 1999.

DOCTORAL DISSERTATIONS (SUBSTANTIAL SUPPORT)

I.W.A. Arthawiguna, "Kontribusi Sistem Usahatani Padi Sawah terhadap Pengkayaan Hara Nitrogen, Fosfor dan Kalium Drainase Permukaan Pada Ekosistem Subak di Bali," Instituut Pertanian Bogor, 2002.

John W. Schoenfelder, "Negotiating Poise in a Multi-hierarchical World: An Archaeological Exploration of Irrigated Rice Agriculture, Ideology, and Political Balance in the Coevolution of Intersecting Complex Networks in Bali," Anthropology, UCLA, 2002.

PUBLICATIONS

J. Stephen Lansing, 1987, "Balinese Water Temples and the Management of Irrigation," *American Anthropologist* 89, no. 2: 326–41.

———, 1991, *Priests and Programmers: Technologies of Power in the Engineered Landscape of Bali*, Princeton, N.J.: Princeton University Press.

———, 1993, "Emergent Properties of Balinese Water Temples," *American Anthropologist* 95, no. 1 (March): 97–114. Also published in Christopher Langton, ed., *Artificial Life III*, Redwood City, Calif.: Addison-Wesley and the Santa Fe Institute Studies in the Sciences of Complexity, 1994: vol 10: 201–25.

———, 1994, *The Balinese*. New York: Harcourt Brace.

James N. Kremer and J. Stephen Lansing, 1995, "Modelling Water Temples and Rice Irrigation in Bali: A Lesson in Socio-ecological Communication," in Charles A. S. Hall, ed., *Maximum Power: The Ideas and Applications of H. T. Odum*, Niwot, Colo.: University Press of Colorado, 412 pp.

J. Stephen Lansing and James N. Kremer, 1995, "A Socio-ecological Analysis of Balinese Water Temples," in D. M. Warren, L. Jan Slikkerveer, and David Brokensha, eds., *Indigenous Knowledge Systems: The Cultural Dimension of Development*, London and New York: Intermediate Technology Publications: 258–68.

————, 1996, "Engineered Landscape: Balinese Water Temples and the Ecology of Rice," *Encyclopedia Brittanica Yearbook of Science and the Future.*

J. Stephen Lansing, 1996, "Stella in Bali: Systems-Ecological Simulation Modelling of Irrigation systems," in Jonathan B. Mabry, ed., *Canals and Communities: Small-Scale Irrigation Systems,* Tucson: University of Arizona Press.

————, 1997, "Bali and Daisyworld: Ecological Feedback and the Emergence of Functional Structure in Ecosystems," *Mathematical Social Sciences* 33: 95–96.

————, 1997, "Systems Theory," in Thomas Barfield, ed., *The Blackwell Dictionary of Anthropology,* Oxford: Blackwell Publishers: 462–63.

J. Stephen Lansing, James N. Kremer, and Barbara B. Smuts, 1998, "System-Dependent Selection, Ecological Feedback and the Emergence of Functional Structure in Ecosystems," *Journal of Theoretical Biology* 192: 377–91.

J. Stephen Lansing, 1999, "Anti-Chaos, Common Property and the Emergence of Cooperation," in Timothy Kohler and George Gumerman, eds., *Dynamics in Human and Primate Societies: Agent-Based Modelling of Social and Spatial Processes,* New York: Santa Fe Institute and Oxford University Press.

Vernon L. Scarborough, John W. Schoenfelder, and J. Stephen Lansing, 1999, "Early Statecraft on Bali: The Water Temple Complex and the Decentralization of the Political Economy," *Research in Economic Anthropology* 20: 299–330.

Kremer, J. N, R. C. Murphy, J. S. Lansing, and P. Kremer, 2000, "Bali's Reefs: A Qualitative Survey and Potential Inputs of Land-Derived Nutrients." Report to the World Wide Fund for Nature (WWF) in Indonesia, unpublished.

Vernon L. Scarborough, John W. Schoenfelder, and J. Stephen Lansing, 2000, "Ancient Water Management and Landscape Transformation at Sebatu, Bali," *Bulletin of the Indo-Pacific Prehistory Association* 20: 79–92.

J. Stephen Lansing, Vanda Gerhart, James N. Kremer, Patricia Kremer, Alit Arthawiguna, Suprapto, Ida Bagus Suryawan, I Gusti Arsana, Vernon L. Scarborough, and Kimberly Mikita, 2001, "Volcanic Fertilization of Balinese Rice Paddies," *Ecological Economics* 38: 383–90.

J. Stephen Lansing, 2002, " 'Artificial Societies' and the Social Sciences," *Artificial Life* 8 (October): 279–92.

————, 2002, "Irrigation Societies," *International Encyclopedia of Social and Behavioral Sciences,* Oxford: Elsevier Science: 7910–13.

————, 2003, Comment on "The Precolonial Balinese State Reconsidered: A Critical Evaluation of Theory Construction on the Irrigation, the State, and Ritual" by Brigitta Hauser-Schäublin, *Current Anthropology* 44, no. 2 (April).

J. S. Lansing, T. M. Karafet, M. H. Hammer, A. J. Redd, I. W. Ardika, S.P.K. Surata, J. S. Schoenfelder, and A. M. Merriwether, 2004, "A Foreign Trader in Ancient Bali?" *Antiquity* 78, no. 300 (June): 287–93.

J. S. Lansing and John H. Miller, 2005, "Cooperation Games and Ecological Feedback: Some Insights from Bali," *Current Anthropology* 46(2): 328–33.

Guy s. Marion, Robert B. Dunbar, and David A. Mucciarone, n.d., "Organic Nitrogen $\delta^{15}N$ in Coastal Coral Reef Skeletons Reveals Isotopic Signatures of an Agricultural Revolution," in press, *Pacific Science.*

FILM AND TELEVISION

1988 *The Goddess and the Computer.*
A one-hour ethnographic film, produced and directed by J. Stephen Lansing and Andre Singer. Camera by J. Stephen Lansing and Mike Thomson. Produced by Channel Four London and broadcast over British television November 11, 1988. Acquired for U.S. broadcast on the PBS science series *Nova*, WGBH Television (Boston). British selection for Italian International Festival of Ethnographic Films, Sardinia, 1–3 October 1990. Distributed in the United States by Documentary Educational Resources, Boston, Mass. (tel. 617-926-0492).

1994 *Farmer's meeting, From the Mountains to the Sea, Aftermath of the Green Revolution.*
Three short videos for the Balinese agro-ecology exhibit in The Great Technology Challenge, a traveling exhibition on sustainable technology created by the California Museum of Science and Technology. Videos are shown in a Balinese farmers' meeting pavilion, accompanied by photos and interactive displays based on *Priests and Programmers: Technologies of Power in the Engineered Landscape of Bali.* Available as streaming video from http://www.ic.arizona.edu/~lansing/home.htm.

2003 *The Sacred Balance.*
Sequences on Balinese ecology in a four-part science series hosted by David Suzuki and cofunded by the National Science Foundation. See http://www.sacredbalance.com/web/baliintroduction.html.

Index

abiseka ratu ritual (installation of kings),
    21, 119, 158
adat (legal systems), 62
agrarian kingdoms: forces shaping South-
    east Asian, 23–24; three successive
    phases of, 22–23
Airlangga inscriptions (A.D. 1021,
    1037), 47
Airlangga (Javanese ruler), 47, 48
amrta (Hindu water of immortality), 51
anak wanua (persons of the wanua), 28
Anak Wungcu (Balinese king), 130
ancestral line (purusa), 141
ancestry status, 51–52
Ardika, Wayan, 22, 24, 25, 34
Artaud, Antonin, 1
Asian Development Bank, 12
Athenian democracy, 149–50
Austronesians: artifacts of, 27; coloniza-
    tion of Bali by, 24–25; elaborate funer-
    ary rites of, 57; rites and religious tradi-
    tions of, 29–30; subak as reconciling
    beliefs of Indian and, 48–49, 51; temples
    constructed by, 26
awig-awig (written legal code), 196
Axelrod, Robert, 69

Babad Patisora (religious text), 168
Badung, Guru, 183
bale lantang (temple), 46
Bali: aerial tour of, 24; comparing develop-
    ment of Java and, 42–46, 63–64; com-
    paring development of Mayan sites and,
    32–34, 35fig, 41–42; Dutch colonialism
    of, 57–62, 64–65, 95, 180; early agricul-
    ture in, 24–25; intertwined histories of
    Java and, 53–54; Japanese invasion of,
    180; map showing sites mentioned in
    text, 34fig; modernization drive imple-
    mentation in, 7; modern nationalism/
    political crisis in, 180–83; reconquest
    by Majapahit empire (Java), 55–56;
    replacement of royal temples with village
    temple networks, 53–62; significance of
    water in, 46–54. See also State

Bali Aga/Mula (Original Balinese), 45
balian ketakson (sorcerer's trance),
    139, 160
balians (magic user), 142n.12
Balinese kings: abiseka ratu ritual (installa-
    tion of kings), 21, 119, 158; Brahmani-
    cal tradition on order/prosperity
    through, 196–97; cult role in construct-
    ing, 157–59; divine kingship cult and,
    20–22, 23, 56–57, 65–66, 203; human
    sacrifice/rituals during funerals of,
    56–57, 203–4; maleness of powers and
    obligations of, 197–201, 204; parallels
    between Polynesian chiefdoms and,
    26–27; participation in Ulun Danu Batur
    temple by, 187, 188; powers identified
    with maleness, 197–98; religious tradi-
    tions allowed by, 29–30; rituals to "con-
    struct a king," 21, 202–4; royal inscrip-
    tions by, 28–31, 34, 42–43, 54, 191; tax
    system instituted by, 27–28, 30–31,
    63–64; theater state validating, 20–21,
    22, 147–48, 157–58; water temple net-
    works replacing royal temples of, 53–62,
    64–66. See also State
Balinese priests: comparing perspectives of
    Western science and, 2–3; concern with
    hierarchy, 4–5; dualism as central to
    authority of, 166–70; funeral ceremony
    performed by apprentice of, 1–2; myths
    on role of, 168–69; premade (medium)
    endowing authority onto, 160–61; self-
    perception of, 4; Ulun Danu water tem-
    ple, 155–56, 166–70, 173, 186–89. See
    also Brahmanical tradition; high priests
Balinese religion: aristocratic Brahmanical
    tradition of, 131–36; caste system and
    spiritual progress belief of, 126–27; on
    coherence of universe, 123; cosmological
    dualism doctrine of, 123–26, 129–31,
    148–49, 157–58; cosmological symbol-
    ism of, 123–25; karma doctrine of, 98,
    126–27; metaphysics of, 128–29,
    137–38; reincarnation beliefs of, 166;
    restricted access to religious texts of,

PRINCETON STUDIES IN COMPLEXITY

Series Editors:

Philip W. Anderson (Princeton University); Joshua M. Epstein (The Brookings Institution); Duncan K. Foley (Barnard College); Simon A. Levin (Princeton University); Martin A. Nowak (Harvard University)

Series List: